Supporting Web Servers

ISBN 0-13-085899-4

THE ADVANCED WEBSITE ARCHITECTURE SERIES

DESIGNING WEB INTERFACES
  Michael Rees
  Andrew White
  Bebo White

SUPPORTING WEB SERVERS
  Benay Dara-Abrams
  Drew Dara-Abrams
  Trevor Peace
  Bebo White

ANALYZING E-COMMERCE & INTERNET LAW
  J. Dianne Brinson
  Benay Dara-Abrams
  Drew Dara-Abrams
  Jennifer Masek
  Ruth McDunn
  Bebo White

Supporting Web Servers

Benay Dara-Abrams

Drew Dara-Abrams

Trevor Peace

Bebo White

Prentice Hall PTR
Upper Saddle River, NJ 07458
www.phptr.com

Library of Congress Cataloging-in-Publication Data

Dara-Abrams, Benay.
  Supporting web servers / Benay Dara-Abrams, Drew Dara-Abrams
Trevor D. Peace, Bebo White.
    p. cm.— (Advanced web site architecture)
ISBN 0-13-085899-4
  1. Web site development. 2. Web servers. I. Dara-Abrams, Drew. II. Peace,
  Trevor D. III. White, Bebo, 1945- IV. Title. V. Series.

TK5105.888 .D36 2001
005.7′ 1376—dc21

                                                                     00-054714

Editorial/production supervision: *Jessica Balch (Pine Tree Composition)*
Project coordination: *Anne Trowbridge*
Acquisitions editor: *Karen McLean*
Developmental editor: *Ralph Moore*
Editorial assistant: *Richard Winkler*
Manufacturing manager: *Alexis R. Heydt*
Marketing manager: *Kate Hargett*
Cover design director: *Jerry Votta*
Interior designer: *Meryl Poweski*

©2001 Prentice Hall PTR
Prentice-Hall, Inc.
Upper Saddle River, NJ 07458

Prentice Hall books are widely used by corporations and government agencies for training, marketing, and resale.

The publisher offers discounts on this book when ordered in bulk quantities. For more information, contact: Corporate Sales Department, Phone: 800-382-3419; Fax: 201-236-7141; E-mail: corpsales@prenhall.com; or write: Prentice Hall PTR, Corp. Sales Dept., One Lake Street, Upper Saddle River, NJ 07458.

All products or services mentioned in this book are the trademarks or service marks of their respective companies or organizations.

All rights reserved. No part of this book may be reproduced, in any form or by any means, without permission in writing from the publisher.

Printed in the United States of America
10 9 8 7 6 5 4 3 2

ISBN 0-13-085899-4

Prentice-Hall International (UK) Limited, *London*
Prentice-Hall of Australia Pty. Limited, *Sydney*
Prentice-Hall Canada Inc., *Toronto*
Prentice-Hall Hispanoamericana, S.A., *Mexico*
Prentice-Hall of India Private Limited, *New Delhi*
Prentice-Hall of Japan, Inc., *Tokyo*
Pearson Education Asia Pte. Ltd.
Editora Prentice-Hall do Brasil, Ltda., *Rio de Janeiro*

Dedicated to my family, who believed me when I said that the Internet and the Web would change how we communicate, how we do business, and how we teach and learn.

—B.D-A.

Dedicated to my family, who help enable my dreams and never tire of listening to my grand ideas.

—D.D-A.

To Sandy.

—T.P.

My contributions to this book series are dedicated to my loving and supportive family—Nancy, Andrew, and Christopher—whose tolerance for patience is always severely tested whenever I take on a book project. We did it again!

—B.W.

CONTENTS

From the Editor		xv
Executive Foreword		xvii
Introduction		xix
About the Authors		xxii

CHAPTER 1 Networking Fundamentals for Webmasters — 1

Lab 1.1	Networks and Network Characteristics	3
1.1.1	Identify Different Types of Networks	5
1.1.2	Identify Network Resource-Sharing Facilities	5
	Self-Review Questions	7
Lab 1.2	The Open Systems Interconnection (OSI) Reference Model	8
1.2.1	Identify Where HTTP Fits in the OSI Model	11
1.2.2	Give Examples of Protocols on Different Layers	11
	Self-Review Questions	12
Lab 1.3	Internetworks and Network Topologies	14
1.3.1	Identify Various Network Topologies	16
1.3.2	Understand the Function of Internetworks	17
	Self-Review Questions	19
Lab 1.4	Networks Characterized by Spatial Distance	20
1.4.1	Understand the Benefits of LAN Technology	22
1.4.2	Relate Spatial Characterization to the Internet, Intranets, and Extranets	22
	Self-Review Questions	24
Lab 1.5	Intranets and Extranets	26
1.5.1	Describe the Major Components of an Intranet and an Extranet	29
1.5.2	Understand the Differences Between Intranets, Extranets, and the Internet	30
	Self-Review Questions	31
	Test Your Thinking	33

CHAPTER 2 Architectures, Devices, and Connections — 35

Lab 2.1	Packet-Switched Networks	36
2.1.1	Describe How a Packet-Switched Network Works	37
2.1.2	Compare Packet Switching and Circuit Switching	37
	Self-Review Questions	39
Lab 2.2	The Web Client/Server Model	41
2.2.1	Understand the Difference Between Client/Server, Peer-to-Peer, and Master/Slave Architectures	43
2.2.2	Appreciate the Advantage of Client/Server Architecture for the Web	43
	Self-Review Questions	45
Lab 2.3	Ethernet and FDDI Networks	47
2.3.1	Understand the Advantages of Using Ethernet Technology	48
2.3.2	Compare Ethernet and FDDI Technologies	49
	Self-Review Questions	50
Lab 2.4	Network Devices	52
2.4.1	Distinguish Between Routers, Bridges, and Switches	53
2.4.2	Determine Appropriate Interconnecting Devices for Your Network Architecture	54
2.4.3	Relate LAN Topologies to Switches	54
	Self-Review Questions	55
Lab 2.5	Network Connections	57
2.5.1	Understand Different Modes of Access to Your Internet Service Provider (ISP)	59
2.5.2	Determine Why PPP Is Preferred over SLIP	59
	Self-Review Questions	61
	Test Your Thinking	62

CHAPTER 3 Internet, Network, and Transport Protocols — 63

Lab 3.1	Internet and Internet Protocol (IP)	65
3.1.1	Determine the Organizations Responsible for Domain Name Registration	67
3.1.2	Register a New Domain Name	67
	Self-Review Questions	68

Lab 3.2	IP Addresses	70
3.2.1	Understand the IP Addressing Scheme	73
3.2.2	Know How to Identify a Domain Name by Its IP Address	73
	Self-Review Questions	75
Lab 3.3	Domain Name System (DNS)	77
3.3.1	Understand How Domains Are Associated with IP Addresses	78
3.3.2	Know How a Domain Name Is Resolved	78
	Self-Review Questions	79
Lab 3.4	Transmission Control Protocol (TCP)	81
3.4.1	Determine the Socket Number for "Well Known Services"	84
3.4.2	Understand the Use of Ports for Services	85
	Self-Review Questions	86
Lab 3.5	MAC Addresses	87
3.5.1	Find MAC Addresses of Computers within Your LAN	90
3.5.2	Read and Interpret MAC Addresses	90
	Self-Review Questions	91
Lab 3.6	User Datagram Protocol (UDP)	93
3.6.1	Understand the Difference Between TCP and UDP Protocols	94
3.6.2	List Applications that May Use the UDP Protocol and Understand Why	94
	Self-Review Questions	95
	Test Your Thinking	97

CHAPTER 4 Applications and Protocols   99

Lab 4.1	Hypertext Transfer Protocol (HTTP)	100
4.1.1	Diagram Web Page Retrieval from the Internet	104
4.1.2	Diagram Web Page Retrieval from Cache	104
	Self-Review Questions	106
Lab 4.2	SMTP, MIME, and FTP	108
4.2.1	Understand How Mail Protocols Work	109
4.2.2	Know How to Use File Transfer Protocol	110
	Self-Review Questions	111
Lab 4.3	Push and Pull Technologies	113
4.3.1	Differentiate Between Push and Pull Technologies	114

x   Contents

4.3.2	Consider When Push Technology Is Appropriate	114
	Self-Review Questions	115
Lab 4.4	Streaming Multimedia	117
4.4.1	Know the Delivery Mechanisms Involved in Streaming Media	119
4.4.2	Determine When to Provide Streaming Multimedia Facilities	120
	Self-Review Questions	122
	Test Your Thinking	123

CHAPTER 5 Connectivity   125

Lab 5.1	ISDN, DSL, and T-Carrier Technologies	126
5.1.1	Differentiate Between Various Technologies Offered by Telephone Companies	129
5.1.2	Determine Availability of Network Services in Your Area	129
	Self-Review Questions	131
Lab 5.2	Wireless Networks	132
5.2.1	Differentiate Between Wireless and Wired Networks	133
5.2.2	Understand How Wireless Networks Transmit Data	133
	Self-Review Questions	136
Lab 5.3	Cable Modems	138
5.3.1	Compare Various Network Technologies and Services	139
5.3.2	Differentiate Between Technologies Offered by the Telephone Companies and by the Cable Companies	139
	Self-Review Questions	142
	Test Your Thinking	143

CHAPTER 6 Network Security   145

Lab 6.1	Encryption Systems	146
6.1.1	Understand the Use of Public Key Cryptography	152
6.1.2	Consider the Trade-offs in Encrypting Messages	152
	Self-Review Questions	153
Lab 6.2	Secure Internet Protocols	155
6.2.1	Understand the Function of the SSL Protocol	159
6.2.2	Develop a Privacy Statement	159
	Self-Review Questions	161

Lab 6.3	Firewalls and Sniffers	162
6.3.1	Understand the Functionality of a Firewall	163
6.3.2	Distinguish Between Use of Sniffers by Network Administrators and Hackers	164
	Self-Review Questions	165
Lab 6.4	Proxy Servers, Virtual Private Networks, and Smartcards	167
6.4.1	Understand the Functionality of a Proxy Server	169
6.4.2	Assess the Feasibility of a Smartcard Solution	170
	Self-Review Questions	172
	Test Your Thinking	174

CHAPTER 7 Web Server Support   175

Lab 7.1	Web Server Evaluation Issues	177
7.1.1	Understand the Basic Concepts of Web Hosting	183
	Self-Review Questions	185
Lab 7.2	Web Site Service Models	187
7.2.1	Understand the Basic Web Site Architectures	190
	Self-Review Questions	192
Lab 7.3	Supporting Multiple Servers	193
7.3.1	Choose an Appropriate Web Server Configuration	196
	Self-Review Questions	198
Lab 7.4	Server Security Issues	200
7.4.1	Understand Basic Security Risks	208
7.4.2	Implement Appropriate Security Measures	209
	Self-Review Questions	212
Lab 7.5	Document Root Taxonomies	214
7.5.1	Design Appropriate Document Root Taxonomies	216
	Self-Review Questions	218
Lab 7.6	Access Authorization, Security, and Privacy	221
7.6.1	Understand Basic Security Configuration	225
	Self-Review Questions	227
Lab 7.7	Searching and Indexing Issues	228
7.7.1	Understand Searching and Indexing Issues	234
	Self-Review Questions	236
	Test Your Thinking	237

CHAPTER 8 The Web Programming and Scripting Environment — 239

Lab 8.1	Reasons Why Developers Write Server-Side Script	240
8.1.1	Discuss the Problems of Writing Client-Side Code	241
8.1.2	Explain the "Lowest Common Denominator" Solution	242
	Self-Review Questions	244
Lab 8.2	3-Tiered Web Application Design	245
8.2.1	Understand and Explain the Presentation Layer	246
8.2.2	Understand and Explain the Business Logic Layer	247
8.2.3	Understand and Explain the Persistence Layer	248
	Self-Review Questions	250
	Test Your Thinking	252

CHAPTER 9 Programming and Scripting in a Client/Server System — 253

Lab 9.1	Server-side Programming	254
9.1.1	Identify Key Technologies for Processing Server-Side Code	256
9.1.2	List Advantages and Disadvantages of Server-Side Code	257
	Self-Review Questions	259
Lab 9.2	Client-Side Programming	261
9.2.1	Write Simple Client-Side JavaScript	263
9.2.2	Perform Basic Client-Side Form Validation	264
	Self-Review Questions	267
Lab 9.3	Combining Client-Side and Server-Side Scripting	269
9.3.1	Combine Server-Side and Client-Side Logic	270
9.3.2	Explain How Cookies Are Both Client- and Server-Side Objects	271
	Self-Review Questions	273
	Test Your Thinking	275

CHAPTER 10 Programming and Scripting Security Issues — 277

Lab 10.1	Security Tradeoffs	278
10.1.1	Identify Potential Security Threats	279

10.1.2		Find a Balance Between Restrictive and Functional	279
		Self-Review Questions	282
Lab 10.2		The Importance of Validating User Input	283
10.2.1		Examine User Input	284
10.2.2		Prevent Users from Entering HTML	284
10.2.3		Filter Out Malicious SQL Code	285
		Self-Review Questions	288
Lab 10.3		User versus Webmaster Scripting	290
10.3.1		Identify Web Applications That Are Both Fun and Safe	291
10.3.2		Identify Web Applications That Are Useful but Dangerous	291
		Self-Review Questions	293
		Test Your Thinking	295

CHAPTER 11 Scripting Language Evolution 297

Lab 11.1	ASP		298
11.1.1		Output Basic Variables	299
11.1.2		Code a Basic If-Then Statement	300
11.1.3		Code a While Loop	301
		Self-Review Questions	304
Lab 11.2	Cold Fusion		305
11.2.1		Output Variables	306
11.2.2		Code a Basic If-Then Statement	307
11.2.3		Code a Loop	308
		Self-Review Questions	312
Lab 11.3	PHP		313
11.3.1		Output Basic Variables	314
11.3.2		Code a Basic If-Then Statement	316
11.3.3		Code a While Loop	317
		Self-Review Questions	321
Lab 11.4	Language Evolution		323
11.4.1		Describe Conceptual Building Blocks	324
11.4.2		Identify Emerging and Evolving Technologies	325
		Self-Review Questions	327
		Test Your Thinking	329

CHAPTER 12 Supporting Supplementary Technologies — 331

Lab 12.1	Internet and WWW Standardization Activities	333
12.1.1	Understand the Role of Standards and Standardization	341
12.1.2	Know Which Organizations Impact the Development of WWW Standards	342
12.1.3	Understand the Standardization Process Used by These Organizations	342
12.1.4	Understand How to Use These Organizations as an Information Resource	342
	Self-Review Questions	344
Lab 12.2	Strategies for Evaluating New Technologies	346
12.2.1	Understand the Importance of Standardization When Evaluating New Technology	352
12.2.2	Understand When New Technologies Should Be Introduced in the Web Site Life Cycle	352
	Self-Review Questions	353
Lab 12.3	New Technologies to Watch	355
12.3.1	Understand the W3C Functional Domains	371
12.3.2	Understand the Collaboration between the W3C and the IETF	371
	Self-Review Questions	372
	Test Your Thinking	374

Appendix   Answers to Self-Review Questions — 375

Index — 382

FROM THE EDITOR

As the Internet rapidly becomes the primary commerce and communications medium for virtually every company and organization operating today, a growing need exists for trained individuals to manage this medium. Aptly named *Webmasters,* these individuals will play leading roles in driving their organizations into the next millennium.

Working with the World Organization of Webmasters (WOW), Pearson PTR has developed two book series that are designed to train Webmasters to meet this challenge. These are *The Foundations of Website Architecture Series,* and *The Advanced Website Architecture Series.*

The Webmaster who masters the materials in these books will have working knowledge of Web site management, support, maintenance, organizational strategy, electronic commerce strategy and tools, as well as legal issues surrounding the Web. The Webmaster will be able to implement sound Web site design, navigation and HCI (Human-Computer Interaction) practices. Webmasters will also have a solid understanding of networking, Web servers, Web programming, and scripting, as well as supporting supplementary technologies.

The goal of *The Advanced Website Architecture Series* is to provide an advanced Webmaster training curriculum. *The Advanced Website Architecture Series* offers in-depth coverage of the content, business, and technical issues that challenge Webmasters.

Books in this series are:

> *Designing Web Interfaces*
> *Supporting Web Servers*
> *Analyzing E-Commerce & Internet Law*

The Foundations of Website Architecture Series is designed to introduce and explain the technical, business, and content management skills that are necessary to effectively train the new Webmaster.

From the Editor

Books in *The Foundations of Website Architecture Series* include:

> *Understanding Web Development*
> *Mastering Internet Protocols*
> *Administrating Web Servers, Security, & Maintenance*
> *Exploring Web Marketing & Project Management*
> *Creating Web Graphics, Audio, & Video*

Thank you for your interest in *The Advanced Website Architecture Series,* and good luck in your career as a Webmaster!

Karen McLean
Senior Managing Editor
Pearson PTR Interactive

EXECUTIVE FOREWORD

Within the next few years, you will think about the Internet in the same way you think about electricity today. Just as you don't ask a friend to "use electricity to turn on a light," you will assume the omnipresence of the Web and the capabilities that it delivers. The Web is transforming the way we live, work, and play, just as electricity changed everything for previous generations.

Every indication suggests that the explosive growth of the Web will continue. The question we need to address is, "How can we deliver the most value with this ubiquitous resource?" Today, most of the world's Web sites were created and are maintained by self-taught Webmasters. Why? Because there were limited opportunities to receive formal standards-based education. Quality, accessible, affordable education will help provide the broad range of knowledge, skills, and abilities to meet the demands of the marketplace.

Over the last three years, the World Organization of Webmasters (WOW) has worked with colleges and universities, business and industry, and its own membership of aspiring and practicing Web professionals to develop the Certified Web Professional (CWP) program. Our three-part goal is to provide:

- Educational institutions with guidelines around which to develop curricula.
- An organized way to master technical skills, content development, business proficiency and personal workplace ability.
- An assessment standard for employers to measure candidates.

The Foundations of Website Architecture Series and *The Advanced Website Architecture Series* grew organically from the communities they will serve. Written by working professionals and academics currently teaching the material, and reviewed by leading faculty at major colleges and universities and the WOW Review Board of industry professionals, these books are designed to meet the increasingly urgent need for Web professionals with expertise in three areas: technical development, design and content development, and business.

There is a huge increase in demand for qualified Web professionals, with the number of Web sites projected to grow from about 5 million today to about 25 million by the year 2002. Web professionals with business, technical, design, and project management skills are, and will continue to be, the most in-demand and will receive the highest compensation.

On behalf of WOW and its members, we wish you the best of success and welcome you to this exciting field.

William B. Cullifer
Executive Director-Founder
World Organization of Webmasters
bill@joinwow.org

INTRODUCTION

WHAT YOU WILL NEED

A networked PC with access to the Internet. The faster the connection, the less time you spend on the "World Wide Wait."

A Web browser with as many plug-ins as you can support (to experience as much marketing media as possible) and an e-mail account. In your browser preferences, please enable cookies.

HOW THIS BOOK IS ORGANIZED

In this book, and the others in this series, you are presented with a series of interactive labs. Each lab begins with Learning Objectives that define what exercises (or tasks) are covered in that lab. This is followed by an overview of the concepts that will be further explored through the exercises, which are the heart of each lab.

Each exercise consists of either a series of steps that you will follow to perform a specific task or a presentation of a particular scenario. Questions that are designed to help you discover the important things on your own are then asked of you. The answers to these questions are given at the end of the exercises, along with more in-depth discussion of the concepts explored.

At the end of each lab is a series of multiple-choice Self-Review Questions, which are designed to bolster your learning experience by providing opportunities to check your absorbtion of important material. The answers to these questions appear in the Appendix. There are also additional Self-Review Questions at this book's companion Web site, found at http://www.phptr.com/phptrinteractive/.

Finally, at the end of each chapter you will find a Test Your Thinking section, which consists of a series of projects designed to solidify all of the skills you have learned in the chapter. If you have successfully completed all of the labs in the chapter, you should be able to tackle these projects with few problems. There are not always "answers" to these projects, but where appropriate, you will find guidance and/or solutions at the companion Web site.

The final element of this book actually doesn't appear in the book at all. It is the companion Web site, and it is located at http://www.phptr.com/phptrinteractive/.

This companion Web site is closely integrated with the content of this book, and we encourage you to visit often. It is designed to provide a unique interactive online experience that will enhance your education. As mentioned, you will find guidance and solutions that will help you complete the projects found in the Test Your Thinking section of each chapter.

You will also find additional Self-Review Questions for each chapter, which are meant to give you more opportunities to become familiar with terminology and concepts presented in the publications. In the Author's Corner, you will find additional information that we think will interest you, including updates to the information presented in these publications, and discussion about the constantly changing technology Webmasters must stay involved in.

Finally, you will find a Message Board, which you can think of as a virtual study lounge. Here, you can interact with other *Advanced Website Architecture Series* readers, and share and discuss your projects.

NOTES TO THE STUDENT

This publication and the others in *The Advanced Website Architecture Series* are endorsed by the World Organization of Webmasters. The series is a training curriculum designed to provide aspiring Webmasters with the skills they need to perform in the marketplace. The skill sets included in *The Advanced Website Architecture Series* were initially collected and defined by this international trade association to create a set of core competencies for students, professionals, trainers, and employers to utilize.

NOTES TO THE INSTRUCTOR

Chances are that you are a pioneer in the education field whether you want to be one or not. Due to the explosive nature of the Internet's growth, very few Webmaster training programs are currently in existence. But while you read this, many colleges, community colleges, technical institutes, and corporate and commercial training environments are introducing this material into curriculums worldwide.

Chances are, however, that you are teaching new material in a new program. But don't fret, this publication and series are designed as a comprehensive introductory curriculum in this field. Students successfully completing this program of study will be fully prepared to assume the responsibilities of a Webmaster in the field or to engage in further training and certification in the Internet communications field.

Each chapter in this book is broken down into labs. All questions and projects have the answers and discussions associated with them. The labs and question/answer formats used in this book provide excellent opportunities for group discussions and dialogue between students and instructors. Many answers and their discussions are abbreviated in this publication for space reasons. Any comments, ideas, or suggestions to this text and series will be would be greatly appreciated.

ACKNOWLEDGMENTS

From Benay: My sincere appreciation to my supportive family, particularly my wonderful daughter Cassie, for encouraging me to develop, teach, and write about Web technology.

From Drew: My thanks to my family, who encouraged me to take on this project.

From Bebo: I am grateful to

- Robert Cailliau and Tim Berners-Lee who let me share their visions a decade ago and have continued to support me.
- My book co-authors who worked tirelessly to make this book series the best that it could be.
- Bill Cullifer of WOW for finding in Prentice Hall, a publisher not interested in just another book series on the Web, but a series that dares to address many of the Web management issues that have been previously overlooked or ignored.
- Karen McLean of Prentice Hall for a patient, yet firm, hand that pushed this project to completion.

ABOUT THE AUTHORS

Benay Dara-Abrams (http://www.dara-abrams.com/benay) is CEO of BrainJolt (http://www.brainjolt.com) and designer of the Web-based Online Adaptive Learning Environment™. Benay has been involved in the Internet since ARPANet days in 1970 and in Web development since 1993. She managed the development of the first WYSIWYG HTML Editor and the first commercial Web-based intranet. She served as Curriculum Development Director for the Stanford University Western Institute of Computer Science. Benay has developed and taught intensive courses in Electronic Commerce and Web Business Management and in Networking Fundamentals for Webmasters at Stanford University and the University of Hong Kong. She was co-founder and Director of Engineering for Silicon Valley Public Access Link, a community network ISP. Benay has been involved in electronic commerce since 1980, when she managed public packet-switched network-based services for travel and home banking. She plans to complete her PhD in Computer Science and Educational Psychology in 2001.

Drew Dara-Abrams serves as CTO (Chief Technology Officer) for BrainJolt (http://www.brainjolt.com), an online learning technology start-up venture. He has designed and taught classes on Internet, Web design, programming, and advanced topics in computers to both adults and children. He has also served as Webmaster and Network and Systems Administrator for a number of high-tech start-ups, schools, and summer camps. He can be found on the Internet at drew@drewnet.net and http://drew.dara-abrams.com.

Trevor Peace has a degree in computer science from Carleton College. He is currently working as a computer consultant in the San Francisco area.

Bebo White is a member of the technical staff at the Stanford Linear Accelerator Center (SLAC), the high-energy physics laboratory operated by Stanford University. He also holds academic appointments at the University of California, Berkeley, the University of San Francisco, and Hong Kong University.

He was fortunate enough to become involved with WWW development quite early while on sabbatical at CERN in 1989. Consequently, he was a part of the team instrumental in establishing the first non-European Web site at SLAC in December, 1991.

Bebo has authored and co-authored multiple books and articles. He has lectured and spoken internationally to academic and commercial audiences and has been particularly involved with two major international conference series: the Computing in High Energy Physics (CHEP) Conference and the International World Wide Web Conference. He served as Co-Chair of the Sixth International World Wide Web Conference, co-hosted by SLAC and Stanford University.

In 1996, Mr. White was added to the Micro Times 100 list of those making outstanding contributions to personal computing. He is a member of the IW3C2 (International World Wide Web Conference Committee), a fellow of the International World Wide Web Institute (IWWWI) and is cited by the World Wide Web Consortium.

CHAPTER 1

NETWORKING FUNDAMENTALS FOR WEBMASTERS

CHAPTER OBJECTIVES	
In this chapter, you will learn about:	
✔ Networks and Network Characteristics	Page 3
✔ The Open Systems Interconnection (OSI) Reference Model	Page 8
✔ Internetworks and Network Topologies	Page 14
✔ Networks Characterized by Spatial Distance	Page 20
✔ Intranets and Extranets	Page 26

The Web, email, and voice communications all sit on top of networks. We use networks of many types in our jobs, in our homes, and when we travel. However, many people are uncomfortable with all the acronyms and jargon used in the worlds of telephony, cable, networking, and the Internet. Some people contend that consumer electronics, computing, and telecommunications are all converging. Others (with whom I agree) do not foresee a single point of convergence, with a TV, telephone, PIM (Personal Information Manager), and networked computer all rolled into one appliance. However, there is much confluence occurring among the areas of computing, telecommunications, and consumer electronics. Witness the development of Digital Home Networks; the development of PIMs combining email, calendaring, and even a cellular phone; the availability of set-top boxes to surf the Web on your TV. Given the direction toward everything being networked in some way, it is important that we, as Web professionals, understand the fundamentals of networking. Therefore, in the first section of this book, Chapters 1 through 6, we provide you with an understanding of the terminology, concepts, and technologies involved in networking today.

LAB 1.1

NETWORKS AND NETWORK CHARACTERISTICS

LAB OBJECTIVES

After this lab, you will be able to:

✔ Identify Different Types of Networks
✔ Identify Network Resource-Sharing Facilities

What is a network? A network is a set of nodes interconnected by communication paths. Network nodes may be systems that are functioning as Web servers, email servers, firewalls, Web clients, application servers, or in other capacities. Networks can interconnect with other networks. Networks may also contain sub-networks.

A network may be characterized in terms of:

- Its topology
- The spatial distance it covers
- The data transmission technology it employs
- The type of signal it carries
- Whether it is a public network, or whether access is controlled to the network
- The type of connections that are used
- The type of physical links used

LAB 1.1

Lab 1.1: Networks and Network Characteristics

The topology of a network is its general configuration. Bus, ring, and star topologies are three major network topologies. Network topologies are discussed in greater detail in Lab 1.3.

Networks may cover different spatial distances as described in the name of each type: Local Area Networks (LANs), Metropolitan Area Networks (MANs), and Wide Area Networks (WANs). Spatial distance characteristics are described further in Lab 1.4.

Networks may use various technologies to transmit data. Chapter 5 discusses such technologies as DSL (Digital Subscriber Line) and ISDN (Integrated Services Digital Network).

One characteristic of a network is the type of signals it carries. Does the network carry voice signals, data signals, or a mixture of voice and data signals?

A network may also be described in terms of the people who are allowed to use this particular network. Is the network considered a private network or a public network? Is there access control to allow various levels of public and controlled access to the network?

Networks can be differentiated in terms of the nature of the connections they use. We can describe a network according to the following characteristics:

- Connections between network nodes—dial-up or switched
- Network—switched or dedicated (nonswitched)
- Virtual connections between network nodes—no direct physical connections between nodes

Physical links between nodes characterize networks. Organizations may use optical fiber, coaxial (coax) cable, or copper wire for their physical network connectivity.

In the 1980s, with the rapidly growing installed base of PCs in companies and organizations, LANs (Local Area Networks) were implemented to connect PCs to each other. LANs were also implemented to provide for sharing of resources, such as high-performance or color printers and high-capacity storage on file servers. WANs (Wide Area Networks) were developed to interconnect LANs in the 1980s.

In 1983, to bring about consistency and provide a framework for network protocols, a group of computer and telecommunications companies worked together to develop the Open Systems Interconnection (OSI) model. The OSI model provides a framework to describe how messages should be transmitted between points in a network. The plan was for other groups to take on the task of developing the detailed interfaces. The OSI reference model guides engineers in their development of interfaces between products and network nodes. The International Standards Organization (ISO) standardized the OSI model in 1984, hoping that it would become the standard description of networks, on which interface specifications would be developed. These interface specifications have been developed and turned into standards over time. The OSI model defines seven layers of functions that take place in a communication between points in a network. We'll discuss the OSI model in detail in the next lab.

LAB 1.1 EXERCISES

1.1.1 IDENTIFY DIFFERENT TYPES OF NETWORKS

a) Make a chart of various network characteristics.

b) Based on what you have learned about the characteristics of networks, do you think they can be mixed and matched?

___

___

1.1.2 IDENTIFY NETWORK RESOURCE-SHARING FACILITIES

a) Take a look at the network facilities that you use in your organization today. What resource-sharing facilities do your networks provide?

___

___

LAB 1.2 EXERCISE ANSWERS

1.1.1 ANSWERS

a) Make a chart of various network characteristics.

	Topology		
Characteristic	Bus	Ring	Star
Spatial Distance	LAN	MAN	WAN
Data Transmission Technology	DSL	ISDN	T-carrier
Type of Signal	Voice	Data	Voice and Data
Public or access-controlled	Private	Public	Access Control—levels of public and controlled access
Type of connections	Dial-up or switched	Switched or dedicated	Virtual connections
Type of physical links	Copper wire	Coaxial cable	Optical fiber

b) Based on what you have learned about the characteristics of networks, do you think they can be mixed and matched?

Answer: Yes, in general, but there are some mixtures that are more common than others. For example, a network with the characteristic of large spatial distance, a wide area network, may transmit both data and voice and offer public access via dial-up or switched connections.

1.1.2 ANSWER

a) Take a look at the network facilities that you use in your organization today. What resource-sharing facilities do your networks provide?

Answer: We'll consider a typical organization that has multiple LANs connecting PCs and uses the Internet for Wide Area Networking. The PC client systems may share such resources as high-speed laser printers, color printers, file servers with licensed software, back-up storage, and Internet access.

LAB 1.1 SELF-REVIEW QUESTIONS

In order to test your progress, you should be able to answer the following questions.

1) Network nodes may be systems that are functioning as which of the following? (Select all that apply.)

   a) _____ Web servers
   b) _____ Email servers
   c) _____ Paper shredders
   d) _____ Web clients

2) A large city most likely uses which type of network?

   a) _____ LAN
   b) _____ WAN
   c) _____ MAN
   d) _____ Both b and c

3) The Open Systems Interconnection model was developed to provide a framework for network protocols.

   a) _____ True
   b) _____ False

4) WANs are used to connect which of the following?

   a) _____ MANs
   b) _____ LANs
   c) _____ Individual nodes

5) Connections between network nodes can be which of the following?

   a) _____ Dial-up
   b) _____ Switched
   c) _____ Dedicated
   d) _____ Virtual
   e) _____ All of the above

Quiz answers appear in the Appendix, Section 1.1.

LAB 1.2

THE OPEN SYSTEMS INTERCONNECTION (OSI) REFERENCE MODEL

> **LAB OBJECTIVES**
>
> After this lab, you will be able to:
> - Identify Where HTTP Fits in the OSI Model
> - Give Examples of Protocols on Different Layers

The OSI (Open Systems Interconnection) model of networking was developed by a group of telecommunications companies for their use to advance the implementation of standard interfaces. In order to promulgate the reference model, the development group worked with the International Organization for Standardization, ISO (www.iso.ch). The OSI model of networking is meant to describe the different layered components that together allow users of a shared networking medium to communicate with each other. Though the OSI model is often referred to in the context of networking discussions, it is not a specifically followed set of standards but rather a generalization of the processes and pieces that together make up a computer network.

The OSI model is based on the concept that the process of communications between two end users in a telecommunications network can be divided into layers, with each layer adding special related functions. The central concepts supported by the OSI model are based on three major components: services, interfaces, and protocols. In a message between users, the model describes the flow of data

Lab 1.2: The Open Systems Interconnection (OSI) Reference Model

through each layer at one end down through the layers in that computer. When the message arrives, the model describes the flow of data up through the layers in the receiving computer. The flow of data eventually reaches the end user.

The model is composed of seven layers of functionality, employing a hardware/software combination that includes the operating system, applications (often including a browser), TCP/IP, and the signal on the line. The telecommunications process is divided into seven layers, with the layers divided into two major tiers. The top tier consists of the upper four layers and is responsible for handling the message passing from and to the user. The bottom tier, which consists of the lower three layers, handles the message passing through the host. Messages intended for this host computer pass to the upper layers. Messages for another host are not passed to the upper layers but are instead forwarded to another host.

The OSI model is defined as a layered architecture consisting of the following seven layers, as shown in Figure 1.1.

The top layer, layer 7, provides facilities to identify communication partners. In addition, the quality of service (QOS) expected or required for this particular transmission is identified. User authentication and privacy are also considered in layer 7. Layer 7 functionality is responsible for identifying any constraints on the data syntax. While some applications may perform the application layer functions, layer 7 does not include the application itself.

OSI Layer 6 provides presentation facilities. Layer 6 is usually part of the operating system. Layer 6 converts incoming and outgoing data from one presentation format to another. For this reason, layer 6 is sometimes called the syntax layer. An example of layer 6 processing is a text stream updated in a pop-up window with text that has just arrived.

Layer 5 is called the session layer. The session layer sets up conversations. In this layer, exchanges are communicated. In addition, layer 5 handles the termination of dialogs between applications at each end. The session layer's task is to coordinate connections and the beginning and end of a dialogue.

Layer 7	Application
Layer 6	Presentation
Layer 5	Session
Layer 4	Transport
Layer 3	Network
Layer 2	Data Link
Layer 1	Physical

Figure 1.1 ■ **The OSI model.**

The upper layers (5–7) of the OSI model are often grouped together and referred to as the application layer. In this context, the upper layers would refer generically to a "program," such as a web browser. This program is written in some common computer language such as C and compiled into an application. The program, as written in C, encompasses the functionality of layers 5 through 7. Discerning between the individual layers can sometimes be difficult.

Layers 1 through 4 are, for the most part, well differentiated in typical computer networks.

Layer 4 is called the transport layer. The transport layer is very important, managing end-to-end control of the communication. One example of layer 4 processing is to determine whether all packets have arrived. Layer 4 also manages error checking and ensures complete data transfer. The dominant protocols in layer four are TCP (Transmission Control Protocol) and UDP (User Datagram Protocol). At the present time, TCP is the dominant protocol at layer 4 and UDP is a lesser-known but also used layer 4 protocol. Both TCP and UDP sit on top of the dominant layer 3 protocol, IP (Internet Protocol).

Layer 3, the network layer, handles the routing of data. Layer 3 processing includes the sending of data in the right direction and sending the transmission to the right destination. Layer 3 receives the transmission at the packet level. Routing and forwarding are also included in layer 3 processing. The function of layer 3 is to integrate the many different types of layer 2 technologies into a common interface for the upper layers. Layer 3 has its own addressing scheme, distinct from layer 2. Though IP is the dominant protocol in layer 3 today, there have been some successful predecessors.

Layer 2 is the data link layer. The data link layer handles error control. Layer 2 also provides facilities for synchronization, addressing, and modulation for the physical level. OSI layer 2 manages the transmission protocol. The transmission scheme consists of addressing, modulation, and synchronization. The transmission scheme is often tied to a particular physical medium on the layer 1 level. The most common example of a layer 2 technology is Ethernet. Ethernet has a well-defined addressing scheme that is entirely its own. The Ethernet addressing scheme should not be confused with the IP addressing scheme on layer 3. Other commonly used data link technologies are PPP (Point-to-Point Protocol), used for modem connections, and FDDI (Fiber Distributed Data Interface), which is used over fiber optic cables.

Layer 1 is the physical layer. The physical layer conveys the bit stream through the network. Layer 1 provides the hardware mechanism to transmit the message, via electrical and mechanical means. The physical layer sends the data on the carrier and also receives the data on the carrier. Layer 1 consists of the set of wires and fiber optic cables that transmit electronic or optical signals from one point to the next. Layer 1 also defines the type of connectors and various other hardware

Lab 1.2: The Open Systems Interconnection (OSI) Reference Model   **11**

characteristics. Examples of layer 1 technology include coaxial, fiber optic and twisted pair cable, telephone wires, microwave transceivers and dishes, as well as infrared technology.

LAB 1.2 EXERCISES

1.2.1 IDENTIFY WHERE HTTP FITS IN THE OSI MODEL

a) Take a look at the OSI model. Where do you think HTTP (Hypertext Transfer Protocol) fits in the OSI model?

_____

_____

1.2.2 GIVE EXAMPLES OF PROTOCOLS ON DIFFERENT LAYERS

Review the layers of the OSI model.

a) Give examples of protocols operating at different layers.

_____

_____

LAB 1.2 EXERCISE ANSWERS

1.2.1 ANSWER

a) Take a look at the OSI model. Where do you think HTTP (Hypertext Transfer Protocol) fits in the OSI model?

Answer: HTTP, the Hypertext Transfer Protocol, operates on top of TCP. TCP/IP is the protocol (along with TCP's cousin UDP) on which all Web traffic rides. In particular, HTTP is built upon TCP (Transmission Control Protocol). Much of the Internet's success is due to the fundamental strength and scalability of these lower layer protocols. Though TCP/IP is commonly referred to as the layer 3 protocol of the Internet, a more careful statement would include both UDP and TCP as higher layer processes that take advantage of the Internet Protocol (IP). When we refer to TCP/IP as the transmission protocols of the Internet, we implicitly include UDP.

Lab 1.2: The Open Systems Interconnection (OSI) Reference Model

1.2.2 Answer

Review the layers of the OSI model.

a) Give examples of protocols operating at different layers.

Answer: In layer 4, the transport layer, the main protocols are: TCP (Transmission Control Protocol) and UDP (User Datagram Protocol). IP (Internet Protocol) is the main protocol for layer 3, the network. The PPP (Point-to-Point) protocol operates on layer 2.

LAB 1.2 SELF-REVIEW QUESTIONS

In order to test your progress, you should be able to answer the following questions.

1) The OSI model is _____.

   a) _____ a specifically followed set of standards
   b) _____ a generalization of the processes and pieces that together make up a computer network
   c) _____ LAN protocols
   d) _____ WAN protocols

2) The OSI model includes _____.

   a) _____ hardware
   b) _____ software
   c) _____ firmware
   d) _____ both a and b

3) Put the following layers of the OSI model in order (highest to lowest).

   a) _____ Data Link
   b) _____ Presentation
   c) _____ Network
   d) _____ Transport
   e) _____ Physical

4) What is the most common example of technology used in the data link layer?

   a) _____ Point-to-Point Protocol
   b) _____ Fiber Distributed Data Interface
   c) _____ Ethernet
   d) _____ Extranet

Lab 1.2: The Open Systems Interconnection (OSI) Reference Model

5) What kind of facilities does OSI layer 6 provide?

    a) _____ Conversion of incoming data
    b) _____ Security
    c) _____ Presentation functionality
    d) _____ ISDN
    e) _____ All of the above
    f) _____ Both a and c

Quiz answers appear in the Appendix, Section 1.2.

LAB 1.2

LAB 1.3

INTERNETWORKS AND NETWORK TOPOLOGIES

> **LAB OBJECTIVES**
>
> After this lab, you will be able to:
> - Identify Various Network Topologies
> - Understand the Function of Internetworks

The proliferation of LANs resulted in significant problems. Isolated LANs led to a duplication of resources, defeating the purpose of connecting systems for sharing resources. Major problems started to arise from the lack of network management across LANs. There were discussions of islands of automation and islands of information reducing the overall effectiveness of networking in organizations. Lacking a centralized method of troubleshooting, it became increasingly expensive and difficult to support large numbers of isolated local area networks across a large organization. Enter internetworks.

An internetwork is a collection of individual networks. Intermediate networking devices provide connections between the network nodes between networks. On the Internet, these intermediate networking devices are routers that determine the next network point to which a packet should be forwarded toward its destination. An internetwork functions as a single large network. An advantage of an internetwork is that it can span disparate technologies. In addition, different sites may use different types of media. Different sites may operate at varying speeds. An internetwork provides consistent, reliable access to resources, connecting the islands created by departmental LANs.

Network topologies are the general configurations of networks. Three major network topologies are: bus, ring, and star topologies.

In the bus topology, the bus is considered to be the transmission path. In the bus network configuration, signals are dropped off or picked up at every device attached to the line. Only the devices addressed by the signals pay attention to the signals. Other devices simply discard the signals as they are transmitted through the network. A bus network is a network topology or circuit arrangement in which all devices are attached to the line directly. All signals pass through each device. In the network, each device has a unique identity, and each device recognizes signals intended for it.

A ring network is defined as a network topology or circuit arrangement in which each device is attached along the same signal path to two other devices. A ring network forms a path in the shape of a ring. Each device in a ring network has a unique address. Information flow in a ring network is unidirectional. A ring network includes a controlling device, which is responsible for intercepting and managing the flow to and from the ring.

Various types of access methods can be implemented by means of different physical-level topologies. The most prevalent form of ring network topology is a token ring network. A token ring network is a type of local area network (LAN) in which all workstations are connected in a ring or star topology. A bus topology LAN can also use a token-passing scheme. The token-passing scheme prevents collision between two workstations that want to send messages at the same time. In the token-passing scheme, empty information frames are continuously circulated on the ring. When a workstation wants to send a message, it inserts a token into an empty frame. Inserting a token into a frame may simply consist of changing the value 0 to the value 1 in the token bit part of the frame. Then the workstation inserts a message and a destination identifier (ID) into the frame. As it moves around the network, the frame is examined by each workstation. If the workstation is the destination for this message, the workstation copies the message from the frame. The workstation then changes the token back to the value of 0 to indicate that there is no message in the frame. Then the frame is sent back to the originator. When the originating workstation sees that the token has been changed to the value 0, it knows that the message has been copied and received at its destination. The originating workstation then removes the message from the frame. After this, the frame continues to circulate as an "empty" frame. In this way, the empty frame is ready for a workstation to use when it has a message to send. The standard for token ring protocol is the IEEE 802.5 standard. The best known implementation of the token ring protocol is the IBM Token Ring Network, which is widely used in corporate LANs. Another example of a token ring network is the Fiber Distributed-Data Interface (FDDI), a newer network configuration developed to transmit data throughout larger campus environments across fiber optic links.

In a star topology, all attached devices are wired directly to a central network hub. The hub establishes the network connections. The hub is also responsible

16 *Lab 1.3: Internetworks and Network Topologies*

for maintaining and breaking connections. In a star topology, it is easy to isolate problem nodes. However, if a network hub fails, the entire system is affected.

A star topology, such as 10Base-T Ethernet, is the type of network configuration that is best suited for campuses comprised of multiple buildings. The star topology is an appropriate topology for fiber optic links.

LAB 1.3 EXERCISES

1.3.1 IDENTIFY VARIOUS NETWORK TOPOLOGIES

a) Draw a diagram of a bus network topology.

b) Draw a diagram of a ring network topology.

c) Draw a diagram of a star network topology.

1.3.2 UNDERSTAND THE FUNCTION OF INTERNETWORKS

a) Consider your organization. What internetworks are in operation within your organization?

___

b) What internetworks are in operation between your organization and other organizations?

___

c) What function do these internetworks serve?

___

LAB 1.3 EXERCISE ANSWERS

1.3.1 ANSWERS

a) Draw a diagram of a bus network topology.

Answer:

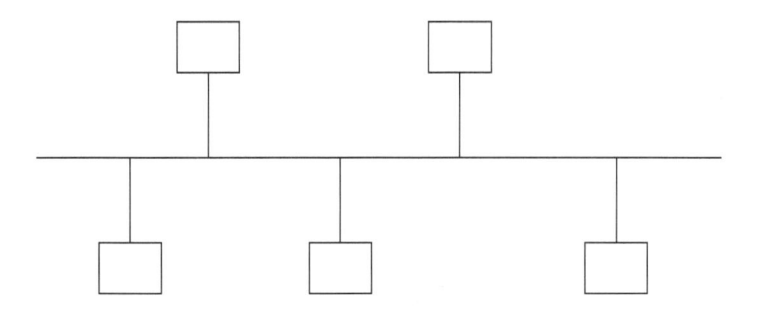

Lab 1.3: Internetworks and Network Topologies

b) Draw a diagram of a ring network topology.

Answer:

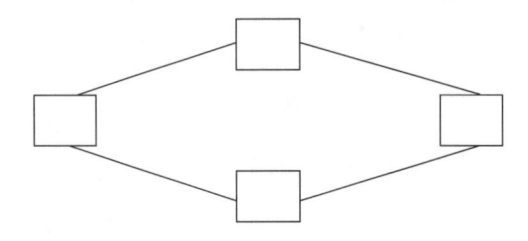

c) Draw a diagram of a star network topology.

Answer:

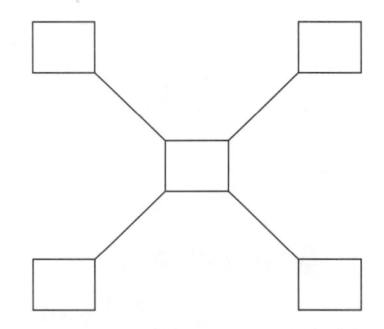

1.3.2 ANSWERS

a) Consider your organization. What internetworks are in operation within your organization?

Answer: In our start-up organization, there is an internetwork that connects all the PCs and Linux servers to the router. The router connects all the devices to the Internet.

b) What internetworks are in operation between your organization and other organizations?

Answer: In a larger organization, there are internetworks between regional sales offices with their local networks connecting PCs and print servers and the corporate headquarters local network containing its PCs, print servers, and mainframes with enterprise databases.

Lab 1.3: Internetworks and Network Topologies

c) What function do these internetworks serve?

Answer: The internetwork in the start-up organization serves to provide Internet access to all devices via one common router, which is then one point of expense. In the large organization where the internetwork connects the regional sales offices to the corporate headquarters, the internetwork provides access to enterprise databases in a consistent fashion to all the regional sales offices.

LAB 1.3 SELF-REVIEW QUESTIONS

In order to test your progress, you should be able to answer the following questions.

1) Each device on a ring network has its own unique address.

   a) _____ True
   b) _____ False

2) Internetworks can do which of the following?

   a) _____ Span disparate technologies
   b) _____ Span different types of media
   c) _____ Provide consistent access to resources
   d) _____ All of the above

3) In a bus network, which of the following are true?

   a) _____ Only the devices addressed by the signals pay attention to the signals.
   b) _____ Devices pass the signal around in a circle until it is claimed by a device.
   c) _____ All devices are attached to a central hub.
   d) _____ None of the above.

4) Internetworks are necessary to support Web sites.

   a) _____ True
   b) _____ False

5) Which of the following are true of the star network topology? (Select all that apply.)

   a) _____ Each device is wired to the next one in the network.
   b) _____ The hub provides network connections.
   c) _____ The failure of the network hub doesn't affect other nodes on the network.
   d) _____ The star network topology is well-suited for corporate campuses with multiple buildings.

Quiz answers appear in the Appendix, Section 1.3.

LAB 1.4

NETWORKS CHARACTERIZED BY SPATIAL DISTANCE

> **LAB OBJECTIVES**
>
> After this lab, you will be able to:
>
> ✔ Understand the Benefits of LAN Technology
> ✔ Relate Spatial Characterization to the Internet, Intranets, and Extranets

We have seen that we can characterize networks in terms of their topologies or configurations. Now let's consider networks in terms of the spatial distances that they span.

In terms of spatial distance characteristics, the three major types of networks are:

- Local Area Networks (LANs)
- Metropolitan Area Networks (MANs)
- Wide Area Networks (WANs)

LAN is the acronym that stands for Local Area Network. A LAN consists of a network of interconnected workstations or servers. In a LAN, the workstations are connected to each other so that they are able to share the resources of a single processor or server. When LANs were first installed and configured, they were built to serve a relatively small geographic area. Physical limitations limited the area that they could serve and LANs were thus used to support small organizations or departments within larger organizations. With FDDI technology, LANs are able to extend over much wider areas.

LANs can serve as few as four or five users who want to share resources within their group. Using any LAN access technology such as FDDI, Ethernet, Token Ring, or ATM (asynchronous transfer mode), LANs can serve as many as several thousand users. Note that ATM is a high-performance, cell-oriented switching and multiplexing technology utilizing fixed-length packets in order to carry different types of traffic.

Some examples of technologies used to implement LANs include: Ethernet, FDDI (Fiber Distributed Data Interface), and token ring.

We will discuss Ethernet and FDDI technologies in Chapter 2, "Architectures, Devices, and Connections." We discussed token ring technology in the last section.

Although the terms LAN and WAN are used quite often to describe networks, the term MAN is used less frequently. The acronym MAN stands for Metropolitan Area Network. A MAN interconnects users with computer resources. Although there is no precise definition of capacity, a MAN is larger than a LAN but smaller than a WAN. A MAN groups LANs together and offers an efficient way to connect to a WAN. A MAN provides facilities for the interconnection of LANs into a campus-wide network. MANs are designed for bridging LANs with backbone lines.

A MAN may provide the backbone lines for the interconnection of networks in a city into a single larger network. This is the case in the state of Pennsylvania, whose government decided to provide facilities to interconnect all state agencies in the region in and around Harrisburg, the state capital of Pennsylvania. In the Harrisburg MAN, there are more than 25,000 individual users working in state agencies interconnected to other users within the state agency system. Another example of a MAN can be found in Trieste, Italy, where the community hosts a MAN for individual users within Trieste boundaries.

A WAN is the term used to indicate a Wide Area Network. WANs provide services to geographically dispersed users. WANs are also used to interconnect LANs. A WAN may be privately owned by a single corporation or large organization. Alternatively, a WAN may be leased or rented from a telecommunications vendor. Individual users may connect via a WAN using normal home or business telephone lines, sometimes referred to as POTS (Plain Old Telephone Service). The WAN or WANs used by the members of an organization usually includes public or shared user networks. At this point, the shared WAN is most often the Internet accessed via the ISP (Internet Service Provider) the organization uses for its router or the ISPs to which individual users subscribe.

LAB 1.4 EXERCISES

1.4.1 UNDERSTAND THE BENEFITS OF LAN TECHNOLOGY

Consider a local area network (LAN) in operation in your organization.

    a) What functions does/can the LAN serve?

_____

_____

    b) What benefits can your organization gain from using a LAN?

_____

_____

1.4.2 RELATE SPATIAL CHARACTERIZATION TO THE INTERNET, INTRANETS, AND EXTRANETS

    a) Do the terms LAN, MAN, or WAN imply the use of a particular technology to implement the network connectivity?

_____

_____

LAB 1.4 EXERCISE ANSWERS

1.4.1 ANSWERS

Consider a local area network (LAN) in operation in your organization.

    a) What functions does/can the LAN serve?

        Answer: A LAN server can host a suite of application programs. In this case, users download a specific application, such as FrameMaker, a desktop publishing system. Each user runs selected applications on his or her own desktop. In the case of a large application, users can offload components of the application onto the server. The LAN server can also provide version control for an application, providing all users access to the same revision of the application. When new releases become available, the server application is updated.

LANs are also used to share laser printers or color printers. Printers can be connected to the LAN server and used throughout the group served by the LAN. Another important function of the LAN server is to provide a facility for message exchange. The LAN server acts as an intermediate transmission point between the main gateway and the outside world, forwarding messages to individual desktop systems. The LAN server may also function as a file server, allowing multiple users to share files with each other via the file server. In addition, a LAN server may function as a departmental or even organizational Web server.

b) What benefits can your organization gain from using a LAN?

Answer: Having a LAN server host a suite of application programs is a useful way to share access to large, expensive application programs. In a shared application server environment in which I worked, a group of software engineers and managers shared access to several copies of the FrameMaker publishing system. A license server ran on the shared server, which was also used as an intermediate mail server, passing on email from the corporate gateway through the LAN server onto individual workstations. When an individual wished to use FrameMaker, he or she accessed the license server to obtain a temporary license. Once in a while, more users wished to simultaneously use FrameMaker than the number of licenses that were available, but this did not happen very often. In most situations, the licenses were shared with no problem and the company was able to license one copy of the software for every ten people in the group, saving the company a fair amount of money. Also, since FrameMaker was a large application, users did not want to always store it on the desktop machines and they were happy to offload components of the application onto the server. In addition, by storing the FrameMaker application on the server, all the users have the same revision of the application. It is not necessary to update individual workstations when new releases of the application become available.

LANs are also used to share expensive laser printers or color printers. Printers can be connected to the LAN server and shared throughout the group served by the LAN. This reduces organizational expenses. In addition, printers can then be accessed in a common room rather than kept in individual offices. Another important function of the LAN server is to provide a facility for message exchange. The LAN server may be an intermediate transmission point between the main gateway and the outside world, with the LAN server forwarding messages to individual desktop systems. With IMAP (Internet Message Access Protocol) mail protocols, messages are stored on a server and can be accessed from individual workstations but are not kept on the individual systems themselves. This facilitates access to email by users who are in and out of the office, traveling and needing mobile access to email via their laptops. The LAN server may also function as a file server, allowing multiple users to share files with each other via the file server. File sharing can reduce expenses by sharing storage media among members of the group as well as increase communication through easy sharing of documents. The LAN administrator is responsible for maintaining read and write access to specific files residing on the file server. Back-up and recovery facilities can reduce the loss or corruption of important information. In addition, a LAN server may function as a departmental or even organizational Web server, offering access to shared information via the Web. This is another facility that can facilitate communication and sharing of information among members of a work group as well as between a work group and the rest of the organization. If the LAN server doubles as a Web server, it is important to develop a plan to protect both the data and applications that are stored on the LAN server.

1.4.2 ANSWER

a) Do the terms LAN, MAN, or WAN imply the use of a particular technology to implement the network connectivity?

Answer: No, LANs, MANs, and WANs may use whatever network technologies are available and meet the needs of the organizations using these networks. With the popularity of Ethernet and the Internet, a LAN may use Ethernet to connect individual users and workstations to an intranet, and a WAN most often uses the Internet. A MAN may be an extranet, with shared access to resources by a community of interest. All may thus use Internet technologies but in different configurations and with different physical links. We will discuss intranets and extranets in the next lab.

LAB 1.4 SELF-REVIEW QUESTIONS

In order to test your progress, you should be able to answer the following questions.

1) LANs are used to _____.

    a) _____ connect MANs
    b) _____ share printers
    c) _____ share files
    d) _____ host application programs
    e) _____ none of the above

2) Put in order of size from largest to smallest.

    a) _____ WAN
    b) _____ LAN
    c) _____ MAN

Lab 1.4: Networks Characterized by Spatial Distance

3) FDDI is used to implement LANs.

   a) _____ True
   b) _____ False

4) License servers are used in the following ways: (Select all that apply.)

   a) _____ They run on servers on a LAN.
   b) _____ They provide access to shared applications.
   c) _____ They use the HTTP protocol for application sharing.
   d) _____ They reduce the expense of licensing certain applications.

5) A MAN is a necessary component of a network configuration.

   a) _____ True
   b) _____ False

Quiz answers appear in the Appendix, Section 1.4.

LAB 1.4

LAB 1.5

INTRANETS AND EXTRANETS

> **LAB OBJECTIVES**
>
> After this lab, you will be able to:
>
> ✓ Describe the Major Components of an Intranet and an Extranet
> ✓ Understand the Differences Between Intranets, Extranets, and the Internet

Sun Microsystems has an extensive intranet, providing employees with information on such company-internal information as benefit plans. Hewlett-Packard supports electronic commerce transactions through its extranet. An intranet can be defined as a network that employs standard Internet protocols, such as TCP/IP and HTTP, to connect a set of clients within an organization or group of associated clients supporting a community of interest. Here the focus is on the network protocols and on the clients served by the network. Another way to define an intranet is as a network using the Internet Protocol (IP) to connect multiple nodes behind a firewall. Here, the emphasis moves to the internal aspect of the network, one of the key characteristics that distinguish an intranet from an extranet or the Internet. Intranets caught on quickly; in fact, many organizations moved forward with their intranet plans, with or without serving publicly accessible content on the Internet. Now let's take a look at intranets and extranets.

Another way to define an intranet is in terms of the services it provides. An intranet can then be defined as pseudo-Internet services inside an organization, in-house or on a LAN, that may span the organization's information network. These services include the use of Internet technologies and may also include such services as: PC-to-host connectivity, mobile communications, client/server networks, and the integration of data warehouses.

We can map out a rough correspondence between the components of an intranet and the architecture of a multi-tier client/server system, as shown in Figure 1.2.

Lab 1.5: Intranets and Extranets

Client Layer

- Web Browser
  e.g., Netscape Communicator, Internet Explorer, Opera, Lynx

Business Logic Tier

- Web Server — e.g., Microsoft IIS
- Web Server — e.g., Apache
- Web Server — e.g., Netscape Enterprise Server
- Java Servlets
- Web Application Server — e.g., Cold Fusion
- Web Application Server — e.g., Netscape Application Server

Middleware

- CGI — e.g., PERL or TCL scripts
- JDBC (Java Data Base Connectivity) Driver
- ODBC (Open Database Connectivity)
- Application Server API

Transaction Management Layer

- Component Transaction Server (×4)

Backend Data Storage

- Database Server — e.g., Oracle
- Database Server — e.g., SQL Server

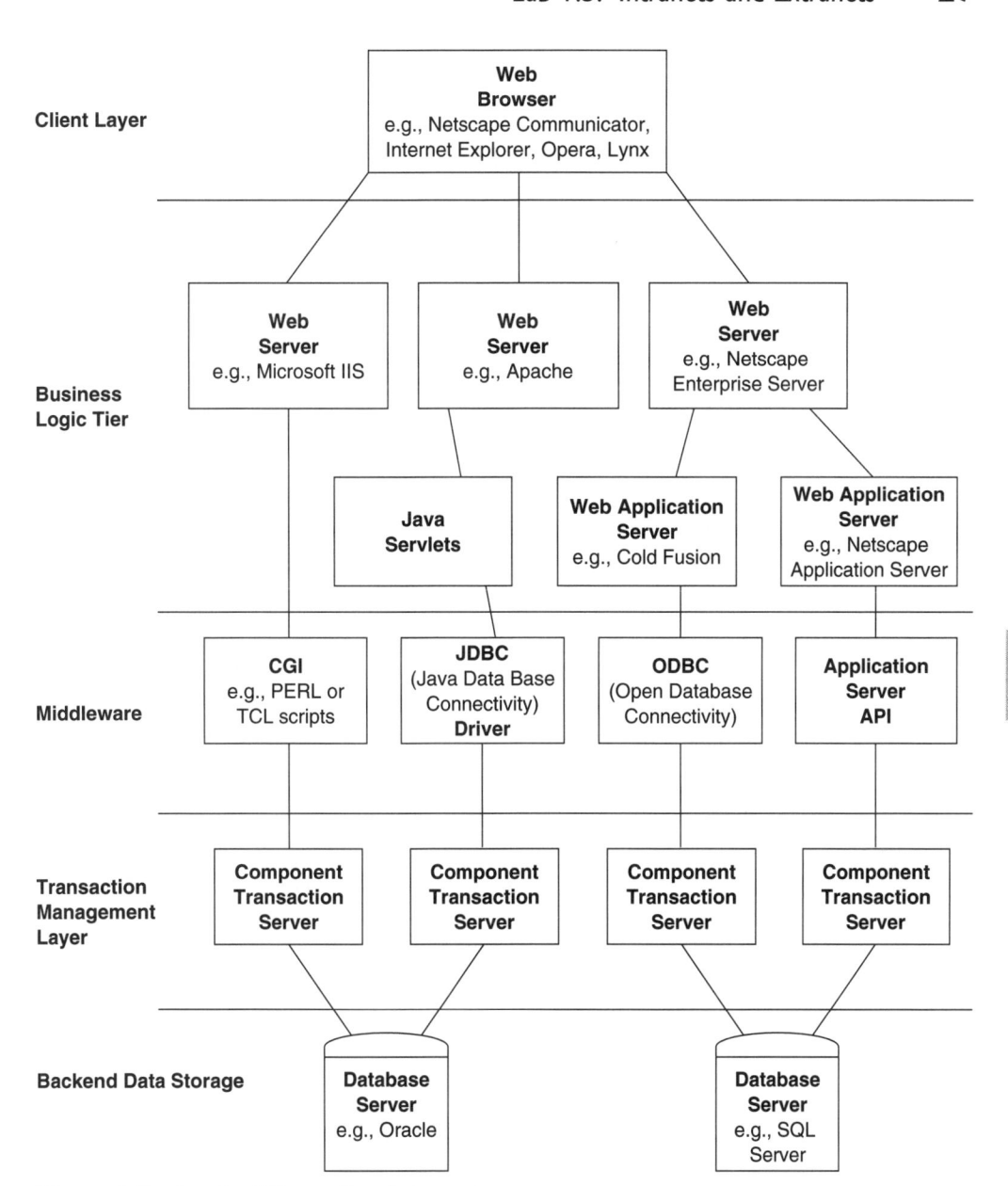

Figure 1.2 ■ Logical View of an Intranet.

- In the top tier, the browser corresponds to the client layer.
- In the second tier, the Web server and optional application server(s) are part of the business logic tier.
- The third tier is the middleware layer, which most commonly contains CGI scripts. The middleware layer may also include JDBC drivers as well as specific application server APIs, most often developed in-house to connect to operational applications.
- The lower level is the transaction manager layer, which may consist of a component transaction server. Component transaction servers function as interfaces to the back-end database servers.
- Database servers are often connected into the intranet via transaction servers. Therefore, the lowest tier constitutes the back-end data stores, or in intranet parlance, the database servers, such as Oracle and SQL Server.
- Search and retrieval tools developed for the Internet can be used on the intranet to locate specific pieces of data. One of the important advantages of using Internet technology for your intranet is that you can use the same tools you use to access information outside your organization when you're accessing information within and across your organization.

In 1996, when organizations started to realize the benefit from working with their trusted partners using the Internet infrastructure, Bob Metcalfe, inventor of the Ethernet, coined the term extranet. An extranet is defined as a network using Internet communication protocols that runs over a Virtual Private Network and supports a community of trading partners. An extranet uses Web browser technology to provide support to members of the community it supports on a "community controlled" basis. An extranet provides Internet-like connectivity with the added advantage of providing isolation from general Internet users and traffic. However, all members of the extranet need to have compatible applications for shared use.

Extranets are very similar to intranets in terms of their components. The key components include:

- IP-based network connectivity.
- Hardware, usually including at least one Web server and at least one firewall.
- Software including network facilities, Web server (HTTPD—HTTP daemon), and business application software to be used by an organization and its partners and that can be used through their firewalls.
- Network security facilities and defined measures.

The network connection is IP (Internet Protocol)-based. The network connection can be provided via various types of connections:

- Dial-up line
- Leased or private line
- Secure tunnel on the Internet, providing end-to-end encryption

The hardware includes at least one Web server and at least one firewall, both of which may run on standard PCs with off-the-shelf components. The software includes shared applications that can be used on the extranet. Extranet server software is available to handle access control, security, and transaction and site management. Applications must be compatible between partners to allow for shared use.

The simplest form of security is browser-based encryption, which can be provided by an SSL (Secure Sockets Layer)-enabled Web commerce server. Specific pages that are highly confidential or all pages can be transmitted using SSL. SSL is commonly used for electronic commerce applications and is incorporated into secure online ordering on many Web sites. However, for shared use of applications, browser-based encryption is not sufficient. Shared applications require a VPN (virtual private network) or tunnel.

There are two basic forms of extranets: hub extranets and mutual extranets. A hub extranet is hosted by one organization offering access to trusted external partners. Hub extranets are used to support an organization and its suppliers, key customers, or collaborative partners. A mutual extranet allows multiple organizations to access designated areas on each other's intranets. Mutual extranets are used to support virtual communities and vertical industries.

LAB 1.5 EXERCISES

1.5.1 DESCRIBE THE MAJOR COMPONENTS OF AN INTRANET AND AN EXTRANET

Think about the logical components of both an intranet and an extranet.

a) Which components are found in most intranets?

_____

_____

Lab 1.5: Intranets and Extranets

b) Which components of an intranet are optional?

c) What are the key components of an extranet?

1.5.2 UNDERSTAND THE DIFFERENCES BETWEEN INTRANETS, EXTRANETS, AND THE INTERNET

For this exercise, you will compare the internet, an intranet, and an extranet.

a) How are the Internet, an intranet, and an extranet the same?

b) How does an intranet differ from the Internet? How does an extranet differ from the Internet?

LAB 1.5 EXERCISE ANSWERS

1.5.1 ANSWERS

Think about the logical components of both an intranet and an extranet.

a) Which components are found in most intranets?

Answer: An intranet usually contains at least one Web browser and at least one Web server.

b) Which components of an intranet are optional?

Answer: Additional Web servers, application servers, CGI scripts, JDBC drivers, application server APIs, component transaction servers, and database servers are all optional. They add power and flexibility to the intranet, but some of these components may not be appropriate to your organization's intranet configuration.

c) What are the key components of an extranet?

Answer: An extranet includes IP-based network connectivity, hardware including at least one Web server and at least one firewall, software including network facilities and shared business application server, and network security facilities and policies.

1.5.2 ANSWERS

For this exercise, you will compare the Internet, an intranet, and an extranet.

a) How are the Internet, an intranet, and an extranet the same?

Answer: The Internet, an intranet, and an extranet all use the same protocol, IP (Internet Protocol).

b) How does an intranet differ from the Internet? How does an extranet differ from the Internet?

Answer: An intranet serves an organization or a community of interest and restricts access to members of the organization or community. An extranet serves a community of interest that includes an organization's trusted partners. A secure extranet provides access to a protected area that is not inside the firewall of the organization but is also protected from the publicly accessible areas of the Internet. The Internet is the public network of networks and servers connected via IP (Internet Protocol) around the world.

LAB 1.5 SELF-REVIEW QUESTIONS

In order to test your progress, you should be able to answer the following questions.

1) A network connection can be provided by _____. (Select all that apply.)
   a) _____ leased line
   b) _____ dial-up line
   c) _____ private line
   d) _____ power line

Lab 1.5: Intranets and Extranets

2) Put the following layers in order from client to back-end.

   a) _____ Transaction Management Layer
   b) _____ Client Layer
   c) _____ Business Logic Tier
   d) _____ Backend Data Storage

3) ODBC is an example of a _____.

   a) _____ client
   b) _____ backend data storage package
   c) _____ middleware package
   d) _____ none of the above

4) Which of the following use the Internet Protocol (IP)?

   a) _____ Internet
   b) _____ Extranet
   c) _____ Intranet
   d) _____ All of the above

5) JDBC is able to do which of the following?

   a) _____ Connect databases to Web servers
   b) _____ Run on an intranet
   c) _____ Provide middleware functionality
   d) _____ a and b
   e) _____ b and c
   f) _____ All of the above

Quiz answers appear in the Appendix, Section 1.5.

CHAPTER 1

TEST YOUR THINKING

In this chapter, you have learned about intranets. We have considered intranets in terms of client/server systems and the various layers of functionality in an intranet. Let's suppose that you are creating an intranet for an organization from scratch. You may use any commercially available packages.

1) Draw a multi-tiered diagram of the client/server system.
2) Differentiate between the layers in the system, indicating what software packages you would use at each layer.
3) You do not need to use multiple packages at the business logic level, but at lower levels, you should use different packages as you will need to connect to multiple legacy databases.

CHAPTER 2

ARCHITECTURES, DEVICES, AND CONNECTIONS

CHAPTER OBJECTIVES

In this chapter, you will learn about:

- Packet-Switched Networks — Page 36
- The Web Client/Server Model — Page 41
- Ethernet and FDDI Networks — Page 47
- Network Devices — Page 52
- Network Connections — Page 57

In order to understand how the Internet functions, it is important to understand the operational structure of a packet-switched network. To understand how the Web operates, it is also important to understand the client/server architecture on which the Web is based. The majority of organizations now use Ethernet to connect their desktop systems, servers, and workstations, so we will also examine how standard LAN configurations can be extended to campus-wide networks with fiber optic lines. In addition, we will discuss the various types of hardware devices that are used for connecting networks and how you can connect your PC to the Internet using standard protocols.

LAB 2.1

PACKET-SWITCHED NETWORKS

> **LAB OBJECTIVES**
>
> After this lab, you will be able to:
> - Describe How a Packet-Switched Network Works
> - Compare Packet Switching and Circuit Switching

When people talk about networks and data transmission, they often use the term packet without knowing what a packet really is. Let's take a look at the terms packet and packet-switching so that we know what we are talking about. A packet is a unit of data routed between an origin and a destination on the Internet or on another packet-switched network. The term datagram is similar in meaning to the term packet. Datagram is the term used in the protocol known as UDP (User Datagram Protocol), an alternative to TCP (Transmission Control Protocol). We'll discuss UDP in Chapter 3 when we investigate various network protocols. Let's look at how packet switching works when you send a file from one place to another on the Internet. The file may be in the form of an email message, an HTML (hypertext markup language) page, a GIF (graphics image format) image, or a URL (uniform resource locator) request. The TCP layer divides the file into "chunks" (packets), in an efficient size for routing on the network.

Each of the packets is individually numbered. An individual packet includes the destination Internet address to which the original file or message was sent. Including the destination address in each individual packet allows the individual packets comprising a given file to travel via different routes through the Internet. When all packets in a file or message have arrived, the TCP layer at the receiving end reassembles the individual packets into the file that was sent. A packet-switching scheme is an efficient way to handle transmissions on a connectionless network, such as the Internet. The alternative to packet-switching is known as circuit-switching, which is generally used for voice transmissions. In a circuit-switching network, the lines in a network are shared among many users. In a circuit-switched network, each connection requires the dedication of a particular path for the duration of the connection. When you call someone on the telephone with your regular telephone company, the connection is maintained on a particular circuit until the end of your phone call. However, when you use Internet telephony to make a phone call, you use the same packet-switching method for your phone call as you would for an email message.

LAB 2.1 EXERCISES

2.1.1 DESCRIBE HOW A PACKET-SWITCHED NETWORK WORKS

a) Draw a representation of a file being transmitted via a packet-switched network.

2.1.2 COMPARE PACKET SWITCHING AND CIRCUIT SWITCHING

a) Create a table comparing packet switching and circuit switching. Indicate the state of the connection, the method of data transmission, and the major use of each type of network.

Lab 2.1 Exercise Answers

2.1.1 Answer

a) Draw a representation of a file being transmitted via a packet-switched network.

Answer:

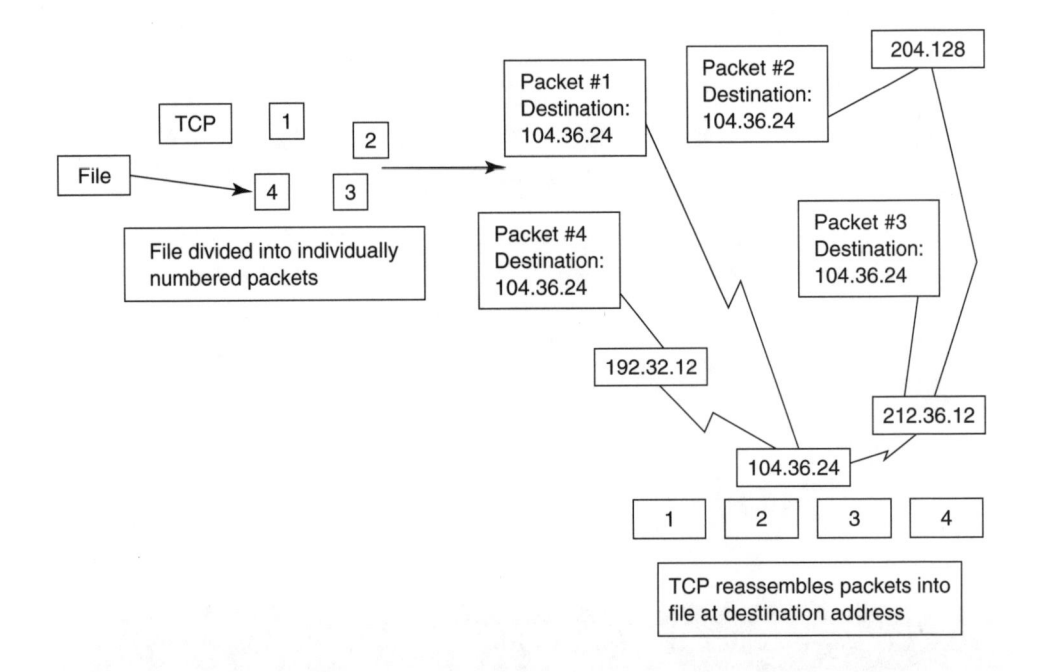

[Diagram: File → TCP → File divided into individually numbered packets (1, 2, 3, 4) → Packets routed through network with destinations (Packet #1, #2, #3, #4 Destination: 104.36.24) via routers 204.128, 192.32.12, 212.36.12 → arrive at 104.36.24 → reassembled as 1, 2, 3, 4 → TCP reassembles packets into file at destination address]

2.1.2 Answer

a) Create a table comparing packet switching and circuit switching. Indicate the state of the connection, the method of data transmission, and the major use of each type of network.

Answer: See the table on p. 39 for an example.

Characteristics	Connection	Transmission Method	Main Use
Packet switching	Used for connectionless networks since individual packets sent via different routes	TCP layer divides file into "chunks" called packets. Each packet is individually numbered and includes destination address so packets can be sent via different routes. TCP reassembles packets into file at other end.	Data networks, e.g., Internet
Circuit switching	Connection maintained on a particular circuit through duration of transmission	Lines of network shared among many users. Particular path is dedicated to a particular connection until the end of the transmission.	Voice networks, e.g., telephone calls

LAB 2.1 SELF-REVIEW QUESTIONS

In order to test your progress, you should be able to answer the following questions.

1) A packet-switching scheme is an efficient way to handle transmissions on the Internet.

   a) _____ True
   b) _____ False

2) Which of the following is true of an individual packet?

   a) _____ It is numbered.
   b) _____ It includes the destination Internet address.
   c) _____ It can travel through multiple hosts to reach its final destination.
   d) _____ All of the above

3) All of the packets that make up an individual file have to take the same route from the sending computer to the receiving computer.

   a) _____ True
   b) _____ False

Lab 2.1: Packet-Switched Networks

4) Packet switching can be used for voice and data.

    a) _____ True
    b) _____ False

5) Which of the following is/are true of the Internet? (Select all that apply.)

    a) _____ The Internet is a connectionless network.
    b) _____ The Internet requires a dedicated path for a connection.
    c) _____ The TCP layer reassembles packets.
    d) _____ The Internet can transmit voice signals.
    e) _____ All of the above

Quiz answers appear in the Appendix, Section 2.1.

LAB 2.2

THE WEB CLIENT/SERVER MODEL

LAB OBJECTIVES

After this lab, you will be able to:

- Understand the Difference Between Client/Server, Peer-to-Peer, and Master/Slave Architectures
- Appreciate the Advantage of Client/Server Architecture for the Web

The client/server model describes the relationship between two different computer programs, which may reside on the same or different computers. In a client/server architecture, the client makes a service request, and the server fulfills the request. The client/server architecture is the central concept that underlies network computing. A client/server architecture is a convenient way to interconnect programs. In this way, programs can be distributed efficiently across a network. It is also an efficient way to distribute the workload and functions of programs even if they are running on the same computer.

TCP/IP, which we'll discuss in greater detail in Chapter 3, is actually composed of two separate protocols—TCP and IP. These are the most commonly used network protocols today because they are used to transmit traffic across the Internet. The pair of protocols, TCP and IP, use the client/server model, in which the server software is often referred to as a daemon in UNIX parlance. When a server is activated, it awaits client requests. There may be and usually are multiple client programs running simultaneously, each requesting services from the same server or set of servers. These multiple client programs share the services of a common server program, which may be running on a single computer, or on multiple computers on a network. Models that contrast with the client/server model include those in which there is a master program providing direction to a slave program, with the two programs tied together in a master/slave relationship. Master/slave models are used at times for disk drives, when additional disk drives are controlled by the disk controller running the primary disk drive. Another possible model is a peer-to-peer architecture, in which programs communicate with each other by passing messages back and forth and functions are performed by various programs working together. This means that each peer program is required to provide some of the same functionality in order to be able to work with another peer program. Therefore, a peer-to-peer architecture is often not as efficient as the client/server model in which you can centralize functionality used by all programs in a single server program.

The World Wide Web was designed as a client/server architecture. In the Web architecture, the Web browser serves as a client. The client program requests services. Although the Web is most often known for HTTP access to files, it was designed both to handle local and remote access to files and systems and to standard Internet protocols. In this way, a Web browser may request such services as access to files located on remote servers via HTTP (Hyptertext Transfer Protocol) or FTP (File Transfer Protocol), access to local files on the same system, or access to other systems via the telnet protocol. The Web server processes the request for access to a Web page, a file, or another system, whether the server is located in the same computer, on the same network, in the same building or organization, or at some remote location on the Internet. The Web server software is also sometimes referred to as HTTPD, the Hypertext Transfer Protocol Daemon.

The original Web server was the CERN HTTPD developed at the European Center for High-Energy Physics in Switzerland where the World Wide Web was developed. When the Web was first developed, a number of browsers, both text-based and graphical, were developed. All the initial browsers, including Mosaic developed by the National Center for Supercomputing Applications (NCSA), used the CERN HTTPD as their Web server. With the CERN Hypertext Transfer Protocol Daemon running on a UNIX workstation, a browser could run on a UNIX workstation, an IBM-compatible PC, or an Apple Macintosh and any of these browsers could request services from the same Web server running on another computer on the Internet. That is the beauty of the client/server model and of the World Wide Web architecture. Using the Internet's TCP/IP protocol combination, a client program can request files from FTP servers directly through FTP. Before the advent of the Web, files were uploaded to FTP servers for distribution on the Internet. FTP is still used to place large files on another server or to upload Web pages that were developed on an individual's system onto the Web server system.

Lab 2.2 Exercises

2.2.1 Understand the Difference Between Client/Server, Peer-to-Peer, and Master/Slave Architectures

a) Create a chart comparing client/server, peer-to-peer, and master/slave architectures in terms of their communication methods and how they are used.

2.2.2 Appreciate the Advantage of Client/Server Architecture for the Web

a) Add a column to the table to the chart listing the major advantage and disadvantage of each architecture.

Lab 2.2 Exercise Answers

2.2.1 Answer

a) Create a chart comparing client/server, peer-to-peer, and master/slave architectures in terms of their communication methods and how they are used.

44   Lab 2.2: The Web Client/Server Model

Answer:

Architecture/Comparison	Communication Method	Example of Use
Client/Server	Client makes request, which is passed to the server. Server then fulfills the request (e.g., retrieves a requested Web page from the Internet) and passes back information to client.	WWW, client = Web browser, server = Web server
Peer-to-Peer	Programs work together; communicate through message-passing.	PCs exchanging documents with each other.
Master/Slave	Programs tied together within one directory with one program issuing commands to the other.	PC accessing and controlling printer to output a print job.

2.2.2 ANSWERS

a) Add a column to the table to the chart listing the major advantage and disadvantage of each architecture.

Answer:

Architecture/Comparison	Communication Method	Example of Use	Advantage/Disadvantage
Client/Server	Client makes request, which is passed to the server. Server then fulfills the request (e.g. retrieves a requested Web page from the Internet) and passes back information to client.	WWW, client = Web browser, server = Web server	Centralizes functionality needed and used by all client programs in a single server program. However, this makes the server a critical resource, a good reason for back-up Web servers and mirrored sites.

(continued)

Architecture/ Comparison	Communication Method	Example of Use	Advantage/ Disadvantage
Peer-to-Peer	Programs work together; communicate through message-passing.	PCs exchanging documents with each other.	No single peer is a critical resource, so it's okay if one goes down or is unavailable. However, this means that functionality may be duplicated in peer programs.
Master/Slave	Programs tied together within one directory with one program issuing commands to the other.	PC accessing and controlling printer to output a print job.	Simpler to implement but it ties slave function to that of the master.

LAB 2.2 SELF-REVIEW QUESTIONS

In order to test your progress, you should be able to answer the following questions.

1) The World Wide Web was designed as which of the following?

   a) _____ Client/server architecture
   b) _____ Peer-to-peer architecture
   c) _____ All of the above
   d) _____ None of the above

2) The Web server software is sometimes referred to as which of the following?

   a) _____ httpd
   b) _____ smtpd
   c) _____ wwwd
   d) _____ http://

3) Web servers can be considered to be which of the following? (Select all that apply.)

   a) _____ Location-dependent
   b) _____ Critical resources
   c) _____ Location-independent
   d) _____ No more critical than client programs
   e) _____ All of the above

Lab 2.2: The Web Client/Server Model

4) Advantages of client/server architecture over peer-to-peer or master/slave include which of the following? (Select all that apply.)

    a) _____ Error handling
    b) _____ Centralization of functionality
    c) _____ Efficient resource usage
    d) _____ Message passing
    e) _____ All of the above

5) Which method of communication is used for peer-to-peer architecture?

    a) _____ PC-to-PC
    b) _____ LAN-based
    c) _____ Packet switching
    d) _____ Message passing

Quiz answers appear in the Appendix, Section 2.2.

LAB 2.3

ETHERNET AND FDDI NETWORKS

> **LAB OBJECTIVES**
>
> After this lab, you will be able to:
> - Understand the Advantages of Using Ethernet Technology
> - Compare Ethernet and FDDI Technologies

Ethernet is now the most widely installed technology for LANs. The Ethernet protocol has been standardized by the IEEE (Institute for Electronic and Electrical Engineers) as IEEE Standard 802.3. In an Ethernet configuration, devices are connected to cables for network connectivity. Special grades of twisted pair wires connect devices in a bus topology. Data bits are transmitted along the Ethernet using an approach called Carrier Sense Multiple Access with Collision Detection (CSMA/CD). In this transmission scheme, devices compete for access.

The most commonly installed Ethernet configurations use 10Base-T technology. This means that the network can carry data bits at transmission speeds up to 10 Megabits per second (10 Mbps). Fast Ethernet is called 100Base-T and offers transmission speeds up to 100 Megabits per second (100 Mbps). 100Base-T Ethernet is generally used for LAN backbone systems, which support workstations with 10Base-T cards in them. This is a cost-effective combination, providing lower speed connections between the workstations and the LAN backbone, with the higher speed reserved for traffic along the LAN backbone. Gigabit Ethernet has been introduced and has begun to be installed for even faster transmission along the backbone of a network. Gigabit Ethernet transmits data at speeds up to 1000 Megabits per second (1000 Mbps).

Lab 2.3: *Ethernet and FDDI Networks*

Another acronym that is becoming more widely used is FDDI. FDDI stands for Fiber Distributed-Data Interface and is the standard for data transmission along fiber optic lines in a LAN. While LANs have provided cost-effective sharing of resources in organizations, they have been limited in terms of the geographic area that they could serve. With FDDI, LANs can be extended over a much wider area. This allows a LAN to serve several thousand users, often distributed throughout an organizational campus.

Now that we know what the token ring protocol is, it makes sense to say that the FDDI protocol is based on the token ring protocol. An FDDI network actually contains two token rings, the primary ring and the secondary ring. The primary ring has a 100 Mbps capacity, the same as 100Base-T Ethernet. The secondary ring can be used for backup if the primary ring fails. In addition, the secondary ring can be used to provide an additional 100 Mbps capacity if it is not needed for backup purposes. With the two rings in operation, FDDI networks can transmit data at speeds up to 200 Megabits per second, twice that of fast Ethernet networks. In addition, FDDI networks can span larger areas than Ethernet networks. A single ring extends the network across 200 kilometers (km) or 124 miles. With the secondary ring in use, an FDDI network can extend an additional 100 kilometers or 62 miles.

There are two standards that use token-passing rings:

- Token ring (IBM standard)
- FDDI

The FDDI protocol has been standardized by ANSI (American National Standards Institute) as the ANSI X3-T9 standard. FDDI conforms to the OSI model and provides a layer 2 network protocol on the data link layer. FDDI can be used to interconnect LANs that employ other protocols. This allows for the interconnection of disparate networks, which is an important facility in today's world of mix-and-match devices, systems, and network protocols. FDDI-II is an enhanced version of FDDI that adds circuit-switched service for voice signals. With FDDI-II, an organization can use the same fiber optic lines for voice and data transmission.

LAB 2.3 EXERCISES

2.3.1 UNDERSTAND THE ADVANTAGES OF USING ETHERNET TECHNOLOGY

a) Why do you think that Ethernet is the most widely used technology for LANs today?

Lab 2.3: Ethernet and FDDI Networks   49

2.3.2 COMPARE ETHERNET AND FDDI TECHNOLOGIES

a) What do Ethernet and FDDI technologies have in common?

_____

_____

b) How do these two technologies differ?

_____

_____

LAB 2.3

LAB 2.3 EXERCISE ANSWERS

2.3.1 ANSWER

a) Why do you think that Ethernet is the most widely used technology for LANs today?

Answer: Ethernet is an industry standard technology. LAN technologies, which were developed prior to the introduction of Ethernet, were built on proprietary protocols, connecting the devices and workstations from one single vendor. An example of the difference in long-term viability of proprietary versus open standards for technology can be seen in the case of Sun Microsystems and Apollo Computer in the 1980s. Sun Microsystems offered standard UNIX workstations connected via Ethernet, whereas Apollo Computer provided Apollo Domain networking to link Apollo workstations. While the Apollo domain network offered Apollo an early lead in the workstation market, Sun gradually increased its market share, linking its workstations via a standard protocol, which also allowed devices from other vendors to be connected to the Ethernet network. Apollo Computer was acquired by Hewlett-Packard, while Sun Microsystems now leads the market in UNIX workstations.

2.3.2 ANSWERS

a) What do Ethernet and FDDI technologies have in common?

Answer: Ethernet and FDDI technologies are both used to provide technology for local area networks.

Lab 2.3: Ethernet and FDDI Networks

b) How do these two technologies differ?

Answer: The difference between the two technologies is in the physical layer of the network. Twisted pair or coaxial cable is used to connect devices on an Ethernet network, whereas fiber optic lines are used to connect devices on an FDDI network. With the difference in the physical layer, layer 1, of the network, there comes a difference in the speed of data transmission as well as the geographic distance that can be covered by such a network. Ethernet is currently available in 10Base-T, 100Base-T, and Gigabit technologies, providing data transmission speeds of up to 10 Mbps, 100 Mbps and 1000 Mbps, respectively. FDDI with its fiber optic links can transmit data along its lines as fast as 100 Mbps using only the primary ring. If the secondary ring is not required for backup, transmission speeds can range up to 200 Mbps. FDDI can be used to span a distance of up to 200 kilometers (km) or 124 miles.

LAB 2.3 SELF-REVIEW QUESTIONS

In order to test your progress, you should be able to answer the following questions.

1) Ethernet uses which type of topology?

   a) _____ Bus
   b) _____ Star
   c) _____ Ring

2) Which of the following is generally used for LAN backbone systems?

   a) _____ 1Base-T
   b) _____ 10Base-T
   c) _____ 100Base-T
   d) _____ 1000Base-T

3) FDDI allows LANs to do which of the following? (Select all that apply.)

   a) _____ Extend over a much wider area
   b) _____ Make wireless connections with laptops
   c) _____ Serve several thousand users
   d) _____ Support Windows-based computers

Lab 2.3: Ethernet and FDDI Networks

4) Which of the following is/are true for CSMA/CD? (Select all that apply.)

    a) _____ CSMA/CD is a transmission scheme.
    b) _____ CSMA/CD is used for data bits along an Ethernet.
    c) _____ Devices do not have to compete for access in this scheme.
    d) _____ Speed is dependent on the number of users.
    e) _____ All of the above

5) FDDI can be used on copper wire networks.

    a) _____ True
    b) _____ False

Quiz answers appear in the Appendix, Section 2.3.

LAB 2.4

NETWORK DEVICES

LAB OBJECTIVES

After this lab, you will be able to:

✔ Distinguish Between Routers, Bridges, and Switches
✔ Determine Appropriate Interconnecting Devices for Your Network Architecture
✔ Relate LAN Topologies to Switches

A router is a hardware/software combination or a software package running on standard hardware, such as a PC or UNIX workstation. Whether a router is a device or a program, its function is to determine the next network point. Once it has determined the next point in the network, the router forwards a packet of data on toward the destination address. In order to perform its routing function, a router must be connected to at least two networks. With these connections, the router is tasked with deciding which direction to send each information packet. The router makes its decision based on its current understanding of the state of the networks to which it is connected. A router is located at the juncture of two or more networks or at a network gateway. This juncture or gateway may be located in a network facility, which connects users to the Internet. Such a network facility is known as an Internet point-of-presence, or a POP.

A router may be a separate device, but often a router is included in a network switch. In other words, the network switch handles both the switching function and the routing function. In order to perform its routing function, a router creates or maintains a table of available routes. The router keeps track of route conditions, distance, and cost algorithms. Based on this information, the router determines the best route for a given packet. A single packet may travel through multiple network points via multiple routers before it reaches its final destination.

Another type of network device is a bridge. We hear more about routers than bridges these days because of the need for organizations to connect to the Internet. However, many organizations still use bridges since organizations rely on LANs to connect systems and users within their organizations. A bridge connects two LANs with the same protocol. A bridge examines each message on the LAN. It then passes on messages in the same LAN and forwards those messages on interconnected LANs to the other LANs. The way in which a bridge functions is to copy a data frame from one network to the next one. Network node addresses do not relate to their physical locations. Therefore, a bridge develops a learning table for forwarding messages to the correct location. Bridges operate at the data link layer, layer 2 of the OSI model.

A switch is a network device that selects the path or circuit for sending a unit of data to the next destination. Switches are used in the telephone network to send messages across telephone lines, which are also referred to as circuits. A switch may also include the function of a router. The function of a switch is to determine the adjacent network point to which the data should be sent. Switches are generally simpler and faster than routers. An IP (Internet Protocol) switch is a packet-switching switch that uses the Internet Protocol. An IP switch has the ability to determine routing. An IP switch performs functions on OSI layer 3. A hop is defined as a trip from one switch point to another in a network.

Latency is defined as the amount of time a switch takes to figure out where to forward a data unit. Latency is the price of the flexibility that switches provide at the backbone and gateway levels of network where one network connects with another. On the subnetwork level, data is forwarded close to its destination or its origin.

LAB EXERCISES 2.4

2.4.1 DISTINGUISH BETWEEN ROUTERS, BRIDGES, AND SWITCHES

a) Create a table listing the function and advantage of each type of network device.

2.4.2 DETERMINE APPROPRIATE INTERCONNECTING DEVICES FOR YOUR NETWORK ARCHITECTURE

a) Consider the networks in your organization. Which device do you think is most appropriate for each network connection?

_____
_____

2.4.3 RELATE LAN TOPOLOGIES TO SWITCHES

a) Recall what you learned about different topologies. Which LAN topologies do not require switches and why don't they?

_____
_____

LAB 2.4 EXERCISE ANSWERS

2.4.1 ANSWER

a) Create a table listing the function and advantage of each type of network device.

Answer:

Device/Use	Function	Advantage
Switch	Determines adjacent network point to send data.	Simpler and faster than router.
Router	Determines best path for packet to take.	Efficient routing of packets because router keeps track of network conditions.
Bridge	Connects two LANs with same protocol.	Uses learning table to know where to forward messages from one LAN to another.

2.4.2 ANSWER

a) Consider the networks in your organization. Which device do you think is most appropriate for each network connection?

Answer: You probably have a router to provide access to the Internet for members of the organization. You may have a bridge between two LANs of the same protocol type or between two LANs using different physical media, such as coax cable for an Ethernet for the office PCs and a wireless LAN for laptop computers. If you use dial-up modem access, you will likely use the switch provided by the telephone company.

2.4.3 ANSWER

a) Recall what you learned about different topologies. Which LAN topologies do not require switches and why don't they?

Answer: Not all LANs require switches. Let's recall what we learned about different topologies. When LANs are configured in ring or bus topologies, they do not require switches. In a bus or ring topology, all destinations inspect each message. Since each destination reads only those messages intended for that destination, there is no need for a switch to make that determination.

LAB 2.4 SELF-REVIEW QUESTIONS

In order to test your progress, you should be able to answer the following questions.

1) Which of the following best represents a router's function?

   a) _____ Connects individual nodes to a network.
   b) _____ Determines the next network point on a data unit's path.
   c) _____ Connects two LANs that use the same protocols.
   d) _____ None of the above.

2) Latency is defined as the amount of time a switch takes to figure out where a data unit came from.

   a) _____ True
   b) _____ False

3) LANs configured in ring or bus topologies require switches.

   a) _____ True
   b) _____ False

Lab 2.4: Network Devices

4) IP switches operate on which OSI network layer?

   a) _____ Layer 2
   b) _____ Layer 3
   c) _____ Layer 4
   d) _____ None of the above

5) Bridges operate on which OSI network layer?

   a) _____ Layer 2
   b) _____ Layer 3
   c) _____ Layer 4
   d) _____ None of the above

Quiz answers appear in the Appendix, Section 2.4.

LAB 2.5

NETWORK CONNECTIONS

> **LAB OBJECTIVES**
>
> After this lab, you will be able to:
>
> ✔ Understand Different Modes of Access to Your Internet Service Provider (ISP)
> ✔ Determine Why PPP Is Preferred over SLIP

An ISP is an Internet Service Provider that provides access to the Internet for email and Web access. Some ISPs also provide Web hosting services. Some ISPs have become ASPs (Application Service Providers), offering shared use of specific applications as services. Other ISPs offer electronic commerce hosting services and are referred to as CSPs, or Commerce Service Providers. ISPs offer the use of their equipment and access to telecommunications lines. ISPs establish and maintain Points-of-Presence (POPs) on the Internet to allow for access to services through telephone lines that are local to the area that each POP serves. When you send an email message to a person with a different ISP, ISPs need to interconnect so that they can pass on such messages to the intended recipient, no matter what ISP he or she uses. ISPs interconnect through IP switching centers known as MAEs, or Metropolitan Area Exchanges. These IP switching centers are now managed by MCI WorldCom. The acronym MAE is now a service mark of MCI WorldCom. ISPs exchange traffic through peering arrangements using the MAEs, which are centers for switching traffic between ISPs. MAE-East, located in Washington, DC, handles network traffic from the east coast and Europe. MAE-West is located in San Jose, CA, and handles traffic from the west coast and Asia. There are regional tier-2 MAEs located in Chicago, Dallas, Houston, Los Angeles, and New York City. In addition to serving as switching centers, the MAEs provide co-location space for ISPs.

The MAEs provide the infrastructure for the national commercial Internet backbone. In addition, NSF (National Science Foundation) has identified NAPs

(Network Access Points). Now that we know what switches are, we can see that the MAEs operate as giant LAN switches. The only ISP device that can interconnect to a MAE switch is a router or a computer host acting as a router.

It is the responsibility of the ISPs to work out their own peering agreements and manage their own routing tables. The routers at the two major MAEs require very large routing tables. Therefore, they use large routers, such as one from the Cisco 7xxx series routers. A regional MAE uses an Ethernet switch and an FDDI concentrator. In the regional MAEs, you will most likely find smaller routers, such as the Cisco 4500-M.

Dial-up access to the Internet employs your normal analog telephone connection. A dial-up connection is established and maintained for a limited amount of time. This connection is set up in a system of many lines shared by many users. Because the telephone lines are used at different times by different users, they are sometimes referred to as switched lines. Remember that we discussed circuit-switched lines used for telephone service as opposed to packet-switched network connections used to move data throughout the Internet. The dial-up line, a circuit-switched line, may be used for the user's connection to his or her ISP's POP even though the Internet itself will move data along its transmission paths as packets in a packet-switched manner. The dial-up connection may be initiated manually or automatically via a modem. Sometimes modems are programmed to make an automatic connection at specific times of the day to transmit large amounts of data to a network destination. The alternative to switched connections is a dedicated connection, one that is continuously in place. A dedicated line is sometimes called a nonswitched line. Large corporations sometimes invest in a dedicated line for their network traffic. However, with less costly alternatives available now, some of these organizations have switched to other network technologies, which we'll discuss in Chapter 5.

Now, let's consider the protocol used for the dial-up connection. The older connection that was most frequently used by ISPs is SLIP, which stands for the Serial Line Internet Protocol. SLIP is the TCP/IP protocol used for communication between two preconfigured systems. If your ISP provides you with a SLIP connection, your data is transmitted from your system to the server via a serial line. In this case, the ISP's server responds to requests from your system, the client. The ISP's server then passes your requests on to the Internet. When the designated server on the Internet responds to your requests, the responses are forwarded back to you via the serial line used for your connection.

The SLIP protocol is not as fast as the newer PPP (Point-to-Point) protocol, which is used more often now by ISPs. The PPP protocol is a full-duplex protocol, with the ability to handle traffic in both directions simultaneously, unlike SLIP, which can only handle transmission in one direction at a time. PPP handles the communication between two computers using a serial interface. Typically, PPP is the protocol used to connect a PC by phone line to a server. When an ISP provides a

PPP connection to you, the ISP's server responds to requests from your computer and passes these requests along to the Internet. Once a response is received from the destination server, the ISP's server forwards responses back to your system. The PPP protocol uses IP and can handle other protocols as well. PPP is a member of the TCP/IP suite of protocols. In the OSI model, PPP operates as a layer 2 (data link layer) service. PPP is a flexible protocol in terms of the physical media across which it can transmit data. This layer 2 service can sit on top of various types of layer 1 technologies, including twisted pair, fiber optic, and satellite transmission.

PPP is a variation of the High-speed Data Link Control (HDLC) protocol for packet encapsulation. PPP is preferred over the earlier de facto standard SLIP. PPP handles synchronous as well as asynchronous transmission. PPP can also share a line with other users. In addition, PPP includes error detection facilities that SLIP lacks. If there is a choice of protocols, PPP is preferred over SLIP.

LAB EXERCISES 2.5

2.5.1 UNDERSTAND DIFFERENT MODES OF ACCESS TO YOUR INTERNET SERVICE PROVIDER (ISP)

    a) Draw a diagram showing how SLIP and PPP work through your ISP.

2.5.2 DETERMINE WHY PPP IS PREFERRED OVER SLIP

    a) Use a dial-up connection and determine whether it uses a SLIP or PPP connection.

Lab 2.5: Network Connections

b) Why do you think users prefer PPP over SLIP?

_____
_____

LAB 2.5 EXERCISE ANSWERS

2.5.1 ANSWER

a) Draw a diagram showing how SLIP and PPP work through your ISP.

Answer:

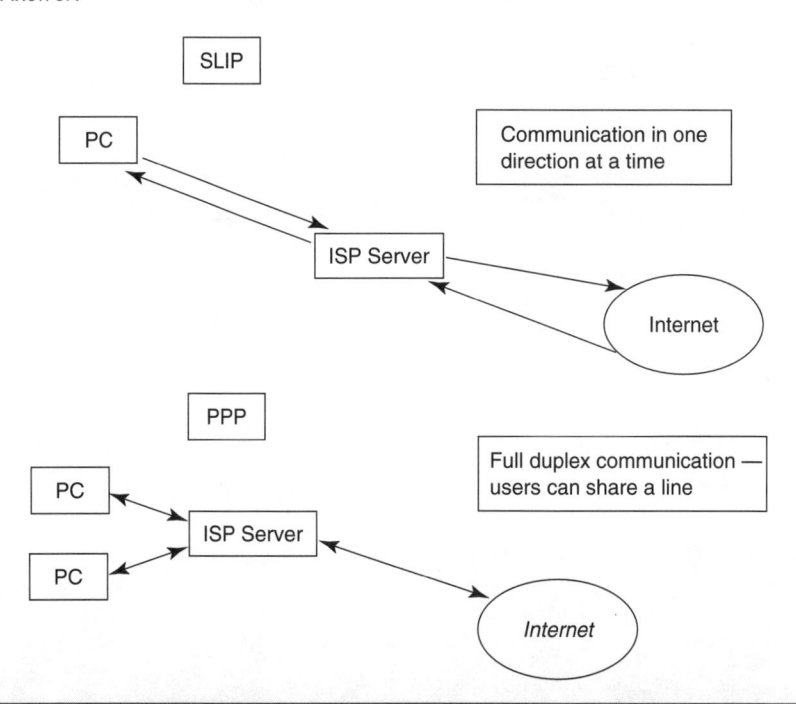

```
           SLIP

   PC ←———————————→          Communication in one
                              direction at a time
         ↘   ↗
         ISP Server ←————————→ Internet


           PPP

   PC ←——→                    Full duplex communication —
         ISP Server ←————————→ users can share a line
   PC ←——→              ↘
                         Internet
```

2.5.2 ANSWERS

a) Use a dial-up connection and determine whether it uses a SLIP or PPP connection.

Answer: If it's a newer service, most likely you will get a PPP connection. Ask your ISP or check on your ISP's Web site, if you can't figure out whether you have a SLIP or a PPP connection.

b) Why do you think users prefer PPP over SLIP?

Answer: PPP, the Point-to-Point Protocol, is faster than SLIP, the Serial Line Interface Protocol. PPP is a full-duplex protocol, transmitting data in both directions simultaneously rather than SLIP, which can only transmit data in one direction at a time. PPP allows users to share a single line and also provides error detection facilities that are not found in SLIP.

LAB 2.5 SELF-REVIEW QUESTIONS

In order to test your progress, you should be able to answer the following questions.

1) The MAEs connect which of the following together?

   a) _____ Email programs
   b) _____ Telephone lines
   c) _____ Printers
   d) _____ ISPs

2) The MAEs only handle a small percentage of Internet traffic.

   a) _____ True
   b) _____ False

3) SLIP is slower than PPP.

   a) _____ True
   b) _____ False

4) Which of the following can operate in full-duplex mode?

   a) _____ PPP
   b) _____ SLIP
   c) _____ MAEs
   d) _____ All of the above

5) HDLC is used for which of the following? (Select all that apply.)

   a) _____ SLIP
   b) _____ Packet encapsulation
   c) _____ PPP
   d) _____ All of the above

Quiz answers appear in the Appendix, Section 2.5.

CHAPTER 2

TEST YOUR THINKING

You have learned about various types of networks. Review the different types of network characteristics and how network nodes are connected. Use the tables and diagrams of characteristics that you created in the lab exercises to help you.

1) Diagram the networks of a hypothetical corporation. You will draw a number of diagrams, each of which shows the overall network at different "zoom levels." For instance, the first diagram will show a WAN, and the second diagram will show an individual LAN as a node in the WAN from the previous diagram.
Use boxes to represent nodes on the network as well as any routers and switches. Use lines to represent connections between nodes. Make sure to label each item.
2) Draw a diagram of a national corporate WAN. Make sure you show individual LANs and MANs. Use fiber backbones to connect nodes.
3) Draw a diagram of one of the LANs at a company building. Include routers, hubs, switches, and departmental servers. Use fiber, token ring, and Ethernet to connect nodes.
4) Draw a diagram of an individual LAN of a department. Include connections to the LAN for the entire building, servers, workstations, and printers. Do not forget to label the connections. Use coax cable or twisted pair wiring, 10Base-T, and 100Base-T to connect nodes.

CHAPTER 3

INTERNET, NETWORK, AND TRANSPORT PROTOCOLS

CHAPTER OBJECTIVES

In this chapter, you will learn about:

- Internet and Internet Protocol (IP) — Page 65
- IP Addresses — Page 70
- Domain Name System (DNS) — Page 77
- Transmission Control Protocol (TCP) — Page 81
- MAC Addresses — Page 87
- User Datagram Protocol (UDP) — Page 93

The success of the World Wide Web, and the Internet in general, can be attributed not only to the attractiveness of applications such as Web browsers and email, but also to the scalability and robustness of the underlying technologies that allow the applications to work. Previous to the meteoric growth of the Internet, many different networking technologies existed, but none had the features that would facilitate the exponential growth that the Internet has experienced, as TCP/IP has done.

TCP/IP is the protocol (along with TCP's cousin UDP) on which all Web traffic rides. In particular, HTTP is built upon TCP (Transmission Control Protocol). Much of the Internet's success is due to the fundamental strength and scalability of these lower layer protocols. Though TCP/IP is commonly referred to as the layer 3 protocol of the Internet, a more careful statement would include both UDP and TCP as higher layer processes that take advantage of the Internet Protocol (IP). When we refer to TCP/IP as the transmission protocols of the Internet, we implicitly include UDP.

LAB 3.1

INTERNET AND INTERNET PROTOCOL (IP)

> **LAB OBJECTIVES**
>
> After this lab, you will be able to:
> - Determine the Organizations Responsible for Domain Name Registration
> - Register a New Domain Name

Before we dive into a technical discussion of Internet Protocol (IP), let's take a brief tour of the history of the Internet. The precursor to the Internet was ARPANET, which was built in the late 1960s to provide support for defense-related and government-funded projects performed in research institutions and universities. The original AUP (Acceptable Use Policy) specified that commercial applications were not allowed on the ARPANET or the original version of the Internet. By the 1980s, the AUP had been relaxed and large corporations were allowed to use the facilities of the Internet.

There were only a few major ISPs, which provided service and connectivity, and they were set up to handle relationships with large corporations. BARRNET (Bay Area Regional Research Network) initially supported Stanford University. After the AUP was modified to allow for use by industry, BARRNET also provided access to Hewlett-Packard and Amdahl Corporation, among many other high-technology companies. On the east coast, the major ISP was BBN (Bolt Beranek and Newman) that supported MIT and other universities in the Boston area. Just as BARRNET began providing Internet access to large high-tech companies on the West Coast, BBN did the same for companies on the East Coast.

Lab 3.1: Internet and Internet Protocol (IP)

In the 1980s, Internet facilities included UNIX-based utilities for "techies," such as email, FTP, and telnet. UNIX commands were typed on the command line to initiate and carry out a telnet or FTP session. Researchers and developers started to build search and retrieval tools on top of the UNIX and Internet infrastructure, including gopher, developed at the University of Minnesota, and WAIS (Wide Area Information Server), developed by a group at Thinking Machines in Boston. Librarians wishing to provide access to research and other library materials started using gopher and WAIS. WAIS was standardized as the Z39.50 standard used by the library and information services community.

A parallel development was the World Wide Web, conceived of as a document management system for high-energy physicists at CERN, the European Particle Physics Laboratory. By 1993, the library and research communities were using gopher and WAIS extensively and some Internet users had started developing and using graphical browsers to access the World Wide Web. Several browsers were developed, the most popular of which was the Mosaic browser, developed at NCSA (National Center for Supercomputing Applications). Mosaic offered a graphical user interface to not only the HTTP protocol and the World Wide Web but also to other Internet protocols, such as FTP and telnet. Developers wrote Web interfaces to gopher and WAIS so that the library community could continue to use these tools, but new collections were organized and made available on the Web through the HTTP protocol. With a graphical user interface rather than the command line interface that intimidated novice users, the Mosaic browser became popular very quickly. The Mosaic browser was then commercialized by Netscape Communications, fueling widespread adoption of browsers and the World Wide Web. Now let's consider the underpinnings of the World Wide Web, the Internet, and Internet Protocol.

The Internet uses the protocol known as IP or Internet Protocol. IP is a layer 3, networking, protocol. IP or Internet Protocol is the method by which data is sent from one computer to another on the Internet. Each Internet host has a unique address on the Internet, called its IP address. We'll consider IP addresses and the IP addressing scheme in greater detail in the next section.

When you want to send or receive a Web page or an email message, the page or message is divided into chunks called packets. As we discussed in the previous chapter, each packet contains the sender's Internet address and the receiver's Internet address. On the Internet, a packet is sent first to a gateway computer. The gateway computer reads the destination address and forwards the packet to the adjacent gateway. Next, the adjacent gateway reads the packet's destination address. When a particular gateway recognizes a packet as destined for a computer in the immediate neighborhood or domain of the gateway computer, the gateway then forwards the packet directly to the computer with the specified address.

Lab 3.1: Internet and Internet Protocol (IP)

When a message is divided into packets, each packet is numbered. Therefore, a major advantage accrues from being able to send each packet by a different route across the Internet.

The task of the IP protocol is merely to deliver the packets in whatever order they arrive. Thus, packets may arrive in a different order from the order in which they were sent or in which they appeared in the original message. In the section on TCP (Transmission Control Protocol), we will discuss how TCP puts the packets back in the right order so that the Web page or email message can be read correctly. In addition, we should remember that another advantage of IP is that it is a connectionless protocol. Once the communication is initiated, there is no requirement on IP to maintain a connection between the end points that are communicating. As packets travel through the Internet, each packet is treated as an independent unit of data without any relation to other units of data.

There are two versions of the Internet Protocol in use today, IPv4 and IPv6. IPv4, Internet Protocol Version 4, is the generally accepted Internet Protocol in use on today's networks. Some vendors are starting to provide support for IPv6, which provides a scheme to accommodate longer addresses. Since we're starting to talk about different addressing schemes, in the next section, we'll consider the addressing scheme IP employs.

LAB 3.1 EXERCISES

3.1.1 DETERMINE THE ORGANIZATIONS RESPONSIBLE FOR DOMAIN NAME REGISTRATION

a) Now that Network Solutions is not the only organization registering domain names, see if you can find a list of organizations with which you can register new domain names.

3.1.2 REGISTER A NEW DOMAIN NAME

a) Check out one of the registrars and read the information provided to determine how to register your own domain name.

Lab 3.1 Exercise Answers

3.1.1 Answer

a) Now that Network Solutions is not the only organization registering domain names, see if you can find a list of organizations with which you can register new domain names.

Answer: The Internet Corporation for Assigned Names and Numbers (ICANN) is the nonprofit corporation that was formed to assume responsibility for IP address space allocation, protocol parameter assignment, domain name system management, and root server system management functions. ICANN maintains a list of accredited registrars on its site (www.icann.org).

I found the current list at: http://www.icann.org/registrars/accredited-list.html.

You can also go to the InterNIC site (www.internic.net). I found the accredited registrar directory at: http://www.internic.net/regist.html. I also found an alphabetical listing of currently accredited domain name registrars at: http://www.internic.net/alpha.html.

3.1.2 Answer

a) Check out one of the registrars and read the information provided to determine how to register your own domain name.

Answer: If you go to the InterNIC site (www.internic.net), you can check out the FAQs (http://www.internic.net/faq.html). The information provided on the FAQs explains the registration process as follows. To register a domain name, you will be asked to provide the registrar you select with the various contact and technical information that makes up the registration. The registrar will then keep records of the contact information and submit the technical information to a central directory known as the "registry." This registry provides other computers on the Internet the information necessary to send you email or to find your Web site. You will also be required to enter a registration contract with the registrar, which sets forth the terms under which your registration is accepted and will be maintained.

Lab 3.1 Self-Review Questions

In order to test your progress, you should be able to answer the following questions.

1) Two computers can have the same IP address without causing problems.

    a) _____ True
    b) _____ False

2) Packets travel in a group and cannot be separated.

   a) _____ True
   b) _____ False

3) Internet Protocol is the method by which _____.

   a) _____ Email addresses are looked up
   b) _____ Packets are put back into their right order
   c) _____ Data is sent from one computer to another over the Internet
   d) _____ None of the above

4) IP and TCP can function separately.

   a) _____ True
   b) _____ False

5) On which layer(s) do TCP and IP function?

   a) _____ TCP on layer 2 and IP on layer 3.
   b) _____ Both on layer 3.
   c) _____ TCP on layer 3 and IP on layer 4.
   d) _____ TCP on layer 4 and IP on layer 3.

   Quiz answers appear in the Appendix, Section 3.1.

LAB 3.2

IP ADDRESSES

> **LAB OBJECTIVES**
> After this lab, you will be able to:
> ✓ Understand the IP Addressing Scheme
> ✓ Know How to Identify a Domain Name by Its IP Address

IP addresses are the names that networked computers use to talk to each other. In the current Internet Protocol addressing scheme, referred to as IPv4 (Internet Protocol version 4), an IP address is represented by 4 bytes of data. IPv6, Internet Protocol version 6, has been developed to provide longer addresses, allowing more hosts. Let's consider how IP addresses are constructed and how they are used on the Internet. The scheme of forming IP addresses is another one of the successes that has allowed the Internet to grow to the size that it is today. With IPv6, Internet developers hope that the Internet can grow much larger without any difficulty in locating particular systems on the network.

An IP address can be expressed in a number of different formats. The most commonly used format is the dotted octal (base 8). An example of an IP address expressed in dotted octal format is:

    123.234.23.21

The numbers offset by the dot range from 0 to 255. This is the equivalent of 0 to 2^8, or 2*2*2*2*2*2*2*2. Where does this come from, you may ask? Well, recall the computer terminology of bits and bytes.

A bit is a single placeholder with two values, either 0 or 1. A byte is composed of eight bits.

Bit: 0 or 1

Bytes: 00000000
        11111111
        01010101
        10011001
        etc....

The total number of possible combinations for a single byte is 2^8 = 2*2*2*2*2*2*2*2 = 256.

An IP address is then made up of four bytes, or a series of 32 bits. The total number of possible IP addresses that can be used on the Internet then is 2 times itself 32 times. Calculating that out shows that there are 2^{32} = 4,294,967,296, or just over four billion IP addresses available in IPv4.

This is about 20 percent smaller than the total number of people on the planet at the time the Internet Protocol was first conceived, yet many people are justifiably worried about what to do when we run out of Internet addresses. In the early days of the Internet, the body that allocates IP addresses to institutions needing them would hand out large chunks of the overall IP address space. Today an organization requesting IP addresses from one of the governing bodies must carefully justify the use of each and every address.

SUBNET MASKS

To properly specify the identity of a machine on the Internet we need two pieces of information: the IP address and the associated subnet mask.

The Internet is made up of many separate but connected networks. In the context of the overall Internet, each of these separate networks is referred to as a subnet—that is, a network complete in and of itself but yet part of a larger network, namely, the Internet.

An IP address can be used to indicate both a particular machine and the subnet to which it belongs. To simplify the business of finding individual machines on the Internet (the task of routers and switches), we first locate the subnet that the machine is a part of, and then go about finding the particular machine.

A subnet mask basically splits an IP address into two portions: the network number and the host number. A simple example illustrates this.

1. Consider the IP address given above: 123.234.23.21

   A subnet mask could be associated with this address to simply specify that the first three octets (123.234.23) represent the network of the machine and the last octet (21) the host identifier. This subnet would have space for 255 hosts, since the last octet is completely left to specify hosts. The network identifier in this case would properly be written 123.234.23.0.

2. The subnet mask for such a configuration would be 255.255.255.0.

   Another possibility would be a network consisting of the first two octets (123.234) and a host identifier consisting of the last two octets (23.21). In this case the subnet would have space for 255*255 or 65025 hosts. The network identifier in this case would be written as 123.234.0.0.

3. The subnet mask for such a configuration would be 255.255.0.0.

   Now, we may want a subnet that is smaller than 65025 but larger than 255. In this case we must split the network and host identifier along a boundary that doesn't line up with the dots in the octal representation of the IP address. For example, a subnet with 1024 hosts would have a subnet mask of 255.255.248.0.

   Recall that each octet (the number between the dots) represents one byte, which is eight bits. In this case we have allocated the first two octets plus six of the eight bits in the third octet to the network number. The remaining ten bits (two from the third octet and eight from the last octet) comprise the host space. Therefore, we have (2*2)*(2*2*2*2*2*2*2*2) = (4) * (256) = 2^{10} = 1024 hosts in this subnet.

As we mentioned earlier, the task of locating a given IP address on the Internet is carried out in two separate stages. First, the proper network is found, and then the given machine is located. This simplifies the amount of information that Internet routers must remember since they deal only with network identifiers. If the size of the "average" subnet on the Internet is 1,000 hosts, then there are 1,000 times fewer networks than there are hosts and a Internet router has 1,000 times fewer addresses with which to concern itself.

Lab 3.2: IP Addresses 73

LAB 3.2 EXERCISES

3.2.1 UNDERSTAND THE IP ADDRESSING SCHEME

Use the winipcfg utility on your PC.

a) Check the IP address of your PC.

_____

_____

b) Now see what the subnet mask of your PC is.

_____

_____

c) Check your host name to see if it is what you think it should be.

_____

_____

3.2.2 KNOW HOW TO IDENTIFY A DOMAIN NAME BY ITS IP ADDRESS

a) Use the ping utility to check to see if a domain is up. Try out a popular domain, such as yahoo.com, mapquest.com, or barnesandnoble.com. *Find the IP address* of each domain that you check.

_____

_____

b) Now *find the IP address* of the Web site www.yahoo.com.

_____

_____

LAB 3.2

Lab 3.2: IP Addresses

c) Type the IP address of the Web site into your Web browser and check to see if you get the main page of the site.

LAB 3.2 EXERCISE ANSWERS

3.2.1 ANSWERS

Use the winipcfg utility on your PC.

a) Check the IP address of your PC.

Answer: From your PC, go to the Start menu and select Run. When the window comes up, type in the command winipcfg. You will see a box that lists the IP address of your machine.

b) Now see what the subnet mask of your PC is.

Answer: In the box that comes up when you run winipcfg, you will also see a subnet mask for your PC.

c) Check your host name to see if it is what you think it should be.

Answer: If you select the button for "More info," you will see your host name.

3.2.2 ANSWERS

a) Use the ping utility to check to see if a domain is up. Try out a popular domain, such as yahoo.com, mapquest.com, or barnesandnoble.com. Find the IP address of each domain that you check.

Answer: From your PC, go to the Start menu and select Run. When the window comes up, type in the ping command with the domain name—e.g., ping barnesandnoble.com. When I "pinged" the yahoo.com domain, I found that the IP address was: 216.115.108.232 though the company may move the domain to another address between the time that I checked the address and when you do.

b) Now find the IP address of the Web site www.yahoo.com.

Answer: Go back to the Start menu and select Run. Type in "ping www.yahoo.com" or try another domain. If you'd like the window to stay up for a while so you can read it more easily, you can use the –t option by typing "ping www.yahoo.com –t". This will continue the "pinging" process. To end the ping, type in Control-C (press the control and the C keys at the same time). Now, the address I see for www.yahoo.com is 204.71.200.75.

c) Type the IP address of the Web site into your Web browser and check to see if you get the main page of the site.

Answer: Open your Web browser and type in the IP address that you read from the result of the ping command. When I typed in 204.71.200.75, the front page of the Yahoo Web site came up.

LAB 3.2 SELF-REVIEW QUESTIONS

In order to test your progress, you should be able to answer the following questions.

1) At the moment, there is a(n) _____ of IP addresses.

   a) _____ Excess
   b) _____ Shortage

2) Which of the following is looked up first when finding an individual computer on the Internet?

   a) _____ Subnet
   b) _____ Individual computer
   c) _____ None of the above

3) What would be the subnet mask for a network of 255 hosts?

   a) _____ 255.0.0.255
   b) _____ 0.0.0.255
   c) _____ 255.255.255.0
   d) _____ 255.255.248.255
   e) _____ 255.0.255.255.255

4) Which are differences between IPv4 and IPv6? Select all that apply.

   a) _____ IPv4 allows for more bytes of data than IPv6.
   b) _____ IPv6 will be written in 6 groups of three hexadecimal digits.
   c) _____ IPv6 allows for 16-byte addresses while IPv4 allows for 4-byte addresses.
   d) _____ All of the above

Lab 3.2: IP Addresses

5) A single byte can represent how many possible combinations of numbers?

a) _____ 8
b) _____ 64
c) _____ 128
d) _____ 256
e) _____ 512

Quiz answers appear in the Appendix, Section 3.2.

LAB 3.3

DOMAIN NAME SYSTEM (DNS)

> **LAB OBJECTIVES**
>
> After this lab, you will be able to:
> - Understand How Domains Are Associated with IP Addresses
> - Know How a Domain Name Is Resolved

Each Internet host has a unique IP address. The Domain Name System (DNS) provides an association between each name and a specific IP address. When you specify the complete DNS name, for example, benay.asilomar.dara-abrams.com or drew.africa.drewnet.net, this name maps into a particular IP address on the Internet. The IP address provides a way to translate a logical domain name, with a name that can be remembered by humans, into an IP address, a physical address that can be used by the Internet Protocol addressing scheme. When you use a domain name in a URL or as an email address, this domain name—e.g., prenhall.com—is translated into a specific IP address on the Internet.

Thus, the domain name functions in the same way as a CB (citizens band) radio "handle" for an IP address. The domain name scheme provides a logical name for an IP address. However, it is impractical to build and maintain a central list of domain names and their corresponding IP addresses. As with other aspects of the Internet, the workload is distributed across the network. A list of correspondences between IP addresses and domain names is distributed in a hierarchy of authority. For resolving addresses when you send or receive messages or Web pages, your system uses a DNS server in close proximity to your ISP. This DNS server maps domain names in your Internet requests or forwards them to other Internet servers.

IP addresses are essentially the names that networked computers use to talk to each other. Since computers aren't able to differentiate each other using properties

78   Lab 3.3: Domain Name System (DNS)

such as the sound of one's voice or the look of one's face, each computer on the Internet must have a unique IP address.

By the same token, while computers are good at keeping track of lots of large numbers, humans are not as proficient at this task. We generally prefer something more descriptive in terms of a name. Many of us have networked computers on our desks that, if connected to the Internet, also have an IP address, but we rarely know what this address is. To help deal with this difference in understanding between humans and computers, the Domain Name System (DNS) was invented.

Simply put, DNS allows for the association of a name with every IP address. In this way we can refer to our computers simply with names such as Asilomar, Pebblebeach, or Pajaro, using beach names on Monterey Bay. As in real life, we often refer to those close to us using less than their complete names. To assure the uniqueness of a DNS name we must specify it completely. A given computer may therefore be named pajaro.dara-abrams.brainjolt.com.

Where pajaro is a unique name within the context of the domain "dara-abrams," dara-abrams is unique within "brainjolt," and brainjolt within "com." Thus, there may be many "pajaros" on the Internet, but only one pajaro.dara-abrams.brainjolt.com.

LAB 3.3 EXERCISES

3.3.1 UNDERSTAND HOW DOMAINS ARE ASSOCIATED WITH IP ADDRESSES

a) On a UNIX system, issue the command, nslookup, with a random IP address. What results do you get?

3.3.2 KNOW HOW A DOMAIN NAME IS RESOLVED

a) Use the "whois" utility to find the IP address of the name server of a popular domain, such as amazon.com or yahoo.com.

LAB 3.3 EXERCISE ANSWERS

3.3.1 ANSWER

a) On a UNIX system, issue the command, nslookup, with a random IP address. What results do you get?

Answer: The command, nslookup, lists the domain name server used to look up the IP address. Then it lists the DNS entry that the server returns for the IP address you provided.

3.3.2 ANSWER

a) Use the "whois" utility to find the IP address of the name server of a popular domain, such as amazon.com or yahoo.com.

Answer: You can use the "whois" utility on the InterNIC site (www.internic.net). Type in the domain name amazon.com (and select domain) and you will get the name server. I got the following information for the name server: NS2.PNAP.NET. Then I typed in the name server listed and selected Nameserver. Then I saw the following information:

Server Name: NS2.PNAP.NET

IP Address: 206.253.194.97

Registrar: NETWORK SOLUTIONS, INC.

Whois Server: whois.networksolutions.com

Referral URL: www.networksolutions.com

Therefore, the IP address of the primary name server for amazon.com is: 206.253.194.197.

LAB 3.3 SELF-REVIEW QUESTIONS

In order to test your progress, you should be able to answer the following questions.

1) Computers address each other by _____ when talking to each other.

   a) _____ Domain name
   b) _____ IP address
   c) _____ Subnet mask
   d) _____ All of the above

Lab 3.3: Domain Name System (DNS)

2) DNS associates _____ with _____.

    a) _____ IP address, domain name
    b) _____ IP address, subnet mask
    c) _____ Domain name, subnet mask

3) If there is a computer with the domain name of "darwin.millenniumpark.org," can there be a computer with the domain name of "darwin.brainjolt.com"?

    a) _____ Yes
    b) _____ No

4) If you don't know the DNS address, you can't find a Web page.

    a) _____ True
    b) _____ False

5) Machine names must be unique for domain names to be unique.

    a) _____ True
    b) _____ False

Quiz answers appear in the Appendix, Section 3.3.

LAB 3.4

TRANSMISSION CONTROL PROTOCOL (TCP)

LAB OBJECTIVES

After this lab, you will be able to:

- Determine the Socket Number for "Well Known Services"
- Understand the Use of Ports for Services

As its name implies, the Transmission Control Protocol (TCP) has built-in features to control the flow of data (packets) between sender and receiver. This flow control has provided support for the exponential growth of the Internet.

The most important feature of TCP is its accounting for the delivery and acceptance of each packet at its final destination. If a single packet is unable to be delivered successfully to the final destination, the user (a higher layer protocol) is notified.

The Whole Truth

The following terms are used interchangeably with respect to TCP:

socket is the equivalent of *port*

and

connection is the equivalent of *session*

SOCKETS

TCP controls and accounts for the delivery of packets by creating a "connection" or "session" for each TCP communication. TCP is referred to as a "connection-oriented" protocol. Sessions in TCP are created between two endpoints. The endpoints are defined by the IP address and socket number of the session for each machine. Every TCP session is uniquely defined by these two parameters.

When a session is initiated between two endpoints, TCP sends a request to synchronize (a packet called a "syn") to the address of the machine targeted for the connection. This packet includes information about the socket number with which the first machine wishes to connect. The target machine then sends an acknowledgment (an "ack") back to the initiating machine, letting it know that the "syn" was received and that the socket requested is available. In addition (in the same transmission), the second machine sends a "syn" request of its own, stating the socket number that it wishes to send packets back to the initiating machine on. The packet is called a "syn-ack" because it is ack-ing the first packet as well as synching. Finally, the initiating machine sends an "ack" back to the second machine, letting it know that the socket requested in the "syn-ack" is available for communication.

At this point, the TCP session is set up. It can be identified by the unique set of endpoints, the IP address and socket number of the first machine, and the IP address and socket number of the second machine. At any one time, this combination is unique.

> **The Whole Truth**
>
> When a client requests an HTTP connection to a server, it makes the request to the IP address of the server on port 80. The server then picks a random port above 1023 and sends a packet back to the requestor, asking if it can send response packets to the requestor's IP address on the randomly chosen port. If the client has this port available, it acknowledges the request and begins listening on the agreed-on port.
>
> In this way, a client may request multiple simultaneous TCP sessions with a given server and still maintain a unique set of identifiers for each session. There is a random assignment of the port on which the server talks to the client because the port on which the server talks to the client is assigned arbitrarily for each session. If the client is currently using the port suggested by the server, it will deny the request and the server will suggest another port, until a port is agreed upon.

Lab 3.4: Transmission Control Protocol (TCP)

In the IP protocol, two bytes of data are used to define the TCP (or UDP) socket number. This means that there are a total of $(2^8)*(2^8)$ = 255 * 255 = 65,025 possible socket numbers.

Port or socket numbers from 0 to 1023 are reserved for defined processes. In other words, every machine running IP must allow only certain protocols to run on these ports. Ports above 1023 (from 1024 to 65025) are not assigned to specific protocols and may be used for any protocol.

The WWW protocol, HTTP is defined as running on port 80. In other words, the only port between 0 and 1023 that can run HTTP is port 80. However, HTTP daemons are allowed to run on other ports in addition to port 80 as long as the port number is in the range of 1024–65025. While it is perfectly acceptable to run an HTTP daemon on port 8080, it is not allowed to do so on port 25. A common situation is one in which a development Web site is run on an HTTP daemon on port 8080, and the production Web site is run on an HTTP daemon on port 80.

The services that run on ports 0 to 1023 (i.e., the programs that respond to requests on these ports) are referred to as "well known services." It is "well known" that email (SMTP) responds to queries on port 25 and HTTP on port 80. In a UNIX system, you can look in the /etc/services file to see the port number assignments. The telnet service is associated with port 23. The /etc/services file also contains references to UDP sockets. There are references to ports larger than 1023 in the /etc/services file. In this file, there may also be references to other services such as: listen, nterm, kpop, ingreslock, tnet, cfinger.

You may occasionally see examples of port numbers in URLs, set off from the name of the target machine by a colon, e.g., http://www.slac.stanford.edu:80/. In this case, the port number could be left out of the URL and it would work just as well, since all HTTP traffic defaults to port 80 unless otherwise specified. On the other hand, the URL, http://www.slac.stanford.edu:8080/ would not be the same as if the 8080 were left out. Including the 8080 means that the initiating machine will request a connection with an HTTP daemon on www.slac.stanford.edu running on port 8080.

TCP is used for much more than just HTTP. Other common applications that make use of TCP are telnet, FTP, and SMTP (email). In order to differentiate one TCP connection from another, TCP connections are often said to connect to a given "port." Just as a ship destined for the United States must eventually decide which port it will be docking in, a TCP connection must specify the port to which it is destined. The port is specified with an integer number that can represent a specific service (e.g., telnet, FTP, and HTTP). When TCP initiates a connection from one machine to another, it specifies the port to which it wishes to connect, thus telling the other computer which service it wishes to use.

Successful delivery of all packets often requires that TCP retransmit packets that initially fail to reach their destination. In order to minimize the retransmission of packets, TCP has a mechanism to allow it to sense the reliability and potential bandwidth of a given connection. What TCP does is start slowly and work up to the maximum speed it deems possible for a given connection. This mechanism is commonly referred to as the TCP slow-start algorithm. Basically, TCP has a fixed number of packets that it transmits to the destination initially, and then it stops and waits for the receiver to acknowledge successful receipt of the packets. If the first group of packets is successfully acknowledged ("ack-ed"), then another, larger group of packets is sent. If the first group of packets is not successfully ack-ed, TCP retransmits a smaller number of packets in hopes that they will reach the destination successfully and be ack-ed. This pattern of acceleration and deceleration continues until a maximum transmission rate is determined, or all of the packets are sent and successfully ack-ed. If TCP is unable to successfully deliver the packets at any rate, it returns an error to the higher layer application.

The number of packets that TCP sends in a given burst (before stopping and waiting for the ack) is referred to as the TCP window size. The initial window size is a configurable parameter that can be set by a system administrator.

TCP's ability to retransmit packets and account for the successful delivery of each packet introduces overhead in the overall amount of data that must be transmitted by the application, thus increasing the total amount of time required to transmit the data. The tradeoff of this overhead for reliability is one that most applications are willing to suffer. However, there may be times when an application wishes to minimize processing overhead, and is willing to risk a reduction in the reliability of the transmission. We will discuss a lower-overhead protocol, UDP, later in this chapter.

LAB 3.4 EXERCISES

3.4.1 DETERMINE THE SOCKET NUMBER FOR "WELL KNOWN SERVICES"

Find a UNIX system that you can use and look at the file /etc/services on the machine.

    a) What is the port number associated with the application "telnet"?

Lab 3.4: Transmission Control Protocol (TCP)

b) Does /etc/services contain references for only TCP sockets?

___

3.4.2 UNDERSTAND THE USE OF PORTS FOR SERVICES

Take another look at the file /etc/services on the UNIX machine.

a) Are there any references to ports larger than 1023 in the /etc/services file?

___

LAB 3.4 EXERCISE ANSWERS

3.4.1 ANSWERS

Find a UNIX system that you can use and look at the file /etc/services on the machine.

a) What is the port number associated with the application "telnet"?

Answer: telnet is associated with port 23.

b) Does /etc/services contain references for only TCP sockets?

Answer: /etc/services also contains references to UDP sockets.

3.4.2 ANSWER

Take another look at the file /etc/services on the UNIX machine.

a) Are there any references to ports larger than 1023 in the /etc/services file?

Answer: Yes, there are references to ports larger than 1023 in the /etc/services file. The one on the server I just checked has references to: listen, nterm, kpop, ingreslock, tnet, cfinger.

LAB 3.4 SELF-REVIEW QUESTIONS

In order to test your progress, you should be able to answer the following questions.

1) Put the following packets in order, first to last.

   a) _____ syn-ack
   b) _____ syn
   c) _____ ack

2) The TCP slow start algorithm minimizes _____.

   a) _____ Network downtime
   b) _____ Retransmission of packets
   c) _____ DNS server queries
   d) _____ All of the above

3) Multiple HTTP sessions always use the same port.

   a) _____ True
   b) _____ False

4) Ports and sockets refer to which of the following? (Select all that apply.)

   a) _____ Different services
   b) _____ The same thing
   c) _____ IP addresses
   d) _____ None of the above

5) Well known services run on ports less than 256.

   a) _____ True
   b) _____ False

Quiz answers appear in the Appendix, Section 3.4.

LAB 3.5

MAC ADDRESSES

> **LAB OBJECTIVES**
>
> After this lab, you will be able to:
> - Find MAC Addresses of Computers Within Your LAN
> - Read and Interpret Media Access Control (MAC) Addresses

The Internet is often said to be "a network of networks." These many different networks that interconnect to make up the Internet are built using a wide variety of networking technologies (e.g., Ethernet, FDDI, SONET, and ATM). Note that SONET (Synchronous Optical Network) technology is the ANSI standard for synchronous data transmission on optical media. ATM (Asynchronous Transfer Mode) is a high-performance, cell-oriented switching and multiplexing technology carrying different types of traffic via fixed-length packets. Each of these protocols was designed to be used independently of the Internet. Therefore, these protocols were not designed with the Internet addressing scheme in mind. In fact, many of these technologies came into existence before the Internet was in common use.

To facilitate communication between two entities sharing any given networking medium, an addressing scheme must be developed. Thus, each of the different technologies mentioned above was designed with its own addressing scheme specific to the particular technology. Remembering that earlier we described these technologies as layer 2 in the OSI model, these addresses are often called layer 2 addresses. The Media is the physical part of the network, e.g., an Ethernet wire or an FDDI fiber optic cable. The Access Controller is the device in your computer or a router or a switch that controls the access of packets to and from the Media. Thus, another name for a layer 2 address is a Media Access Control (MAC) address.

Lab 3.5: MAC Addresses

When an IP packet crosses the Internet, it will likely cross individual networks of multiple types. This means that the packet will, at different times during its travels, be provided with different layer 2 source and destination addresses.

Figure 3.1 represents the communication between two computers on separate Ethernet segments. On each of these Ethernet segments, there is a router. The routers are also connected together via an FDDI ring. A packet passing from one computer to the other will be assigned three different source and destination addresses as it crosses this network. First, the packet will have a source MAC address of computer A and a destination MAC address of router 1, interface X. Second, the packet will have a source MAC address of router 1, interface Y, and a destination address of router 2, interface X. Last, the packet will have a MAC source address of router 2, interface Y, and a destination MAC address of the end computer, B. During the entire transmission, however, the layer 3 source and destination addresses, the IP source and destination addresses, will be those of the computers A and B respectively.

Another way to understand MAC addresses is to think of a packet as an egg with multiple shells. Initially, an application has some data that it wants to communicate to another computer. This data is encased in a shell that contains the IP address of the machine the data is destined for as well as the IP address of the machine itself, i.e., the source IP address. If the packet is then to be transferred across an Ethernet (to stick with our example above), another shell must be put on the egg, containing the MAC destination address of the "next hop" device along the path to the final destination, in this case, the router. The source MAC address is included as well. When the "frame," as the packet is now called, reaches the router, it strips off the first layer of the shell to expose the IP source and destination address. It then determines where to send the packet and puts a new shell on it with the proper source and destination MAC addresses for the next hop in the packet's journey.

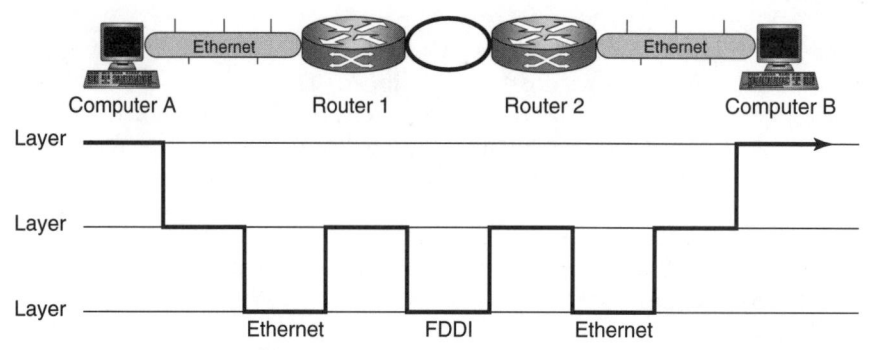

Figure 3.1 ■ **Communication Between Computers on Separate Ethernet Segments.**

This process is repeated until the packet (or datagram) reaches its final destination. At this point, the IP shell is stripped off the packet as well as the MAC shell and the data portion of the packet is handed off to the appropriate application.

MAC ADDRESSES AND ETHERNET

Today, Ethernet is the predominate layer 2 technology used in most Local Area Networks (LANs). In order to ensure that any two computers are able to communicate with each other on an Ethernet segment, every Ethernet adapter manufactured is given a unique MAC address by the vendor at the time of fabrication. These addresses are very much like IP addresses except that they are composed of six different numbers ranging from zero to 255, often delimited with colons. One possible representation of an Ethernet MAC address would be: 01:00:198:234:43:45. More often though, Ethernet MAC addresses are represented using hexadecimal characters. The same MAC address would be written in hexadecimal as 01:00:C6:EA:2B:2D. For those of you who are unfamiliar with hexadecimal (base 16) numbers, the correspondence between hexadecimal and decimal numbers is as follows: 1–9 are the same in hexadecimal and decimal (base 10). Additional numbers in base 16 are indicated by letters, as follows: A=10, B=11, C=12, D=13, E=14, and F=15.

In order for each manufacturer to produce unique MAC addresses when it fabricates Ethernet adapters, the MAC address is broken into two parts: the vendor field and the serial number. The first half of each MAC address is a unique number that is assigned to the manufacturer. The second half of the address is simply a counter that ranges from 00:00:00 to FF:FF:FF (in decimal mode, from 0 to 16,581,375). If a vendor wishes to manufacture more than 16.5 million Ethernet cards, it must apply for a second vendor code. There are a total of over 270 trillion possible MAC addresses, compared with only just over four billion possible IP addresses.

While we have focused on Ethernet MAC addresses, it is important to remember that MAC addresses exist (in one form or another) for each of the different transmission media that make up the Internet.

BROADCAST ADDRESSES

Sometimes a computer will want to communicate the same thing to every other computer on the LAN. Rather than doing this by addressing multiple packets with the same data to each of the machines individually, a special Ethernet MAC address has been defined as a "broadcast" address. Any Ethernet adapter that sees this address as the destination of a frame will read the packet. This special broadcast address is simply the highest possible Ethernet MAC address, that is, FF:FF:FF:FF:FF:FF. Other times, a machine may want to send data to a subset of

Lab 3.5: MAC Addresses

the machines on a given network. This is called "multicasting" and again, there is a special mechanism to handle this type of addressing.

LAB 3.5 EXERCISES

3.5.1 FIND MAC ADDRESSES OF COMPUTERS WITHIN YOUR LAN

a) On your PC, go into DOS and issue the command arp –a. Note: arp stands for Address Resolution Protocol. What results do you get, and what do they mean?

___

___

3.5.2 READ AND INTERPRET MAC ADDRESSES

The physical address of a system is listed as: 00-04-C0-3C-D8-94.

a) What is the vendor code of the machine in decimal notation?

___

___

b) What is the serial number of the machine in decimal notation?

___

___

LAB 3.5 EXERCISE ANSWERS

3.5.1 ANSWER

a) On your PC, go into DOS and issue the command arp –a. Note: arp stands for Address Resolution Protocol. What results do you get, and what do they mean?

Answer: If you have a computer with an Ethernet card on a LAN, you may be able to see the MAC addresses associated with some of the other computers on your LAN.

Most Windows-based machines have a command called "arp" that stands for "Address Resolution Protocol." Under Windows, the "arp" command can usually be issued from the DOS command line. Commonly, the command arp, when issued with the "-a" option will show all the MAC addresses known to your computer.

3.5.2 ANSWERS

The physical address of a system is listed as: 00-04-C0-3C-D8-94.

a) What is the vendor code of the machine in decimal notation?

Answer: The first set of three numbers indicate the manufacturer, that is, the vendor code. Therefore, the vendor code is 00-04-C0 in hexadecimal, which translates into 00-04-192 in decimal notation (C=12 in decimal; for hexadecimal, multiply 12 by 16 because the numbers are in base 16 notation).

b) What is the serial number of the machine in decimal notation?

Answer: The second set of three numbers indicate the serial number of the machine, that is, 3C-D8-94. Translated into decimal notation, the first set is 3*16=48, the second number is 12, therefore, the first pair represents 60. The second pair is 13*16=208 plus 8, which equals 216. The third set translates into 9*16=144 plus 4, which equals 148. The entire serial number in decimal is then 60-216-148.

LAB 3.5 SELF-REVIEW QUESTIONS

In order to test your progress, you should be able to answer the following questions.

1) Each Ethernet adapter has its own unique MAC address.

   a) _____ True
   b) _____ False

2) MAC addresses are transferred between OSI layers.

   a) _____ True
   b) _____ False

3) In network parlance, MAC stands for which of the following?

   a) _____ Michigan Algorithm Coder
   b) _____ Maximum Allowable Cache
   c) _____ Media Access Control
   d) _____ Macaroni and cheese
   e) _____ None of the above

Lab 3.5: MAC Addresses

4) SONET technology uses which of the following?

- a) _____ ATM technology
- b) _____ Optical media
- c) _____ FDDI
- d) _____ Ethernet
- e) _____ All of the above

5) The MAC address functions at which OSI layer?

- a) _____ Layer 2
- b) _____ Layer 3
- c) _____ Layer 1
- d) _____ None of the above

Quiz answers appear in the Appendix, Section 3.5.

LAB 3.6

USER DATAGRAM PROTOCOL (UDP)

LAB OBJECTIVES

After this lab, you will be able to:

✔ Understand the Difference Between TCP and UDP Protocols
✔ List Applications That May Use the UDP Protocol and Understand Why

UDP stands for User Datagram Protocol. However, many people refer to UDP as Unreliable Datagram Protocol. While the vast majority of UDP packets that are sent do indeed reach their destination reliably, UDP does not include mechanisms to guarantee the successful delivery of a given packet. Therefore, UDP is labeled as "unreliable." Given that TCP ensures the reliable delivery of all packets, why would anyone want to use UDP instead?

There are three major reasons to use UDP:

1. UDP incurs less overhead than TCP because it does not include mechanisms to check or ensure that all packets arrive successfully at their destination.
2. Some applications don't need each and every packet to arrive successfully at the destination address.
3. In a properly performing network, the vast majority of UDP packets actually do arrive successfully at their final destination.

Thus, UDP does not really deserve to be called unreliable.

Lab 3.6: User Datagram Protocol (UDP)

UDP is commonly used in applications that don't require that every single packet arrive at its destination successfully. In addition, there is no reason that an application can't use UDP and still demand that every packet arrives successfully at its final destination. In this case, accounting for the proper delivery of every data packet becomes the responsibility of the higher layer application that is making use of UDP. UDP itself will not take care of this for you.

If an application demands successful transmission of every packet, it can use TCP, which will automatically take care of this requirement. Alternatively, the programmer can choose to use UDP and then build additional functionality into the application to account for each data packet. However, it is generally easier in this case to use TCP.

LAB 3.6 EXERCISES

3.6.1 UNDERSTAND THE DIFFERENCE BETWEEN TCP AND UDP PROTOCOLS

a) What is the major difference between UDP and TCP?

_____

_____

3.6.2 LIST APPLICATIONS THAT MAY USE THE UDP PROTOCOL AND UNDERSTAND WHY

a) List two applications that may use UDP and explain why UDP was chosen.

_____

_____

LAB 3.6 EXERCISE ANSWERS

3.6.1 ANSWER

a) What is the major difference between UDP and TCP?

Answer: UDP does not account for the successful delivery of every packet as TCP does. That is why UDP is sometimes referred to as Unreliable Datagram Protocol. However, it is not that UDP is really unreliable, it just does not do the processing that TCP does to account for every packet. With UDP, it is okay if a few random packets are lost, and UDP offers a faster rate of packet delivery with less overhead processing than TCP. However, some applications require that each packet is delivered successfully and thus, these applications should use the TCP protocol.

3.6.2 ANSWER

a) List two applications that may use UDP and explain why UDP was chosen.

Answer: Consider, for example, a streaming media application. The overall quality of the end experience is dependent on a sufficient number of packets actually being delivered. However, the loss of a few random packets (associated with the loss of a random screen update—resulting in occasional jerkiness of the image) may be acceptable if the tradeoff is an overall improvement in the rate at which packets are delivered.

Another common example of a situation in which UDP is often used involves applications that log statistical information about their performance to a remote server. In the case that the connection to the remote server becomes congested, one may decide not to waste time retransmitting the logging messages (as TCP would do) but rather to let them "drop on the floor" until the connection is back and performing properly. In this way, the logging function is less likely to interfere with the proper performance of the core application.

LAB 3.6 SELF-REVIEW QUESTIONS

In order to test your progress, you should be able to answer the following questions.

1) What is the ideal protocol to use for the following situations? (TCP or UDP)

   a) _____ Email
   b) _____ Web
   c) _____ Streaming media
   d) _____ FTP
   e) _____ Log file transfer

2) With help from a lower level application, UDP can be as reliable as TCP.

   a) _____ True
   b) _____ False

Lab 3.6: User Datagram Protocol (UDP)

3) Which of the following is true for UDP? Select all that apply.

   a) _____ UDP is considered to be unreliable.
   b) _____ UDP guarantees successful delivery of a packet.
   c) _____ UDP is often used for streaming media.
   d) _____ UDP incurs less overhead than TCP.
   e) _____ UDP is more reliable than TCP.

4) For UDP to be as reliable as TCP, which of the following must occur?

   a) _____ A lower level application must take care of tracking packets.
   b) _____ Additional functionality must be built into a higher level application.
   c) _____ Additional code must be written in Java.
   d) _____ UDP can't be as reliable as TCP.

5) The advantage of using UDP is which of the following?

   a) _____ UDP is more reliable than TCP.
   b) _____ UDP incurs less overhead than TCP.
   c) _____ UDP is a nonstandard protocol.
   d) _____ None of the above.

Quiz answers appear in the Appendix, Section 3.6.

CHAPTER 3

TEST YOUR THINKING

Traceroute is a program that can be used to trace the path of packets from one computer to another. On Windows computers, this utility is known as tracert. When starting traceroute or tracert, specify the host that you want on the other end of the path (your computer is the start of the path). Note: In Windows, start tracert by using the Run command off the Start menu. In Windows, you can trace from your computer to the Yahoo! Web server with the following command: tracert www.yahoo.com. Traceroute will then display information on all the hosts that are on the path.

Use traceroute on the server of one of your favorite Web sites. After the program finishes, look for the following by examining the DNS entries on the hosts:

1) Notice the timing of the packet's movement.
    When did the packet leave your ISP's network?
    When did the packet travel over a large backbone?
    When did the packet travel through a MAE (if it did)?
    When did the packet reach the destination Web server's ISP?
2) How much time did each host take to process the packet?
    Which hosts were the slowest?
    Where are the slow hosts located—in your ISP's network or on a backbone?

CHAPTER 4

APPLICATIONS AND PROTOCOLS

> **CHAPTER OBJECTIVES**
>
> In this chapter, you will learn about:
>
> ✓ Hypertext Transfer Protocol (HTTP)　　　　　Page 100
> ✓ SMTP, MIME, and FTP　　　　　　　　　　　Page 108
> ✓ Push and Pull Technologies　　　　　　　　　Page 113
> ✓ Streaming Multimedia　　　　　　　　　　　Page 117

The Hypertext Transfer Protocol (HTTP) is the basic protocol underlying the World Wide Web. In this chapter, we will discuss HTTP protocol along with the major email and file transfer protocols, SMTP, MIME, and FTP. We'll also explore the differences between push and pull approaches to presenting information on the Web. Server-based technologies such as streaming multimedia offer yet another mechanism for high-bandwidth delivery of information via the Web.

LAB 4.1

HYPERTEXT TRANSFER PROTOCOL (HTTP)

> ### LAB OBJECTIVES
>
> After this lab, you will be able to:
> - Diagram Web Page Retrieval from the Internet
> - Diagram Web Page Retrieval from Cache

The Hypertext Transfer Protocol (HTTP) was developed as a set of rules for exchanging files on the Web. One of the advances introduced by the Web was the ability for HTTP to handle data in the form of text, images, sound, video, and other types of mixed multimedia formats. Relative to TCP/IP, HTTP is an application protocol that uses the transport and network protocols of the Internet to transmit data. HTTP is considered a lightweight protocol. Following the client/server model, the Web has a client component, that is, the Web browser, and a server component, the Web server software. Each Web server has an HTTPD or Hypertext Transfer Protocol daemon that waits in attendance for requests to come in from the rest of the Web. In software systems, a daemon is a program whose purpose is to wait for requests to come in and then forward these requests to other processes as appropriate.

When HTTPD was initially developed, it used the terminology of UNIX systems and was referred to as a daemon, a process running on a server. Now, most people refer to the HTTP daemon as a Web server. The HTTPD program is designed to wait for HTTP requests and handle them when they arrive. A request is made in the form of a URL, a uniform resource locator, which identifies the Web page that the client would like the Web browser to retrieve from a Web server on the Internet. Each URL can be translated into an IP address using the Domain Name System (DNS) we discussed in Chapter 3. The Web server can also pass on FTP, Telnet and local file requests when they are indicated in the URL.

Lab 4.1: Hypertext Transfer Protocol (HTTP)

The Web browser, Netscape Navigator or Communicator, Internet Explorer, or a browser from another vendor, acts as the HTTP client. The Web browser sends a request to a server machine. This request is made by the user who types in a URL or clicks on a hypertext link (which points to a URL). The Web browser then builds an HTTP request and sends this request to the IP address indicated by the URL. The destination HTTP daemon receives the user's request and returns the requested file to the client.

The Hypertext Transfer Protocol (HTTP) is the set of rules for exchanging files (text, graphic images, sound, video, and other multimedia files) on the World Wide Web. The HTTP protocol is called a transfer protocol because it supports the concept that files may contain references to other files, the selection of which will in turn spawn additional transfer requests. Any Web server machine contains, in addition to the HTML and other files it can serve, an HTTP daemon, a program that is designed to wait for HTTP requests and handle them when they arrive. Your Web browser is an HTTP client, sending requests to server machines. When you type in a Uniform Resource Locator or URL or click on a hypertext link, your browser builds an HTTP request and sends it to the Internet Protocol address indicated by the URL. The HTTP daemon in the destination server machine receives this request. After any necessary processing, the HTTP daemon on the destination Web server returns the requested file.

A browser is an application program that provides a way to look at and interact with all the information on the World Wide Web. The word "browser" was used prior to the Web as a generic term for user interfaces that let you browse text files online. By 1992, when Mosaic with its graphical user interface was released, the term browser was used to indicate a user interface that lets you browse multimedia files. Technically, a Web browser is a client program that uses the Hypertext Transfer Protocol (HTTP) to make requests of Web servers throughout the Internet on behalf of the browser user. In addition to Netscape Communicator and Navigator and Microsoft Internet Explorer, there are less commonly used browsers, such as Lynx and Opera. Lynx is a text-only browser for UNIX shell and VMS users. Opera Software in Norway has developed a thin browser client that has been catching on with developers of Web content and applications for network appliances and information kiosks.

HTTP 1.1 is the successor to HTTP 1.0. HTTP 1.1 was developed to address such issues as performance and persistence. Instead of opening and closing a connection for each application request, HTTP 1.1 provides a persistent connection that allows multiple requests to be batched or pipelined to an output buffer. The underlying TCP layer can put multiple requests (and responses to requests) into one TCP segment that gets forwarded to the IP layer for packet transmission. Since there are fewer connection and disconnection requests for a sequence of "get a file" requests, fewer packets need to flow across the Internet. Since requests are pipelined, TCP segments are more efficient. The overall result is less Internet traffic and faster performance for the user.

HTTP 1.1 uses the URI (Uniform Resource Identifier), to identify and locate requested points of content. The URI has two forms:

- URL (Uniform Resource Locator) as used by HTTP 1.0
- URN (Uniform Resource Name) introduced with HTTP 1.1 for persistent names

Since there are many points of content on the Internet, a URI is used to identify any of those points of content. These points of content may be a page of text, a video or sound clip, a still or animated image, or a program. The most common form of URI is a Web page address. The Web page address is a URL as used in HTTP 1.0, and the more common form of a URI in HTTP 1.1.

A URI typically describes:

- The mechanism used to access the resource
- The specific computer on which the resource is currently stored
- The specific name of the resource on the computer as indicated by a file name in a directory

This is an example URI:

http://www.brainjolt.com/images/logo.gif

This URI identifies an image that can be accessed using the Web protocol application, HTTP, ("http://"). The image is stored in a file on a computer, which has the name "www.brainjolt.com." This computer name can be mapped to a unique Internet address. In the computer's directory structure, the "logo.gif" image file is located in the directory named "images."

URIs can be also be used to specify FTP addresses and email addresses with character strings. These URIs are also the subset of URIs that are URLs.

The second type of URI is the Uniform Resource Name (URN). A URN is a form of URI that has "institutional persistence." This is the new concept that has been added to the idea of the URL as a locator. With a URN, while the exact location may change in the future, the persistent quality of the URN will allow some agency to find the named resource in the future.

When a browser supporting HTTP 1.1 indicates it can decompress HTML files, a server will compress them for transport across the Internet, providing a substantial aggregate savings in the amount of data that has to be transmitted. Since image files are already in a compressed format, this improvement applies only to HTML and other non-image data types.

In addition to persistent connections and other performance improvements, HTTP 1.1 also provides the ability to have multiple domain names share the same Internet address (IP address). This simplifies processing for Web servers that host a number of Web sites with "virtual domains" through what is referred to as "virtual hosting."

The HTTP protocol is a request/response protocol. A client sends a request to the server in the form of a request method, URI, and protocol version, followed by a MIME-like message containing request modifiers, client information, and possible body content over a connection with a server. The server responds with a status line, including the message's protocol version and a success or error code, followed by a MIME-like message containing server information, entity meta-information, and possible entity-body content.

Most HTTP communication is initiated by a user agent and consists of a request to be applied to a resource on some origin server. In the simplest case, this may be accomplished via a single connection (v) between the user agent (UA) and the origin server (O):

request chain -------------->UA --------------v-------------- O<-------------- response chain

A more complicated situation occurs when one or more intermediaries are present in the request/response chain. There are three common forms of intermediary: proxy, gateway, and tunnel. A proxy is a forwarding agent, receiving requests for a URI in its absolute form, rewriting all or part of the message, and forwarding the reformatted request toward the server identified by the URI. A gateway is a receiving agent, acting as a layer above some other server(s) and, if necessary, translating the requests to the underlying server's protocol. A tunnel acts as a relay point between two connections without changing the messages; tunnels are used when the communication needs to pass through an intermediary (such as a firewall) even when the intermediary cannot understand the contents of the messages.

request chain ---->UA ----v---- A ----v---- B ----v---- C ----v---- O<---- response chain

The chain above shows three intermediaries (A, B, and C) between the user agent and origin server. A request or response message that travels the whole chain will pass through four separate connections. This distinction is important because some HTTP communication options may apply only to the connection with the nearest, non-tunnel neighbor, only to the endpoints of the chain, or to all connections along the chain. Although the diagram is linear, each participant may be engaged in multiple, simultaneous communications. For example, B may be receiving requests from many clients other than A, and/or forwarding requests to servers other than C, at the same time that it is handling A's request.

LAB 4.1 EXERCISES

4.1.1 DIAGRAM WEB PAGE RETRIEVAL FROM THE INTERNET

a) Draw a flow chart illustrating the steps involved in a Web client's making a request for a Web page either by clicking on a hypertext link or by typing in a URL. Illustrate the process of retrieving the requested page from the Internet.

4.1.2 DIAGRAM WEB PAGE RETRIEVAL FROM CACHE

Any party to a Web page communication, which is not acting as a tunnel, may employ an internal cache for handling requests. The effect of a cache is that the request/response chain is shortened if one of the participants along the chain has a cached response applicable to that request.

a) Draw a diagram of the request/response chain that demonstrates retrieving a cached page.

LAB 4.1 EXERCISE ANSWERS

4.1.1 ANSWER

a) Draw a flow chart illustrating the steps involved in a Web client's making a request for a Web page either by clicking on a hypertext link or by typing in a URL. Illustrate the process of retrieving the requested page from the Internet.

Answer:

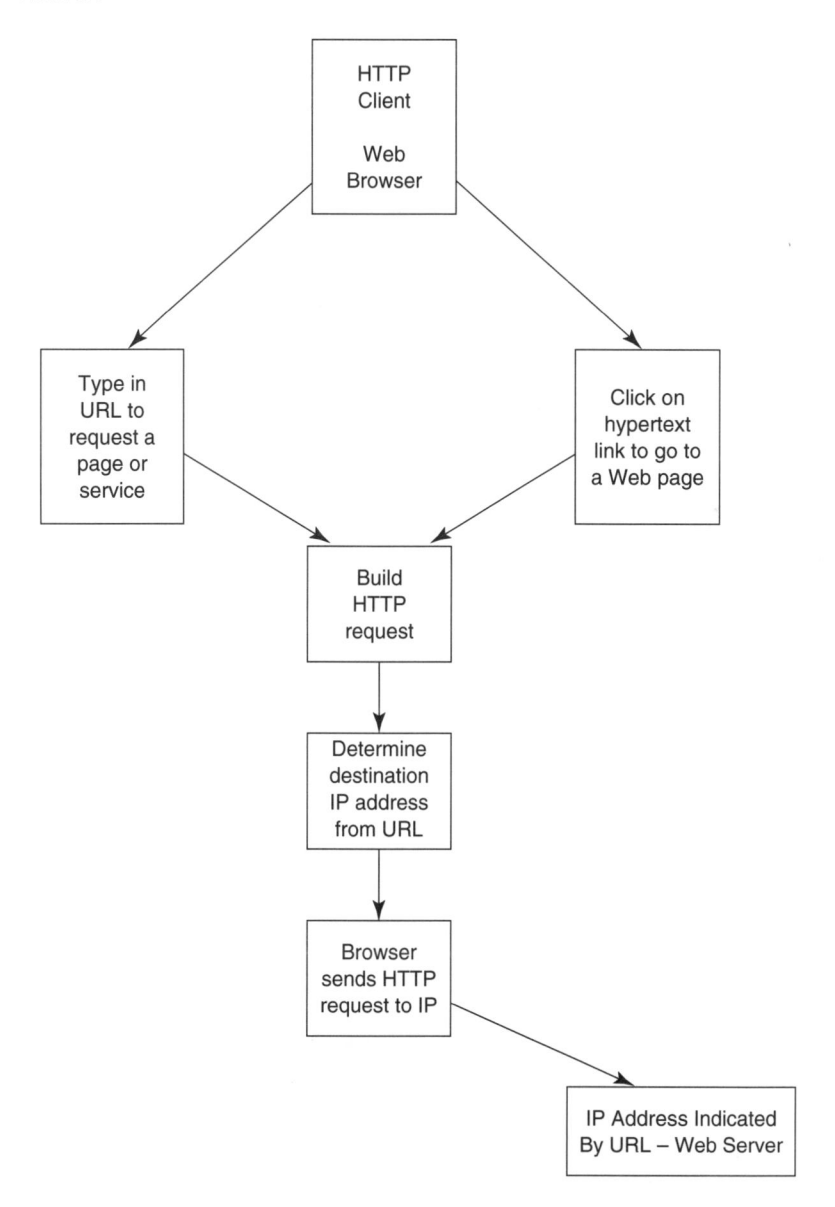

```
          HTTP Client
          Web Browser
         /           \
        /             \
  Type in URL to    Click on hypertext
  request a page    link to go to
  or service        a Web page
        \             /
         \           /
         Build HTTP request
              |
         Determine destination
         IP address from URL
              |
         Browser sends HTTP
         request to IP
              |
         IP Address Indicated
         By URL – Web Server
```

4.1.2 Answer

Any party to a Web page communication, which is not acting as a tunnel, may employ an internal cache for handling requests. The effect of a cache is that the request/response chain is shortened if one of the participants along the chain has a cached response applicable to that request.

a) Draw a diagram of the request/response chain that demonstrates retrieving a cached page.

Answer: The following illustrates the resulting chain if B has a cached copy of an earlier response from O (via C) for a request, that has not been cached by UA or A.

request chain ------->UA -----v----- A -----v----- B ------ C ----- O<------ response chain

Lab 4.1 Self-Review Questions

In order to test your progress, you should be able to answer the following questions.

1) HTTP requests are made in the form of a(n) _____.

    a) _____ IP address
    b) _____ Domain name
    c) _____ URL
    d) _____ All of the above

2) HTTP 1.1 provides a persistent connection.

    a) _____ True
    b) _____ False

3) Which of the following are forms of intermediaries? (Select all that apply.)

    a) _____ Browser
    b) _____ Proxy
    c) _____ Server
    d) _____ Tunnel

4) What is the difference between a Web server and a Web client? (Select all that apply.)

    a) _____ A Web client requests a page while the Web server sends the page.
    b) _____ The Web client displays the information, which the Web server sends.
    c) _____ The Web client is secure but the Web server isn't.
    d) _____ The Web client runs on a PC while the Web server runs on a UNIX system.

5) Compare TCP and HTTP protocols. (Select all that apply.)

   a) _____ TCP operates at a higher layer of the OSI model than HTTP does.
   b) _____ HTTP sits on top of TCP.
   c) _____ TCP is a layer 4 protocol.
   d) _____ HTTP and TCP operate at the same level; neither is on top of the other.

Quiz answers appear in the Appendix, Section 4.1.

LAB 4.2

SMTP, MIME, AND FTP

> **LAB OBJECTIVES**
>
> After this lab, you will be able to:
> - Understand How Mail Protocols Work
> - Know How to Use File Transfer Protocol

As its name implies, SMTP, the Simple Mail Transfer Protocol, is a protocol for transmitting data in the form of email. SMTP uses the TCP/IP protocol to send and receive email. Since message queuing facilities are limited with the SMTP protocol, people often add a protocol to handle message queuing. The two most frequently used message queuing protocols are POP3 and IMAP. POP3 is the Post Office Protocol 3, which handles mail store and forward facilities for such software packages as Eudora. Since more people are accessing email from mobile systems, people have been moving to message queuing that stores messages on remote file servers for access from any system. IMAP, the Internet Message Access Protocol, stores email messages on a remote file server for access from mobile systems. Accessing email through the Netscape browser, you can choose between POP3 and IMAP protocols to operate in conjunction with SMTP. SMTP is standardized in IETF RFC 821. SMTP usually operates over TCP port 25.

MIME stands for Multipurpose Internet Mail Extensions. The MIME protocol provides an extension of the Internet email protocol. With the MIME protocol, you are able to exchange audio, video, images, and applications. Although MIME was originally developed for email extensions, it is now used most frequently on the Web for exchanging various types of file formats. Servers insert the MIME header at the beginning of a Web transmission. Then the clients use the MIME header to indicate the data type, which is known as the MIME type. For built-in types that are understood by the browser, the browser selects the appropriate "player" application for that particular data type. However, if the data type is not understood by the browser, it will ask what player you would like it to use. You can point to the appropriate player so that your browser will use the right type of player to display that data type. You can also download the appropriate player, using downloadable players or plug-ins that are available on certain Web sites.

FTP stands for the File Transfer Protocol. This protocol handles the exchange of files between Internet hosts. FTP is an application protocol that uses Internet's TCP/IP protocols as HTTP and SMTP do. FTP was used by "techies" to exchange files well before the advent of the Web. With FTP, a Webmaster can create Web pages and then transfer the Web page files from the creator's system to a Web server on the Internet. FTP provides the facility to download programs and files from other servers. One problem with FTP is that the text commands to use FTP are intimidating for nontechnical users. Using FTP through a Web browser or through an FTP package with a graphical user interface allows users of various levels of technical expertise to move files from one system to another or to retrieve files from another system.

LAB 4.2 EXERCISES

4.2.1 UNDERSTAND HOW MAIL PROTOCOLS WORK

Go to your browser and check the preferences/options (depending on which browser you use) for mail servers. Notice the request for SMTP server. Experiment with the settings.

    a) What happens if you provide information on the incoming mail server but not on the outgoing mail server?

    b) What information is required so that you can send email from your user account on your mail server?

Lab 4.2: SMTP, MIME, and FTP

4.2.2 KNOW HOW TO USE FILE TRANSFER PROTOCOL

Go to the software archives of Free Software by typing ftp://ftp.freesoftware.com/ into your browser window.

Check out the open source software available via FTP.

a) Try using FTP through your browser or as a utility on your PC. You can use the Windows-based FTP utility, Ws_ftp, to transfer pages to your Web server that you've built on your PC. Find the log, Ws_ftp.log, that tracks the most recent files that were transferred. How can you tell whether the file was moved to the server or moved from the server to the PC?

___

___

LAB 4.2 EXERCISE ANSWERS

4.2.1 ANSWERS

Go to your browser and check the preferences/options (depending on which browser you use) for mail servers. Notice the request for SMTP server. Experiment with the settings.

a) What happens if you provide information on the incoming mail server but not on the outgoing mail server?

Answer: You won't be able to send a Web page or email using your browser. Even if you use a separate email package such as Eudora, it's good to configure your mail server on your browser so that you can forward a Web page to a colleague or friend.

b) What information is required so that you can send email from your user account on your mail server?

Answer: You need to provide the outgoing mail server as well as your user name so that you can send email from your user account on your mail server. If you are traveling, you may have access to another mail server to use for outgoing mail.

Lab 4.2: SMTP, MIME, and FTP

4.2.2 ANSWER

Go to the software archives of Free Software by typing ftp://ftp.freesoftware.com/ into your browser window.

Check out the open source software available via FTP.

a) Try using FTP through your browser or as a utility on your PC. You can use the Windows-based FTP utility, Ws_ftp, to transfer pages to your Web server that you've built on your PC. Find the log, Ws_ftp.log, that tracks the most recent files that were transferred. How can you tell whether the file was moved to the server or moved from the server to the PC?

Answer: In the Ws_ftp.log, there is a list of files that have been transferred in the most recent file transfer. Directional arrows indicate which way the files have been transferred (--> from my PC to the Web server, <-- from the Web server to my PC).

LAB 4.2 SELF-REVIEW QUESTIONS

In order to test your progress, you should be able to answer the following questions.

1) MIME headers are used to identify the _____ of a file.

   a) _____ Size
   b) _____ Data type
   c) _____ Origin
   d) _____ None of the above

2) Messages are stored on the _____ when using the IMAP protocol.

   a) _____ Client
   b) _____ Router
   c) _____ Email server
   d) _____ Web server

3) The _____ protocol is used to send and receive email.

   a) _____ POP3
   b) _____ IMAP
   c) _____ HTTPD
   d) _____ SMTP
   e) _____ FTP

Lab 4.2: SMTP, MIME, and FTP

4) The IMAP mail protocol would help if you're which of the following? (Choose the most appropriate.)

   a) _____ A field sales person
   b) _____ A novice user
   c) _____ A high-tech user
   d) _____ A UNIX programmer

5) The POP3 protocol would help if you're which of the following? (Choose the most appropriate.)

   a) _____ A mobile phone user
   b) _____ A Eudora user
   c) _____ A sales person who travels frequently
   d) _____ A browser user

Quiz answers appear in the Appendix, Section 4.2.

LAB 4.3

PUSH AND PULL TECHNOLOGIES

LAB OBJECTIVES

After this lab, you will be able to:

- Differentiate Between Push and Pull Techniques
- Consider When Push Technology Is Appropriate

Push and pull are two methods to distribute live information to Internet users. The term "push technology" is used in the same way as "push marketing," in which customers are automatically provided with information and services in order to secure their business. On the other hand, in "pull marketing," it is up to the customers to decide that they need particular products or services, perhaps by looking up a company in the yellow pages. Each technology has its own strengths and weaknesses. Both are used to transmit not only text but also images, animations, and video. As its name suggests, push involves a server sending data to a client automatically. Push technology is used to provide live updates to Web sites that feature news, stock quotes, and other frequently changing data. With push technology, a script running on the server delivers information to clients without the clients having to request the information. Pull technology involves a similar script to deliver information. However, the script runs on the client side and automatically requests information for the client from a server.

Originally, Web browsing was set up as a pull technology, providing the information on Web pages and inviting users to request information and peruse the pages that they wanted. If you want to buy a book, you can decide to go to amazon.com or barnesandnoble.com to read reviews and to order the book. You are willing to "pull" the information down since you are actively looking for a particular book. There are other types of information that you would like to have

114 Lab 4.3: Push and Pull Technologies

current and available at all times, such as stock quotes, weather advisories, or news reports. Some companies set up such information with push technology so that the information would be updated without your intervention. Many people started using PointCast as a news service, which is continually updated on their screen.

LAB 4.3 EXERCISES

4.3.1 DIFFERENTIATE BETWEEN PUSH AND PULL TECHNOLOGIES

a) Look on the Web for examples of push and pull technologies. Give an example of each.

4.3.2 CONSIDER WHEN PUSH TECHNOLOGY IS APPROPRIATE

a) When do you think push technology is appropriate to use?

LAB 4.3 EXERCISE ANSWERS

4.3.1 ANSWER

a) Look on the Web for examples of push and pull technologies. Give an example of each.

Answer: In push technology, a script runs on the server to automatically deliver information to clients. You can add weather forecasts (www.weather.com) to your site and use push technology to automatically provide users with current weather reports. In pull technology, a script runs on the client to automatically request information from servers. Any request that you make for a particular Web page on a site makes use of pull technology.

4.3.2 ANSWER

a) When do you think push technology is appropriate to use?

Answer: The use of push technology needs to be considered in light of audience requirements and expectations. Push technology has not been very successful despite the large amount of capital that has been invested in the development and marketing of the technology. The failure of push technology to catch on in the market points out an important issue for Webmasters to consider. Whether we, as technology developers, are excited about a particular Web technology or application, real live users decide whether they want to use certain features, what types of Web functionality is useful to them, and what information is important to them. These real live users make up the audience that we are trying to reach with our Web sites. Market researchers spend lots of time, money, and effort understanding market requirements and audience expectations. It is critical for us as Webmasters to carefully consider who our target audience is for our Web site. We need to know what type of hardware, software, and network facilities our audience is using. If you are hosting a consumer site attracting nontechnical home users, your audience might still be using 28.8K baud dial-up modems. If you are doing business-to-business electronic commerce on the Web, your audience most likely has access to high-speed fiber optic links, T-1, or DSL lines in corporations. Such questions are extremely important to consider when designing the Web site and determining the technology and facilities that will be used. The failure of push technology to catch on beyond the initial interest demonstrates that we need to stay alert to market trends, to what our users and customers want, and to what facilities our users have available to them to access our Web content.

LAB 4.3 SELF-REVIEW QUESTIONS

In order to test your progress, you should be able to answer the following questions.

1) With which technology is content automatically downloaded?

   a) _____ Push
   b) _____ Pull
   c) _____ All of the above

2) Push technology has been successful.

   a) _____ True
   b) _____ False

Lab 4.3: Push and Pull Technologies

3) When you sign up with Amazon.com, they make recommendations for you each time you return to the site and log in. This is an example of which technology?

    a) _____ Push
    b) _____ Pull
    c) _____ Neither of these

4) Suppose you register with Prentice Hall's Web site and request a monthly newsletter informing you of new technologies and recent books. This newsletter is delivered to you via email. This is an example of which technology?

    a) _____ Push
    b) _____ Pull
    c) _____ Neither of these

5) With pull technology, a script running on the server delivers information to clients without the clients having to request the information.

    a) _____ True
    b) _____ False

Quiz answers appear in the Appendix, Section 4.3.

LAB 4.4

STREAMING MULTIMEDIA

> **LAB OBJECTIVES**
>
> After this lab, you will be able to:
>
> ✔ Know the Delivery Mechanisms Involved in Streaming Media
> ✔ Determine When to Provide Streaming Multimedia Facilities

Hypermedia, a term derived from hypertext, extends the notion of the hypertext link to include links among any set of multimedia objects, including sound, motion video, and virtual reality. It can also connote a higher level of user/network interactivity than the interactivity already implicit in hypertext.

The idea behind streaming media is to continually transfer small chunks of a large package so that a narrow pipe can be used for transmission. One major problem with the Internet today is that most users don't have broadband access to the Internet. Many users are also limited by the systems and software to which they have access. Webmasters and creators of Web sites need to consider the type of equipment and network access their users are most likely to have. The importance of designing Web sites appropriate for your user cannot be overemphasized. Designing a site that requires high-speed access for users most likely to access the Web site via dial-up modems will frustrate these users and discourage them from returning to the Web site.

Broadband provides high-speed access to multimedia information that is being streamed from a Web server. The term broadband refers to telecommunication technologies that provide multiple channels of data over a single communications medium. This is typically accomplished by using some form of frequency or wave division multiplexing. Multiplexing is accomplished by sending multiple signals or streams of information on a carrier at the same time in the form of a single, complex signal and then recovering the separate signals at the receiving end. There are different multiplexing approaches depending on whether signals are in analog or digital form. Digital signals are usually multiplexed via time-division multiplexing (TDM). In time-division multiplexing, multiple signals are carried over the same channel in alternating time slots. Frequency-division multiplexing (FDM) is the technique most often used to multiplex analog signals. In frequency-division multiplexing, the carrier bandwidth is divided into subchannels of different frequency widths. Each of the subchannels carries a signal at the same time in parallel with the other subchannels.

Dense wavelength-division multiplexing (DWDM) is the approach that is used for some optical fiber networks. In dense wavelength-division multiplexing, multiple signals are carried together as separate wavelengths of light in a multiplexed signal. Streaming transmission allows users with slow Internet connections to access audio and video files that would normally be too large for them to access.

Broadband access is often dedicated access. Another term for a dedicated line is a nonswitched line. A dedicated line is therefore not a dial-up or switched line, and it is not shared among many users, as dial-up lines are. A dedicated line is a telecommunications path between two points that is available at all times for use by a designated user. Due to cost of renting a line from the telephone company, an individual is not usually the sole user. Most often, companies secure leased lines from the telephone company for high-speed access to the Internet by their staff.

Multimedia information can be downloaded to a user's workstation or personal computer. However, downloading takes a lot of time and a lot of space on the user's system. In addition, there are situations in which the owner of the multimedia information wants to allow users to listen or see the contents of the streamed data but not retain a copy of the contents. Streaming technology allows the Web site administrator to keep the contents on the Web server. Some online courses use a streaming approach not only to allow students to see and hear the contents in a live setting but also to retain ownership of the contents on the server site. It is now possible to stream video data over a 28.8K baud modem. Sophisticated data compression techniques are used to greatly reduce the amount of data that needs to be transmitted. Compression is the reduction in size of data in order to save space or transmission time. For data transmission, compression can be performed on just the data content or on the entire transmission unit (including header data) depending on a number of factors. Content compression can be as simple as removing all extra space characters, inserting a single repeat character to indicate a string of repeated characters, and substituting smaller bit strings for frequently occurring characters. This kind of compression can reduce a text file to 50 percent of its original size. Compression is performed by a program that uses a formula or algorithm to determine how to compress or decompress data. Graphic image, audio, and video file formats are usually designed to compress information as much as possible (since these tend to become very large files).

Streaming video is a sequence of "moving images" that are sent in compressed form over the Internet and displayed by the viewer as they arrive. Streaming media is streaming video with sound. With streaming video or streaming media, a Web user does not have to wait to completely download a large file before seeing the video or hearing the sound. Instead, the media is sent in a continuous stream and is played as it arrives. The user needs a player, which is a special program that uncompresses and sends video data to the display and audio data to speakers. A player can be either an integral part of a browser or downloaded from the software maker's Web site.

Major streaming video and streaming media technologies include RealSystem G2 from RealNetwork, Microsoft Windows Media Technologies (including its NetShow Services and Theater Server), and VDO. Microsoft's approach uses the standard MPEG-4 compression algorithm for video. The other approaches use proprietary algorithms. (The program that does the compression and decompression is sometimes called the codec.) Microsoft's technology offers streaming stereo audio at up to 96 Kbps and streaming video at up to 8 Mbps (for the NetShow Theater Server). However, for most Web users, the streaming video will be limited to the data rates of the connection (for example, up to 128 Kbps with an ISDN connection). Microsoft's streaming media files are in its Advanced Streaming Format (ASF).

Streaming video is usually sent from prerecorded video files, but can be distributed as part of a live broadcast "feed." In a live broadcast, the video signal is converted into a compressed digital signal and transmitted from a special Web server that is able to do multicasting, sending the same file to multiple users at the same time.

Streaming sound is sound that is played as it arrives. The alternative is a sound recording (such as a WAV file) that doesn't start playing until the entire file has arrived. Support for streaming sound may require a plug-in player or come with the browser. Leading providers of streaming sound include Progressive Networks' RealAudio and Macromedia's Shockwave for Director (which includes an animation player as well).

LAB 4.4 EXERCISES

4.4.1 KNOW THE DELIVERY MECHANISMS INVOLVED IN STREAMING MEDIA

a) Imagine that you are going to do a live broadcast of a seminar. What technology can you use to deliver the online broadcast?

4.4.2 DETERMINE WHEN TO PROVIDE STREAMING MULTIMEDIA FACILITIES

Multimedia content can be streamed to the user. Take a look at an online education site to see courses delivered via streaming video.

Go to the Stanford Online site at online.stanford.edu.

Try one of the free online courses. First, you will need to download and install the Microsoft Media Player if you don't have it on your system already. You can download the Microsoft Media Player from the Stanford Online site.

Courses are offered at two levels of compression: Low Bandwidth (28.8 Kbps or greater) or High Bandwidth (Dual ISDN or greater). Try viewing a course at each of the levels if you have access to a high enough bandwidth network connection.

   a) Compare the quality of the video image and the sound. Can you view all the streams at the low bandwidth rate through your network connection? In your mind, how does the quality of the video stream compare to a television image? Do you think the quality and performance are adequate for delivering a college course? Assuming that the video is of comparable quality, would you prefer seeing a course on TV or on your computer?

LAB 4.4 EXERCISE ANSWERS

4.4.1 ANSWER

   a) Imagine that you are going to do a live broadcast of a seminar. What technology can you use to deliver the online broadcast?

   Answer: For broadcasting live events, you need to use live television broadcast equipment (video camera, editing equipment, etc.) along with Internet video streaming technology, including compression software. Stanford uses technology-equipped classrooms with video cameras permanently installed in the room. It is important to realize that the site at which the media is encoded and streamed to users does not have to be the same site as the location where the event actually takes place. Stanford has an editing room where the video is edited. There is a separate facility in an adjoining building where the compression is performed and where the streaming servers are located.

4.4.2 ANSWER

Multimedia content can be streamed to the user. Take a look at an online education site to see courses delivered via streaming video.

Go to the Stanford Online site at: online.stanford.edu.

Try one of the free online courses. First, you will need to download and install the Microsoft Media Player if you don't have it on your system already. You can download the Microsoft Media Player from the Stanford Online site.

Courses are streamed at two different bit rates depending on the bandwidth of your network connection: Low Bandwidth (28.8 Kbps or greater) or High Bandwidth (Dual ISDN or greater). Try viewing a course at each of the levels if you have access to a high enough bandwidth network connection.

 a) Compare the quality of the video image and the sound. Can you view all the streams at the low bandwidth rate through your network connection? In your mind, how does the quality of the video stream compare to a television image? Do you think the quality and performance are adequate for delivering a college course? Assuming that the video is of comparable quality, would you prefer seeing a course on TV or on your computer?

 Answer: The video stream does not provide as high a resolution image as your television screen. There is also a variation in the timing of the delivery of the image (it may be jerky). However, in the case of compressed video streams, students have found the quality and performance to be sufficient for viewing course lectures online. Whether you prefer seeing a course on TV or on your computer depends on a number of factors, including ease of access, availability of content, and comfort level of the setting for course viewing. Comfort level may include such features as having a table on which to take notes when you're viewing a course on a computer. Support features of online courses also add to the desirability of attending a course online via your computer.

Lab 4.4 Self-Review Questions

In order to test your progress, you should be able to answer the following questions.

1) Streaming media involves _____ chunks of a _____ package over a _____ pipe.

   a) _____ Large, large, large
   b) _____ Small, small, small
   c) _____ Small, large, small
   d) _____ Small, large, large

2) Broadband involves technologies that provide (a) _____ channel(s) over (a) _____ communications medium.

   a) _____ Few, multiple
   b) _____ Many, multiple
   c) _____ Multiple, single
   d) _____ Single, single

3) Compression is not required to stream video over a 28.8K baud modem.

   a) _____ True
   b) _____ False

4) A player is which of the following? (Select all that apply.)

   a) _____ A program
   b) _____ An application that uncompresses data
   c) _____ The software that sends video data to the display
   d) _____ The application that sends audio to the speakers

5) A streaming video player can be which of the following?

   a) _____ An integral part of a browser
   b) _____ Provided by the software maker
   c) _____ Available on a Web site
   d) _____ Answers a and b
   e) _____ Answers b and c
   f) _____ All of the above

Quiz answers appear in the Appendix, Section 4.4.

CHAPTER 4

TEST YOUR THINKING

In the email program of your choice open up an old email message. Enable the option to show all the email message headers (see your software's documentation if you do not know how to do this).

1) The "received" fields indicate the hosts through which the email messages passed.
   Do any of the names of the hosts look familiar?
   Do any of the names relate to the name of your ISP or the sender's ISP?
   Did the email pass through many different hosts?
   Does the sender have the same or a different ISP from you?
2) Can you find out the email client that the sender used to create and send the message?
   When was the message sent?
   Does the time given appear to be in the same time zone as your computer?
   What about the same time zone as your ISP?
   The sender's computer? The sender's ISP?
3) Find a site on the Internet that will allow you to download files over either HTTP or FTP. Make sure that you can download the same files from the same server over each of the protocols. Download each file, taking note of how long the download took and the speed of the download.
   Which protocol was faster?
   Which protocol do you think can handle more users based on this experiment?
   What do you think is the preferred protocol for transmitting large files based on this experiment?

CHAPTER 5

CONNECTIVITY

CHAPTER OBJECTIVES

In this chapter, you will learn about:

- ISDN, DSL, and T-carrier Technologies   Page 126
- Wireless Networks   Page 132
- Cable Modems   Page 138

The confluence between telecommunications, consumer electronics, and computing is nowhere more apparent than in the choices that we are now presented with in our connectivity decisions. The telephone companies offer three major types of network service: ISDN, DSL, and T-carrier technologies. Some ISPs, such as Concentric Corporation, offer both DSL and wireless access to the Internet. In some parts of the country, cable modems have caught on as a high-speed access technology, used primarily by consumers at home.

LAB 5.1

ISDN, DSL, AND T-CARRIER TECHNOLOGIES

> **LAB OBJECTIVES**
>
> After this lab, you will be able to:
>
> ✔ Differentiate Between Various Technologies Offered by Telephone Companies
> ✔ Determine Availability of Network Services in Your Area

Telephone companies now offer a variety of services to help you connect to the Internet. There are currently three major types of network service available from the telephone company: ISDN (Integrated Services Digital Network), DSL (Digital Subscriber Link), and T-carrier.

Though ISDN was slow to catch on in the United States, it has become commonplace in European countries. DSL is the latest offering from the telephone companies, and, in some cases, DSL is a cost-effective, high-performing solution for access to the Internet. Corporate customers still generally rely on T-carrier technologies, including T-1 and T-3 lines.

ISDN

ISDN offers high-speed digital data service. With ISDN, you can transmit large quantities of data, voice, and video signals over a single telephone line. ISDN addresses the problem of how to transport digital services across copper wiring that was originally intended to carry only analog signals. ISDN is an international standard through the telecommunications standards organizations, CCITT and ITU.

ISDN consists of a combination of B and D channels on the line. The B channels are called the bearer channels and carry the data and voice services. The D channels are called the delta channels. The D channels are responsible for handling control and signaling functions. The telephone companies offer two levels of ISDN service: Basic Rate Interface (BRI) and Primary Rate Interface (PRI). The Basic Rate Interface service is intended for home or SOHO (small office/home office) use. The BRI interface service provides one or two 64 Kbps B channels along with one 16 Kbps D channel. These are referred to as 1B ISDN service or 2B ISDN service. Transmission speeds depend on the number of B channels and therefore offer 64 or 128 Kbps service (actually 56K or 112K because of the use of some of the data bits for transmission). Larger users may find the Primary Rate Interface (PRI) appropriate for their needs. PRI service in the United States offers 23 B channels and one 64Kbps D channel. In Europe, PRI service offers 30 B channels and one D channel. While ISDN was becoming popular in European countries, few people were using it in the United States. When low-cost ISDN service became available through ISPs, more companies began using ISDN for Internet access.

DSL

The acronym DSL stands for Digital Subscriber Link. DSL is a recent advancement, introduced to the public in 1998. DSL provides high-bandwidth service over copper phone lines. With DSL service, you can receive data at transmission speeds of up to 6.1 Mbps. Typical performance numbers range from 1.544 Mbps to 512 Kbps downstream and 128 Kbps upstream. There are several variations on DSL service, including ADSL (Asymmetric Digital Subscriber Line), HDSL (High bit-rate Digital Subscriber Line), and RADSL (Rate Adaptive Digital Subscriber Line), offering varying levels of performance. DSL carries both data and voice signals, with the data part of the line continuously connected. DSL uses POTS, an old acronym from the world of telephony that stands for "plain old telephone service." In other words, DSL service uses the copper wires in twisted pairs to transmit the signals. DSL combines the transmission of digital and analog signals across the copper wires. Digital signals carry data while analog signals can simultaneously transmit voice over a DSL line. The analog signal uses a small portion of the available amount of information, thereby allowing a maximum of 56 Kbps for data transmission. One of the advantages of DSL is that it assumes that it is transmitting digital data and does not require changing the data into an analog form and back. With DSL, digital data is transmitted directly to your computer. This approach allows the phone company to use a much wider bandwidth for transmitting data. Unfortunately, due to the age and subsequent reduced reliability of the copper wires used to transmit the signals, the distance from the telephone company central office (CO) affects the availability of DSL service in your area. Pacific Bell states that DSL specifications include a two- to three-mile maximum distance from your Pacific Bell central office. Since DSL can separate the signal into part analog and part digital, you can support a phone and a computer on the same line at the same time.

Pacific Bell's press announcement on January 12, 1999 stated that DSL service would be made available to millions of California households and small businesses. On the same date, in a related announcement, Pacific Bell's parent company, SBC Communications, Inc. (SBC), announced plans for the largest rollout of Asymmetrical Digital Subscriber Line (ADSL) service in the United States. By the end of 1999, SBC plans were to provide ADSL service from 526 central offices to 8.2 million residential and 1.3 million business customers. Not only does ADSL service provide higher speeds, the price of the service has been reduced in California to $39/month by the end of 1999. Pacific Bell estimates that as many as 5 million residential and 900,000 business customers will qualify for ADSL service from the 255 central offices.

With ADSL, people can simultaneously use a phone or fax machine while getting downstream connection speeds of up to 1.5 Mbps and an upstream connection speed of 128 Kbps. As we discussed earlier, the disadvantage of DSL is that it is distance-dependent and downstream throughput speeds will vary depending on the customer's distance from the central office. However, at this point, Pacific Bell is guaranteeing ADSL service at a minimum connection speed of 384 Kbps. In addition, Pacific Bell estimates that 75 percent of its customers qualifying for ADSL will actually be able to get downstream connection speeds of 1.5 Mbps. While ISDN was slow to be adopted in the United States, ADSL is catching on quickly. ADSL service was launched in California in May 1998. By September 1998, ADSL service was available to 1.6 million residential customers and 400,000 business customers in the state of California. Market researchers predict a fast rate of acceptance with reduced prices and increases in availability of service. Current ADSL subscribers are estimated at around 50,000, with projections worldwide of up to 5,000,000 subscribers by 2002. It will be interesting to see if these projections come true and if people choose ADSL service over cable modems and other technology options.

T-CARRIER SERVICE

The T-carrier system was introduced by Bell Telephone in the 1960s. The T-carrier system initially supported digitized voice transmission, with speeds of 1.544 Mbps for T-1 service and 44.736 Mbps for a T-3 line. Service is also offered using a fractional T-1 line in which you can rent a portion of 24 channels and leave the other channels unused. The T-carrier system is an entirely digital service. Pulse code modulation, PCM, uses a digital scheme for transmitting analog data. Time-division multiplexing, TDM, sends signals in many segments with short duration, with signals combined for transmission on a single line. Four wires are used so that bits are transmitted in full-duplex mode with two wires receiving and two sending at the same time. Signals are sampled at the rate of 8,000 times/second. Each sample is digitized into an 8-bit word format with 24 channels digitized at the same time. Each 192-bit frame is transmitted 8,000 times/second. With a single bit separating each frame for the 193-bit blocks, data can be transmitted at speeds of 192 bit frames multiplied by 8,000 times/second. There are an additional 8,000 framing bits. Therefore, a T-1 line has a data rate of 1.544 Mbps.

LAB 5.1 EXERCISES

5.1.1 DIFFERENTIATE BETWEEN VARIOUS TECHNOLOGIES OFFERED BY TELEPHONE COMPANIES

Look into DSL network services as well as T-1, T-3, and ISDN.

Compare the T-carrier technologies, ISDN, and DSL technologies.

    a) Create a table listing the advantages and disadvantages of each of the network technologies provided by the telephone companies.

5.1.2 DETERMINE AVAILABILITY OF NETWORK SERVICES IN YOUR AREA

    a) Check the Web site of your local telephone company and find out if you have DSL service available in your area.

    b) If DSL service is available in your area, determine how far you are located from your local telephone company central office (CO) and find out what speed DSL is available to your home.

Lab 5.1: ISDN, DSL, and T-Carrier Technologies

LAB 5.1 EXERCISE ANSWERS

5.1.1 ANSWER

Look into DSL network services as well as T-1, T-3, and ISDN.

Compare the T-carrier technologies, ISDN and DSL technologies.

a) Create a table listing the advantages and disadvantages of each of the network technologies provided by the telephone companies.

Answer: See comparison chart below for advantages and disadvantages of each network technology offered by the telephone companies.

Technology	Bandwidth Comparison	Advantages	Disadvantages
ISDN	56 Kbps–112 Kbps	Symmetric, distance-independent	Slower than other technologies
DSL	128 Kbps upstream, 384 Kbps–1.544 Mbps downstream	Less expensive than T-carrier but in some places can reach same speed downstream	Distance-dependent, asymmetric, not available everywhere
T-carrier	1.544 Mbps (T-1) to 44.736 Mbps (T-3)	Symmetric, high-speed access	Expensive

DSL is a faster and newer technology than ISDN. However, DSL is distance-dependent and its downstream (receiving) performance varies based on the customer's distance from the telephone company Central Office (CO). The fastest DSL service currently available is asymmetric, offering much higher transmission rates downstream than upstream. ISDN is symmetric, providing the same (but slower than DSL) transmission rates in both directions.

5.1.2 ANSWERS

a) Check the Web site of your local telephone company and find out if you have DSL service available in your area.

Answer: I found out that there is DSL service available in my area by visiting the Pacific Bell site at www.pacbell.com.

Lab 5.1: ISDN, DSL, and T-Carrier Technologies 131

b) If DSL service is available in your area, determine how far you are located from your local telephone company central office (CO) and find out what speed DSL is available to your home.

Answer: Since we live approximately four miles from the telephone company central office, we can only get the slowest speed DSL, approximately 384 Kbps downstream and 128 Kbps upstream. On the Pacific Bell site, I can check out available services by providing my local telephone number.

LAB 5.1 SELF-REVIEW QUESTIONS

In order to test your progress, you should be able to answer the following questions.

1) Put the following network services in order by speed (slowest to fastest).

   a) _____ DSL
   b) _____ ISDN
   c) _____ T-3
   d) _____ T-1

2) What would be the best connection for a household of four computer users?

   a) _____ ISDN
   b) _____ DSL
   c) _____ T-3
   d) _____ T-1

3) Access to DSL is limited by a site's distance from the nearest central office.

   a) _____ True
   b) _____ False

4) DSL network services are affected by the telephone service in your area.

   a) _____ True
   b) _____ False

5) Select the statements that are false for ISDN.

   a) _____ ISDN is in more widespread use in Europe than in the United States.
   b) _____ ISDN offers approximately the same bandwidth as DSL.
   c) _____ DSL is catching on quicker in the United States than ISDN did.
   d) _____ ISDN stands for Integrated Digital Services Network.

Quiz answers appear in the Appendix, Section 5.1.

LAB 5.2

WIRELESS NETWORKS

> **LAB OBJECTIVES**
>
> After this lab, you will be able to:
> - Differentiate Between Wireless and Wired Networks
> - Understand How Wireless Networks Transmit Data

Wireless networks are becoming more accepted today. They can provide low-cost, reliable access to the Internet if you are within line-of-sight of a wireless antenna. Living on a hill, we find that our wireless network affords us high-performance at reasonable cost. In a wireless network, electromagnetic waves carry the signal through space rather than along a wire. Radio-frequency (RF) or infrared (IR) waves are used for the signals. Wireless transceivers are used for the connection. The most common use for wireless networks that we see today is for laptop Internet connections without a telephone. However, in Silicon Valley, more and more antennas are visible on rooftops of homes and office buildings. Eventually, wireless networks will link to the Internet via satellites.

Three types of wireless technology are currently available for connecting to the Internet: line-of-sight, wide-area microcellular, and satellite (receive-only).

With line-of-sight wireless technology, an antenna is installed on the roof of your office building or house. This antenna sends radio signals to an antenna operated by your wireless ISP, which is in a direct line, with no obstructions blocking the path between the two antennas. Line-of-sight radio is currently in use for connecting networks in nearby buildings but is not in widespread use yet for Internet service from home or office sites. Most line-of-sight radio solutions can work at about 30 miles in distance and can provide connections at speeds from modem speeds to 10 Mbps. The connection is symmetric, providing the same speed in both directions. The problem with line-of-sight solutions is that they require that there be no obstructions in the path between the two antennas. Often, this is not possible in populated areas.

A wide-area microcellular wireless data network uses radio technology similar to that used in the public switched cellular telephone system. It has limited range and slower speeds since it is transmitting at low power in all directions at once. However, this technology can be useful for wireless modems for laptops or other mobile network appliances. Microcellular radio networks are not useful for connecting servers to the Internet due to the slower speed and the stationary nature of the server. There is little value to using microcellular radio for machines that are fixed in place. Currently, Metricom offers microcellular radio modems that operate at speeds up to 33.6 K baud. Newer products are expected to offer speeds comparable to ISDN service in the near future.

Satellite links offer wireless radio connections but are very expensive at the present time. Satellite connections currently available to the general public operate in receive-only mode. DirecPC offers speeds of 400 KB downstream. You use a modem connection via a different ISP. For outbound transmissions, you need to use a modem connection via a separate ISP. Satellite service is useful in remote locations with few other options available for Internet connectivity.

Figure 5.1 illustrates different options for wireless Internet connectivity.

LAB 5.2 EXERCISES

5.2.1 DIFFERENTIATE BETWEEN WIRELESS AND WIRED NETWORKS

Learn about different network technologies by checking out resources on the Web. The telephone companies provide information on DSL. The Pacific Bell site provides information on DSL at: www.pacbell.com/DSL/.

Learn about high-speed wireless Internet access services on the Wavepath site at: www.wavepath.com.

    a) What is the difference between wired and wireless access solutions for Internet connectivity?

_____

_____

5.2.2 UNDERSTAND HOW WIRELESS NETWORKS TRANSMIT DATA

    a) Take a look at the Metricom site—www.metricom.com—to learn about wide-area microcellular wireless networks.

_____

_____

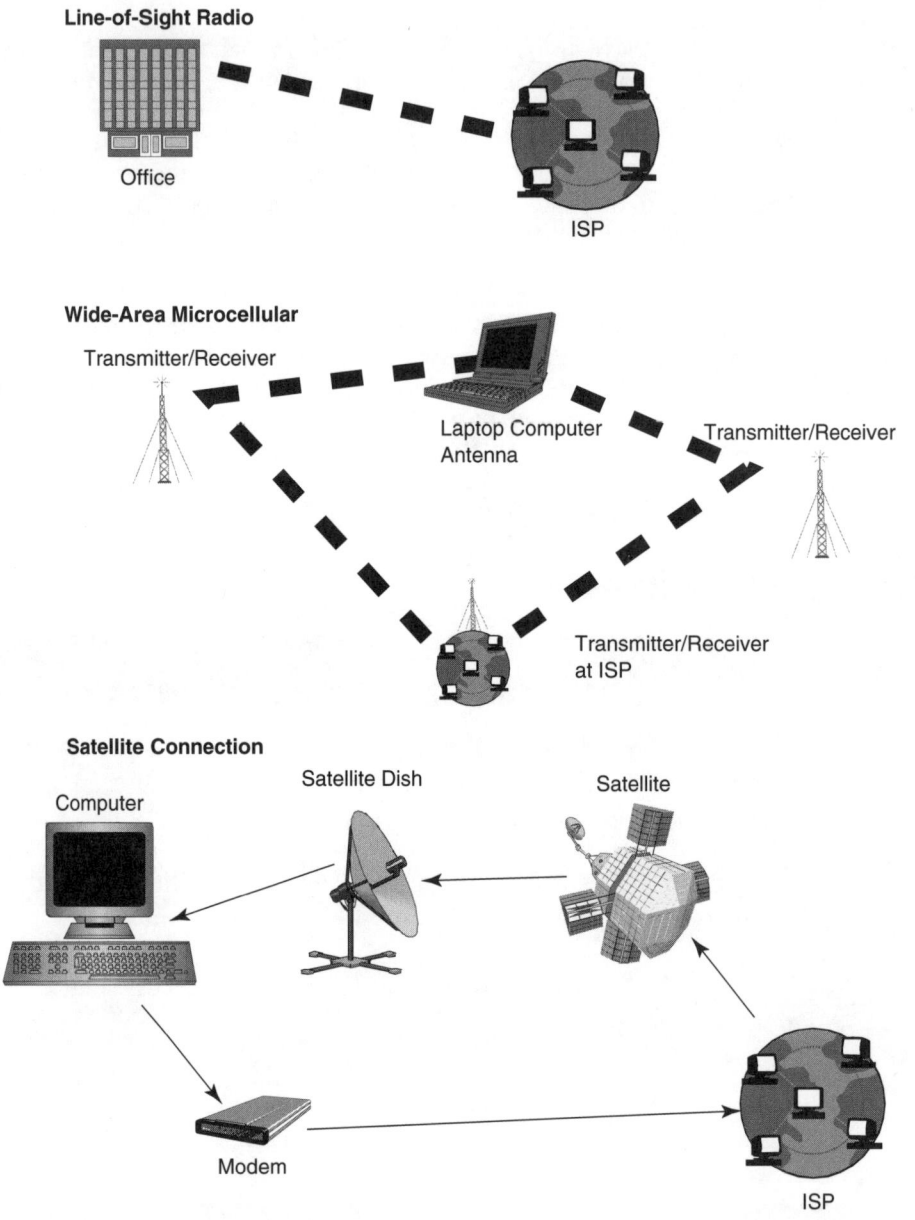

Figure 5.1 ■ Wireless Internet Connection Options.

    b) Refer to the Wavepath site—www.wavepath.com—for information on line-of-sight wireless networks.

ID: 5.2:* *Wireless Networks*

LAB 5.2 EXERCISE ANSWERS

5.2.1 ANSWER

Learn about different network technologies by checking out resources on the Web. The telephone companies provide information on DSL. The Pacific Bell site provides information on DSL at: www.pacbell.com/DSL/.

Learn about high-speed wireless Internet access services on the Wavepath site at: www.wavepath.com.

a) What is the difference between wired and wireless access solutions for Internet connectivity?

Answer: Wireless access solutions use electromagnetic waves to carry signals through space. In wired access solutions, signals are transmitted along wires, such as twisted pair wires. Wireless access solutions such as Wavepath offer higher bandwidth than wired access solutions such as DSL if you have line-of-sight to the Wavepath installation and your home is four miles away from the telephone company central office like ours.

5.2.2 ANSWERS

a) Take a look at the Metricom site—www.metricom.com—to learn about wide-area microcellular wireless networks.

Answer: Looking at the Metricom site, we can see that the basic structure of the Ricochet network consists of microcell radios strategically placed every quarter to half mile in a checkerboard pattern. This "mesh" architecture routes data traffic between the modems and the WAPs (Wired Access Points). A higher density design like this ensures the safe, efficient transmission of data and better indoor penetration of the radio signals. It also offers the reliability and handoff capability necessary to eliminate dropped connections even when moving. The Ricochet mesh architecture provides advantages over the more typical network topology, known as the star topology, in which all communications are required to pass through one or more central base stations or hubs. In this system, congestion and impaired signal communications resulting from weak signal strength are generally addressed by installing another hub, typically a costly and time-consuming process. With the Ricochet network, system congestion is reduced and network coverage and capacity are increased by installing one or more relatively inexpensive poletop or wired access points where needed.

b) Refer to the Wavepath site—www.wavepath.com—for information on line-of-sight wireless networks.

Answer: Looking at the Wavepath site, we see that an iSpeed (WavePath's wireless service) customer is connected to the iSpeed Point of Presence through a special, constant wireless connection. Requests for information are sent from the PC, Mac, or LAN through a conventional 10BaseT Ethernet link to a special modem. The modem then forwards the request to a digital transceiver (transmitter/receiver antenna) at the customer's location. Next, the request is transmitted through the airwaves over Wavepath's private spectrum to one of two iSpeed tower sites in the San Francisco Bay Area, and routed to the iSpeed POP. The data is retrieved from the Internet over iSpeed's high-speed backbone connection. The information is then sent back, from iSpeed's transceiver over private, dedicated frequencies to the digital transceiver installed at the customer's location. The transceiver downloads the data to the special modem, passes the information to the PC, Mac, or LAN. The iSpeed system provides Internet access at speeds of up to 1.5 Mbps to end users through a broadband delivery system utilizing the MMDS spectrum. Owned exclusively by Wavepath in the San Francisco/Silicon Valley area, this spectrum, in the 2.1 to 2.6 gHz range, is ideally suited to data delivery. The frequencies are robust and private. A 6 MHz QAM (Quadrature Amplitude Modulation) transmission is used for the downstream data delivery; a 6 MHz QPSK (Quadrature Phase Shift Keying) transmission is used for the upstream or return path transmission. Sectorization is an architecture which reuses frequency efficiently by using 5 to 10 degree sectors in pie-shaped configurations. In this configuration channels will be reused alternately to afford the iSpeed system the spectral capacity to serve a market the size of the San Francisco Bay Area. Wavepath is the only company in the United States that has been granted a unique authorization in that the current FCC license allows it to transmit digital information over different polarizations on the same frequency from the same geographic area. The license permits upstream sectorization utilizing polarization diversity, which results in over 1000% frequency reuse.

LAB 5.2 SELF-REVIEW QUESTIONS

In order to test your progress, you should be able to answer the following questions.

1) Can a line-of-sight radio connection work in the following situations?

    a) _____ Long distance over wooded and hilly area
    b) _____ Between tall skyscrapers that are next to each other
    c) _____ Hundreds of miles over open plains

2) Most consumer satellite Internet connections are

    a) _____ unidirectional.
    b) _____ bidirectional.

Lab 5.2: Wireless Networks

3) When would a wide-area wireless network be useful? (Select all that apply.)

   a) _____ Laptop around city
   b) _____ Server in office
   c) _____ Laptop around rural area

4) Describe line-of-sight wireless technology. (Select all that apply.)

   a) _____ Line-of-sight wireless technology can be used for Internet access.
   b) _____ Wireless technology is more expensive than T-carrier technology.
   c) _____ Line-of-sight technology operates fine if there are obstructions along the path.
   d) _____ Line-of-sight approaches require a clear path between the user's antenna and the ISP's transceiver.

5) Describe wide-area microcellular wireless technology. (Select all that apply.)

   a) _____ A wide-area microcellular wireless data network transmits radio at high power.
   b) _____ Wide-area microcellular wireless technology transmits radio in all directions at once.
   c) _____ Transmitting in all directions at once reduces the range and speed.
   d) _____ A wide-area microcellular wireless data network uses radio technology similar to that used in the public switched cellular telephone system.
   e) _____ Wide-area microcellular wireless technology can be useful for wireless modems for laptops or other mobile network appliances.

Quiz answers appear in the Appendix, Section 5.2.

LAB 5.3

CABLE MODEMS

> **LAB OBJECTIVES**
>
> After this lab, you will be able to:
>
> ✔ Compare Various Network Technologies and Services
> ✔ Differentiate Between Technologies Offered by the Telephone Companies and by the Cable Companies

Cable modems are one of the latest technologies to provide higher-speed Internet access. Just what do cable modems offer and how do they work? A cable modem enables your PC to use the local cable TV line to receive data at speeds of approximately 1.5 Mbps. Thus, cable modems offer about the same data rate as DSL service. A cable modem can be added to or integrated with a set-top box, thereby turning your TV into an Internet channel. The PC attachment is a cable line split, with part of the line going to the TV and the other part to the cable modem and the PC. In this way, the cable modem functions more like a network interface card (NIC). The cable modem is attached to a cable TV company coaxial cable line and communicates with the Cable Modem Termination System (CMTS) at your local cable TV company office. Cable modems receive and send signals only to or from the CMTS but not to other cable modems on the line. Accessing the Internet over a cable TV line, the available bandwidth is up to 27 Mbps to the subscriber and approximately 2.5 Mbps from the subscriber. Your local provider may have T-1 (1.5 Mbps) service, and, in this case, your likely data rate may be close to 1.5 Mbps. Compared to normal telephone Internet access, cable modems offer a much faster data rate along with a continuous connection.

There is much discussion of the pros and cons of cable modems versus ADSL service. Some people claim that ADSL offers greater reliability, better security, and more consistent speeds, because ADSL service is delivered via a dedicated line from a central office to the individual user's home or office. According to some analysts, accessing the Internet via a cable modem results in inconsistent performance since cable modems depend on shared bandwidth among a group of users, many of whom may be using the cable line at the same time as you are.

LAB 5.3 EXERCISES

5.3.1 COMPARE VARIOUS NETWORK TECHNOLOGIES AND SERVICES

Research network technology alternatives in terms of the services available, their relative cost, speed, and availability.

Compare telephone wire-based, wireless, and cable services.

a) Develop a chart comparing various network technologies and services.

5.3.2 DIFFERENTIATE BETWEEN TECHNOLOGIES OFFERED BY THE TELEPHONE COMPANIES AND BY THE CABLE COMPANIES

Take a look at the chart that you have developed. Check out the tutorial on cable modems at www.cable-modems.org/tutorial/ for all you ever wanted to know but were afraid to ask about cable modems.

a) Which connectivity option listed offers the highest bandwidth?

_____

_____

b) Which connectivity option listed offers the lowest bandwidth?

_____

_____

Lab 5.3: Cable Modems

c) Which connectivity option listed is most affected by the number of people online near you?

_____

_____

LAB 5.3 EXERCISE ANSWERS

5.3.1 ANSWER

Research network technology alternatives in terms of the services available, their relative cost, speed, and availability. Compare telephone wire-based, wireless, and cable services.

a) Develop a chart comparing various network technologies and services.

Answer:

Service	Relative Cost	Speed (approximate)	Availability	Comments
Public Dial-up via Modem	Very Low	28.8 Kbps–56 Kbps	Widespread	Uses existing home or office phone service. Performance limited by speed of actual phone connection.
ISDN	Low–Medium	56 Kbps–128 Kbps	Good	More widespread in Europe than in United States. Needs special ISDN line installed.
DSL	Low–Medium	144 Kbps–1.544 Mbps (DSL can go much faster, but service hard to find)	Fair–Medium	Good choice where available.

(continued)

Service	Relative Cost	Speed (approximate)	Availability	Comments
T-1	High	1.544 Mbps	Good	Standard choice for servers.
T-3	Very High	44.736 Mbps	Good	Costly.
Line-of-Sight Wireless	Medium	384 Kbps–10 Mbps	Poor–Medium	Good choice where available.
Wide-Area Microcellular	Low	22.8 Kbps–128 Kbps	Fair–Medium	Intended for laptops on-the-go.
Receive-only Satellite	Medium	400 Kbps (downstream) modem speed (upstream)	Medium	High price, slow outbound connection.
Cable Modem	Low	128 Kbps (upstream) up to 3 Mbps (downstream)	Fair–Medium	Shared cable, fast speeds cannot scale. As more people connect, speed goes down.

5.3.2 ANSWERS

Take a look at the chart that you have developed. Check out the tutorial on cable modems at www.cable-modems.org/tutorial/ for all you ever wanted to know but were afraid to ask about cable modems.

a) Which connectivity option listed offers the highest bandwidth?

Answer: T-3 leased lines offer the highest bandwidth and most reliable connection, but they are very costly.

b) Which connectivity option listed offers the lowest bandwidth?

Answer: 28.8 K baud modems are the most readily available and cheapest modems available in computers and at computer retailers. Some people, of course, have lower-

speed modems, but generally PCs use 28.8 K baud modems. Many now come with 56 K baud modems.

c) Which connectivity option listed is most affected by the number of people on-line near you?

Answer: While cable modems can be quite inexpensive and can provide very high downstream bandwidth and reasonable upstream bandwidth, their performance is affected by the number of simultaneous users sharing the cable. The performance of your cable modem is reduced dramatically as the number of users on the cable rises.

LAB 5.3 SELF-REVIEW QUESTIONS

In order to test your progress, you should be able to answer the following questions.

1) Cable modems send signals to each other.

   a) _____ True
   b) _____ False

2) Cable modem speed will decrease as more users sign up.

   a) _____ True
   b) _____ False

3) ISDN is much faster than a cable modem.

   a) _____ True
   b) _____ False

4) Which of these statements are true for cable modems? (Select all that apply.)

   a) _____ Cable modems use the cable coming into your house for cable TV.
   b) _____ Cable modems are generally less expensive than ADSL.
   c) _____ Cable modem service is available throughout the United States in 2001.
   d) _____ Cable modem service is shared among a group of customers.

5) Which of these statements are true for DSL? (Select all that apply.)

   a) _____ ISDN is faster than DSL.
   b) _____ DSL can operate as fast as a T-1 line.
   c) _____ DSL bandwidth is affected by your neighbors' use of the telephone line.
   d) _____ DSL is available in all parts of the United States in 2001.

Quiz answers appear in the Appendix, Section 5.3.

CHAPTER 5

TEST YOUR THINKING

You have learned about different connectivity options. Now, take the time to research your Internet connection options.

1) Compare different solutions for home users, small-office/home-office (SOHO) users, medium-sized office users, and corporate users. Obtain information from local and national ISPs.
2) What are the requirements of each of the user groups? For instance, some might need 24-hour, 7-day/week customer support while others require many IP addresses.
3) Develop a table, comparing price, speed, availability, and service.
4) Summarize your findings for each user group.
   What is the best Internet solution for this particular type of user?
   What are the advantages and disadvantages of the solution for each group?

CHAPTER 6

NETWORK SECURITY

> **CHAPTER OBJECTIVES**
>
> In this chapter, you will learn about:
>
> - Encryption Systems — Page 146
> - Secure Internet Protocols — Page 155
> - Firewalls and Sniffers — Page 162
> - Proxy Servers, Virtual Private Networks, and Smartcards — Page 167

A major advantage and a major disadvantage of the Internet is that it is a public network. The World Wide Web has experienced astronomic growth due to the openness and availability of the information presented on Web sites. However, this openness and accessibility becomes a liability in situations where the information is sensitive or when companies move to electronic commerce. In these cases, the openness of the World Wide Web must be supplemented with network security technologies to provide a secure environment for electronic commerce and confidential transactions.

LAB 6.1

ENCRYPTION SYSTEMS

> **LAB OBJECTIVES**
>
> After this lab, you will be able to:
> - Understand the Use of Public Key Cryptography
> - Consider the Trade-offs in Encrypting Messages

When to encrypt? What to encrypt? How much data to encrypt?

Encryption is the conversion of data into a form called a cipher in a way that it isn't intercepted easily by unauthorized parties. Decryption is the conversion of encrypted data back into its original form. Decryption is used to understand the contents of an encrypted message. Encryption and decryption schemes have been used in some form throughout history. During wartime communication, ciphers are often used to keep enemies from understanding the contents of intercepted messages.

Simple ciphers include such schemes as substituting letters for numbers, rotating letters in the alphabet, and inverting sideband frequencies in order to scramble a voice signal.

More complex ciphers include computer algorithms and the rearrangement of digital bits in digital signals. The decryption key is used to recover the contents of an encrypted signal using an algorithm that "undoes" the encryption. It is possible to "break" a cipher with a computer. Complex encryption algorithms are more difficult to break.

It is particularly important to use encryption and decryption in wireless communications since wireless communication is easier to "tap" than hard-wired communication. It is also a good idea to protect sensitive transactions, such as online credit card purchases and internal discussions of sensitive information.

A stronger cipher is harder to break, providing better protection but at a higher cost. There is a controversy in the United States concerning the use of strong encryption. With strong encryption, ciphers are practically unbreakable without the decryption key. Companies and customers view strong encryption favorably, seeing strong encryption as a mechanism to protect secrets and reduce fraud. However, in the view of many government agencies, strong encryption can be used by terrorists in order to evade authorities. Governments, including the U.S. government, have lobbied for the adoption of a key escrow arrangement. In such an arrangement, the government gets a copy of the key when you use a key. The decryption keys are stored in a "secure" place. Only authorities with a court order are allowed access to the keys. Supporters of key escrow arrangements voice the opinion that these arrangements keep criminals from using encryption. However, opponents of such systems contend that criminals can hack into a key escrow database and illegally obtain, steal, or alter keys.

A major concern with encryption via the Internet is that most encryption mechanisms adversely impact performance. RC4 stream encryption provides RC4 ciphers, which are considered to be the fastest ciphers. RC4 is a stream cipher designed by Ronald Rivest (the "R" in RSA) for RSA Data Security, Inc. RC4 is a variable key-size stream cipher with byte-oriented operations. The algorithm for computing the RC4 cipher is based on a random permutation. Analysts have examined the security of the RC4 cipher and have decided that the RC4 cipher is secure. In addition, the cipher should run quickly in software implementations. RC4 is used to encrypt Web traffic to and from secure sites, providing secure communications between sites that use the SSL protocol. RC4 ciphers with 128-bit encryption provide MD5 (message digest) message authentication with 3.4×10^{38} possible keys. A message digest is a form of a hash function that allows authentication to occur without encrypting the entire message. A message digest takes a piece of plain text (not encrypted) and computes a fixed-length bit string from the piece of plain text. The message digest is a useful approach since it is easy to compute the message digest of a particular string of plain text. At the same time, knowing the message digest of a particular string, it is effectively impossible to determine the string of plain text itself. Also, if the hash is at least 128 bits long, two messages cannot be generated that have the same message digest. Message digests can be used to compute faster digital signatures since it is faster to compute a message digest given a piece of plain text than to encrypt a string of plain text with a public key algorithm. Although browsers use 128-bit encryption for electronic commerce transactions within the United States, only 40-bit encryption is approved for export outside the United States. Although the U.S. Department of Commerce discussed lifting export restrictions in the fall of 1999, draft regulations were under discussion at the end of 1999. These rules were intended to ease export restrictions for retail trade, with industry members concerned about the impact on government telecommunications providers outside the United States. There is concern about the security of 40-bit encryption schemes since an RC4 cipher with 40-bit encryption and MD5 message authentication allows for 1.1×10^{12} possible keys. Industry proponents of secure protocols seek to lift export restrictions to allow for the use of 128-bit encryption schemes in international electronic commerce transactions.

Earlier cryptographic schemes included private key cryptography. Private key cryptography involves the creation and sharing of a secret key for the encryption and decryption of messages. However, this scheme can be compromised if the key is discovered or intercepted during transmission. Messages can be decrypted easily once the private key is discovered or intercepted.

PUBLIC KEY CRYPTOGRAPHY

Public key cryptography is also known as asymmetric cryptography. The public key is known, shared, and may be made available in a directory via the Internet. The private key, on the other hand, is protected and not shared with anyone.

In public key cryptography, the public and private keys are created simultaneously using the same algorithm. A Certification or Certificate Authority (CA) is responsible for the creation of the pair of keys. The CA gives a private key to the requestor and provides a digital certificate with a public key. The public key is stored in a publicly accessible directory. The private key is protected, not shared with anyone else and not transmitted across the Internet. The private key is used to decrypt the text that has been encrypted with the sender's public key by another person who retrieves the sender's public key from a directory. To send an encrypted message, it is necessary to contact a central administrator for the public key. To make sure that the recipient of the message knows the identity of the sender who transmitted this message, it is necessary to use the sender's private key to encrypt the digital certificate. The recipient uses your public key to decrypt the digital certificate and authenticate the sender's identity.

The steps in public key cryptography can be summarized as follows:

1. Sender transmits encrypted message using the receiver's public key.
2. Sender transmits the encrypted signature using the sender's key.
3. Receiver decrypts encrypted message using receiver's private key.
4. Receiver decrypts encrypted signature and authenticates the sender with the sender's public key.

While public key cryptography has many advantages over private key cryptography, there are two major problems with public key cryptography. In order to facilitate adoption, procedures and mechanisms must be established for the distribution of keys so that keys are available to the general public. At this time, public directories are not widely available. The major problem, however, stems from the performance impact from using public key cryptography. The speed of the overall transmission is often so degraded that public key cryptography is effectively too slow to use for large documents.

One approach to reducing the impact on performance is to combine asymmetric and symmetric cryptography. In this combined approach, a secret or session key is generated and the message is encrypted using the symmetric algorithm and the session key. The session key is encrypted using the recipient's public key, which becomes what is considered a "digital envelope." The encrypted message and the digital envelope are both sent to the recipient. When the message is received, the recipient uses his or her private key to decrypt the session key. The recipient then uses the session key to decrypt the message.

The elements of the Public Key Infrastructure (PKI) include the following components:

- The Certificate Authority (CA) that issues and verifies digital certificates
- The Digital Certificate, which includes the public key
- The Registration Authority (RA), which verifies the CA before a digital certificate is issued
- A directory containing digital certificates and public keys
- A certificate management system

This public key infrastructure has been slow to catch on. A basic issue that has slowed the acceptance of PKI in industry has been the need for trust in electronic data protection facilities. Trust is essential to the success of Internet commerce. In the physical world, we have many forms of trust, including driver's license or other photo ID, passport, ATM (automatic teller machine) card with PIN (personal identification number), and health club membership cards.

DIGITAL CERTIFICATES

In the electronic world, digital certificates are the analog to these forms of identification to ensure trust. Digital certificates are being promoted as the way to ensure that the parties involved in sensitive transactions, for example, electronic payments—are who they claim to be. A digital certificate is a digital document that attests to the binding of the public key of an individual or entity and verifies the authenticity of the public key. In this way, a digital certificate prevents impersonation through the use of a phony key.

A digital certificate contains the following information:

- Name of certified entity
- Public key
- Name of Certificate Authority (CA)
- Serial number
- Expiration date
- Optional information

There are several types of digital certificates, including the following:

- Email Certificates
- Browser Certificates
- Server (SSL—Secure Sockets Layer) Certificates
- Software Signing Certificates
- Corporate Empowerment Certificates
- SET (Secure Electronic Transaction) Certificates
- EDI (Electronic Data Interchange) Certificates

These types of digital certificates play different roles. Digital certificates establish identity and therefore serve a validation function. Digital certificates may also establish branding and, in this way, establish a relationship between a brand name and the certificate. On the server site, a digital certificate is a component of the security provided by the SSL (Secure Sockets Layer) protocol. SET (Secure Electronic Transaction) includes the use of digital certificates as part of the security and authentication process.

Digital certificates are employed by corporations to authenticate identity for remote access. In addition, digital certificates have been adopted for access to corporate intranets and extranets. Some organizations have adopted digital certificates to provide secure access to the Internet. Access to mainframe facilities and human resource records can be controlled through the use of digital certificates. Some organizations use digital certificates with email, particularly in sensitive communications.

Who uses digital certificates today? Organizations employing digital certificates range from Internet banking firms, brokerages, and content publishers to software publishers, health care organizations, and firms supporting commercial transactions. It is important to note that digital certificates are not only used on the Internet, they are also used for telephone and fax transmissions in some of these organizations.

While there are clear benefits to the security mechanism provided by digital certificates, significant barriers exist today. Barriers to adoption include:

- Portability of digital certificates from one system to another
- Liability of firms issuing digital certificates
- Interoperability between systems employing digital certificates
- Revocation and the lack of accepted mechanisms to control the revocation of digital certificates
- Password-based reliance, which can be compromised
- Market acceptance, which has been slow due to the above issues

The challenges that exist to critical mass adoption of digital certificates range from security technology issues to organizational infrastructure issues. Specific challenges include dealing with the complex authentication process. There is a requirement for secure email and Web methods to request digital certificates. In addition, secure distribution mechanisms need to be put in place for email and Web distribution of digital certificates. The revocation process for digital certificates needs to be defined and implemented. At the same time, a support infrastructure must be put in place to support the issuance, monitor the use, and control the misuse of digital certificates. Dealing with the possibility of compromise is still a major challenge to be addressed.

CERTIFICATE AUTHORITIES

Certificate Authorities have been established to address the issue of how you can trust someone's public key. As in other types of transactions, we rely on third parties to certify. These third parties are known as Certificate Authorities, Certification Authorities, or CAs. A CA validates the identity of an applicant and digitally signs the applicant's certificate.

As a trusted authority, a CA issues a certificate to vouch for the identity of a certificate bearer with a given public key. The CA provides authentication services, which are critical and form the basis of the trust in the bearer of the certificate. Errors in authentication are very costly and authentication services must be provided expeditiously and at a low cost. Various authentication models are currently in use. These models often require physical presence backed by a photo ID. Electronic authentication may be provided by Dun & Bradstreet, TRW, Equifax, or credit bureaus. VeriSign provides 128-bit strong encryption certificates. Validation measures for a corporation include checking articles of incorporation or the bylaws (as banks do when a corporation opens a checking account). Certificate Authorities also check with banks and employees to help authenticate a person's identity before issuing a digital certificate. Biometrics can also help in the authentication process, using retinal scans or fingerprints for identification of individuals to whom digital certificates are being issued.

Cryptographic solutions include a secure hardware box from BBN (Bolt Beranek and Newman) in which a CA stores the certificate root. There are PCMCIA (Personal Computer Memory Card International Association) cryptographic hardware devices, which are FIPS (Federal Information Processing Standard) 140-1 compliant and tamper resistant. Split key techniques increase security. At the top of the trust chain, it is possible to have a 2048-byte key, the largest size key, to increase security.

Physical site security is also important for a Certificate Authority. A CA requires a secure facility, with access control from the outside and guards at all times, 365 days/year, 24 hours/day. Internal strong authentication is also required to safeguard the security of the root keys held by the CA. CAs may employ dual control security devices. Root key generation storage can be protected with biometric access controls.

When the public and private key pair are generated, it is necessary to send the public key to the CA. After the person's identity is verified for the CA, the CA signs and issues a certificate, which is then emailed or placed on a secure Web site for retrieval by the requestor. The requestor uses the certificate to legitimize his or her public key. In order to increase security, it is possible to delegate authority and segregate roles. In this way, it is possible to separate the physical process of issuance, the actual signing of the certification, from the authentication process in which the CA determines the identity and relationship of the public key and the signer. If duties are divided, the CA is responsible for issuing the certificates and the RA (Registration Authority) is responsible for registering other entities and for authenticating certificate receivers.

There are multiple levels of digital certificates:

- Individual Certificates
- Subordinate RA (Registration Authority) Certificates
- Root Certificates

With multiple levels, there exists a hierarchical chaining of certificates in an ordered certificate list.

LAB 6.1 EXERCISES

6.1.1 UNDERSTAND THE USE OF PUBLIC KEY CRYPTOGRAPHY

a) In the case of a start-up developing new Web software and in the case of an established computer company, how do you think each would make use of public key cryptography?

6.1.2 CONSIDER THE TRADE-OFFS IN ENCRYPTING MESSAGES

An established computer company decided to encrypt all messages relating to major contracts but not to encrypt day-to-day communication passing among software engineers.

a) Why do you think the company made this decision?

_____

_____

LAB 6.1 EXERCISE ANSWERS

6.1.1 ANSWER

a) In the case of a start-up developing new Web software and in the case of an established computer company, how do you think each would make use of public key cryptography?

   Answer: *A Web software start-up may decide to use public key cryptography to encrypt messages sent via the Internet regarding its strategic technology and product plans. An established computer company may make use of public key encryption with its trusted partners to transmit purchase orders and confidential reports.*

6.1.2 ANSWER

An established computer company decided to encrypt all messages relating to major contracts but not to encrypt day-to-day communication passing among software engineers.

a) Why do you think the company made this decision?

   Answer: *The company was concerned about competitors' gaining access to information relating to their major accounts. However, the company did not feel that day-to-day communication among software engineers, even when discussing details of development-in-progress, was worth the performance degradation that would be experienced if all messages were encrypted.*

LAB 6.1 SELF-REVIEW QUESTIONS

In order to test your progress, you should be able to answer the following questions.

1) It is important to use encryption and decryption in wireless communication.

   a) _____ True
   b) _____ False

Lab 6.1: Encryption Systems

2) The U.S. government is for heavy encryption.

   a) _____ True
   b) _____ False

3) Put the following steps of public key cryptography in order (first to last).

   a) _____ Receiver decrypts encrypted message using receiver's private key
   b) _____ Sender transmits encrypted message using the receiver's public key
   c) _____ Receiver decrypts encrypted signature and authenticates the sender with the sender's public key
   d) _____ Sender transmits the encrypted signature using the sender's key

4) Digital certificates _____. (Select all that apply.)

   a) _____ are used to identify Internet users
   b) _____ are used by most Internet users
   c) _____ are used in PKI
   d) _____ can be used for branding

5) Select the statements that are true for Certificate Authorities.

   a) _____ Certificate Authorities are also referred to as CAs.
   b) _____ Certificate Authorities are third parties who establish a chain of trust.
   c) _____ The Certificate Authority is not responsible for validating the identity of an applicant.
   d) _____ The digital signature of a Certificate Authority is used for the applicant's certificate.

Quiz answers appear in the Appendix, Section 6.1.

LAB 6.2

SECURE INTERNET PROTOCOLS

> **LAB OBJECTIVES**
>
> After this lab, you will be able to:
> - Understand the Function of the SSL Protocol
> - Develop a Privacy Statement

SSL (SECURE SOCKETS LAYER)

SSL is a general purpose encryption system that was developed by Netscape Communications. SSL is a program layer designed to manage security of message transmissions in a network. Version 2.0 of SSL was released in 1994. The IETF (Internet Engineering Task Force) specification that was adopted is based on version 3.0 of SSL. Both Netscape and Internet Explorer browsers support version 3.0 of the SSL protocol. SSL uses RSA public key cryptography with a 40-bit key size and a RC4 stream encryption algorithm. This is considered adequate for commercial exchange. SSL incorporates the use of a digital certificate.

One factor in the rate of growth of the Web beyond its ease-of-use is the growing acceptance of credit card purchases on secure Web sites. A credit card owner has rights, which protects his or her purchases to a certain degree. Credit card owners feel protected since they have the right to get their money back within a stated length of time. Over the last few years, purchasers have become less concerned about security issues as they visit more and more Web sites, which they perceive to be "secure." These Web sites provide secure payment via SSL.

SSL code is a program layer between the application (Web browser or HTTP) and the TCP/IP layers. HTTP sits on top of SSL and SSL sits on top of TCP/IP. SSL operates at the TCP/IP transport layer and requires the dedicated TCP/IP port designated as port 443. The SSL protocol is referenced via https:// rather than http://. The Netscape browser incorporates the client part of SSL, while the Netscape Commerce Server incorporates the server side of SSL. The Netscape Commerce Server includes the SSLRef program library, which is also downloadable for use with servers that do not incorporate server-side SSL functionality.

When SSL is used, a client opens a connection to the server. The client then lists its capabilities, including the SSL version, cipher suites, and compression method being used. The server responds by telling the client the cipher suite and compression method it will use. The server sends the client a session ID and the server sends its X.509v3 site certificate. The client generates a "premaster secret" and encrypts it using server's public key to create a digital envelope. The client forwards this envelope to the server. After that, the server and client exchange "ChangeCipherSpec" messages for confirmation. Then they both send "finished message" hashes of the entire conversation to that point. For the rest of the session, the client and server use the session key to symmetrically encrypt subsequent messages. SSL supports the use of X.509 digital certificates from the server so that the user can authenticate the sender's identity.

In 1995, there were two well-publicized failures from the use of SSL in Netscape Navigator version 2.0. Unfortunately, a 40-bit secret key is vulnerable to brute force attack. The code for SSL in Netscape Navigator 2.0 used a random number generator to generate the secret keys. This is not sufficient for secure transactions and the algorithm to generate the secret keys was changed to increase security.

SET (SECURE ELECTRONIC TRANSACTION)

SET stands for Secure Electronic Transaction and is a system for ensuring security of financial transactions over the Internet. SET was developed by and for the major credit card companies (Mastercard and VISA) and software companies, including Netscape and Microsoft. In a SET transaction, a user is given an electronic wallet. The electronic wallet contains a digital certificate, and the complete transaction is conducted and verified using digital certificates. For a SET transaction, digital signatures are used among the purchaser, the merchant, and the purchaser's bank to ensure privacy and confidentiality. SET combines the functionality in Netscape's Secure Sockets Layer (SSL), Microsoft's Secure Transaction Technology (STT) and Terisa System's Secure Hypertext Transfer Protocol (S-HTTP). SET also includes some but not all aspects of the Public Key Infrastructure (PKI).

Let's look at what a customer sees. A customer starts out with a SET-enabled Web browser, which can be a Netscape or Microsoft Internet Explorer browser. The transaction provider, either a bank or a store, provides the SET-enabled Web server, which can be a Netscape Commerce Server or another SET-enabled Web server. When the customer opens a Mastercard or Visa bank account, the issuer of the credit card is some kind of bank. Upon opening the account, the customer receives a digital certificate. Then an electronic file representing the digital certificate functions as a credit card for online purchases or other transactions. This digital certificate includes a public key with an expiration date and has been digitally signed by the bank to ensure validity. Third-party merchants also receive digital certificates from the bank, which include the merchant's public key as well as the bank's public key.

When a customer places an order over the Web, the customer's browser receives the merchant's certificate and confirms that the merchant is valid from the certificate. The browser sends order information and the message, transmitting the order information, is encrypted with the merchant's public key. In addition, payment information is encrypted with the bank's public key so that the payment information cannot be read by the merchant. The information required to ensure payment is only used with this order. The merchant then verifies the customer by checking the digital signature on the customer's certificate. After verification, the merchant sends the order message to the bank. This message includes the bank's public key, the customer's payment information, which the merchant cannot decode, and the merchant's certificate. The bank then verifies both the merchant and the message using the digital signature on the certificate. The bank also verifies the payment part of the message. The bank then digitally signs the authorization and sends the authorization to the appropriate merchant. After receiving the bank's authorization, the merchant can then fill the customer's order.

Payment transactions conducted using SET offer more security than those using only SSL. However, with its multiple steps, SET is more complicated than SSL alone. The ease of use of SSL transactions has led to more widespread acceptance of SSL, while SET is much less frequently used than had been expected.

SHTTP (Secure HyperText Transfer Protocol) is a security-enhanced version of HTTP that was developed by Terisa Systems, a spin-off of Enterprise Integration Technology (EIT), the original project managers for the CommerceNet consortium. SHTTP was developed as part of EIT/Terisa's work to develop tools for CommerceNet when it was first established. SHTTP provides server-side functionality for SET. SHTTP was developed in 1994 when Mastercard and VISA decided that they needed a common security mechanism. SSL was not available commercially yet and both major credit card companies determined that the best way for them to encourage adoption of secure electronic credit card transactions was to cooperate on the definition of a common security mechanism. However, soon after, SSL was introduced as a free and easy-to-use facility bundled into the Netscape browser, so we no longer hear very much about SHTTP.

SSL uses HTTPS, also known as the Secure Hypertext Transfer Protocol even though the S is at the end of the acronym. SSL is a Web protocol that was developed by Netscape and built into the Netscape browser, which encrypts and decrypts user page requests as well as pages returned by the Web server. HTTPS uses SSL as a sub-layer under the regular HTTP application layer. When you use a Netscape browser to view a Web catalog, the order form URL will include "https://" instead of "http://." When the page is sent to a retailer's Web site, the browser's HTTPS layer encrypts the page. The catalog server then acknowledges receipt of the page in an encrypted form via a URL that also includes https://. The receipt is then decrypted by the browser's HTTPS sub-layer. Since the functionality of HTTPS is available via normal Web browsers, this operation is transparent to the user. Most users are aware of the SSL operation only when an order form provides the option of using a secure payment mechanism or a straight (unencrypted or plain text) payment or if they notice the https:// in the URL of the Web page that is used by the order form.

NEW PRODUCTS AND ELECTRONIC WALLETS

New products are being introduced by both established and start-up e-commerce ventures. These products are making it easier to use secure services. VeriSign is one company that offers PKI solutions with 128-bit encryption, the strongest encryption on the market in early 2000. Services are being introduced to allow secure transactions without requiring a merchant account. This simplifies SET transaction processing while providing the added security of the SET approach.

Electronic wallets have been introduced but have been slow to catch on. A wallet is a small software program and data that is used for online purchase transactions. Electronic wallets can function as browser add-ons. Currently, CyberCash provides free wallet software that allows several methods of payment to be defined within the wallet—for example, several different credit cards. Payment is accomplished through the electronic wallet in the following way. When you order an item, the order is sent to the merchant. The merchant sends back an invoice via the merchant's server and asks the consumer to launch his or her wallet software. When the customer selects the pay option, the merchant server software sends back a message to the customer's system that activates the wallet software. The customer then selects one of the cards defined in the wallet. The transaction also includes real-time credit card authorization.

PRIVACY AND DATA PROTECTION

TRUSTe is a service offering a "seal of approval" for privacy protection of information on Web sites. Though privacy is different from security, the issue of protection of personal data is related to network security issues and is important to consider in the overall security and privacy plans for an organization. It is important to establish a privacy policy in your company and to post your privacy policy on your Web site. Any information that is being collected from visitors and customers to your Web site should be carefully protected. If information will be used for a particular purpose, this needs to be stated in your privacy policy on your Web site. The TRUSTe Web site (www.truste.org) provides direction in developing and publishing a privacy policy for your Web site.

LAB 6.2 EXERCISES

6.2.1 UNDERSTAND THE FUNCTION OF THE SSL PROTOCOL

Go to a secure electronic commerce storefront, such as www.1800flowers.com. Go through the ordering process (you can cancel out if you don't want to buy something). Walk through the ordering form and review the security policy stated on the site (most sites, including www.1800flowers.com, discuss their use of SSL for secure payment transactions).

    a) How does the secure order form use SSL? Figure out and explain client-side functionality.

    b) Figure out and explain the server-side functionality that supports secure ordering using SSL.

6.2.2 DEVELOP A PRIVACY STATEMENT

Go to the TRUSTe site at: www.truste.org. Take a look at the Privacy Resource Guide and the Site Coordinator's Guide.

    a) Use the model privacy statement (available in HTML and in Word formats) to develop a privacy statement for your organization.

Lab 6.2: Secure Internet Protocols

LAB 6.2 EXERCISE ANSWERS

6.2.1 ANSWERS

Go to a secure electronic commerce storefront, such as www.1800flowers.com. Go through the ordering process (you can cancel out if you don't want to buy something). Walk through the ordering form and review the security policy stated on the site (most sites, including www.1800flowers.com, discuss their use of SSL for secure payment transactions).

> **a)** How does the secure order form use SSL? Figure out and explain client-side functionality.
>
> *Answer: A secure catalog order form uses SSL on the client side when the person purchasing the item from the catalog enters payment information via a secure server.*
>
> **b)** Figure out and explain the server-side functionality that supports secure ordering using SSL.
>
> *Answer: On the server side, SSL is used on one of the "commerce servers" or by downloading the SSLRef program library. A scripted interaction occurs when the client opens the connection to the server and lists its capabilities and the server then responds by indicating the client cipher suite and compression method in use.*

6.2.2 ANSWER

Go to the TRUSTe site at: www.truste.org. Take a look at the Privacy Resource Guide and the Site Coordinator's Guide.

> **a)** Use the model privacy statement (available in HTML and in Word formats) to develop a privacy statement for your organization.
>
> *Answer: In order to meet TRUSTe's guidelines, your privacy statement must at a minimum disclose the following:*
>
> *What personally identifiable information is collected*
>
> *What organization is collecting the information*
>
> *How the information is used*
>
> *With whom the information may be shared*
>
> *What choices are available to users regarding collection, use, and distribution of the information*

What kind of security procedures are in place to protect against the loss, misuse, or alteration of information under the company's control

How users can correct any inaccuracies in the information

LAB 6.2 SELF-REVIEW QUESTIONS

In order to test your progress, you should be able to answer the following questions.

1) SSL sits between the _____ and the _____ layers.

   a) _____ SMTP, HTTPD
   b) _____ HTTPD, TCP/IP
   c) _____ FTP, TCP/IP
   d) _____ TCP, IP

2) SET users use a digital _____.

   a) _____ Handle
   b) _____ Identifier
   c) _____ Wallet
   d) _____ Certificate

3) With SET, a credit card is identified by a digital certificate online.

   a) _____ True
   b) _____ False

4) SET allows merchants to see their customers' credit card information.

   a) _____ True
   b) _____ False

5) SSL uses which of the following protocols?

   a) _____ SHTTP
   b) _____ HTTPS
   c) _____ STCP/IP
   d) _____ SET

Quiz answers appear in the Appendix, Section 6.2.

LAB 6.3

FIREWALLS AND SNIFFERS

> **LAB OBJECTIVES**
>
> After this lab, you will be able to:
> - Understand the Functionality of a Firewall
> - Distinguish Between Use of Sniffers by Network Administrators and Hackers

FIREWALLS

A firewall is a set of related programs, located in a network gateway server. A firewall serves to protect private network resources, such as an organization's intranet that is located behind the firewall. A firewall also allows workers in the organization to gain access to the Internet. At the same time that the firewall prevents outsiders from accessing an organization's private data resources, a firewall can control which outside resources users within the organization can access. While it is useful to share files within the organization, it is not a good idea to allow any file sharing to run on attached systems that are visible on the Internet.

Firewall software works with router software, filtering all network packets and determining whether to forward these packets. In addition, a firewall generally either includes or works with a proxy server to make network requests on behalf of workstation users. A firewall is generally (and should be) installed on a separate system from other network servers so that incoming requests are not allowed to access internal resources. In this way, packet filtering is used to screen requests to determine if they come from acceptable domain names and IP addresses. A firewall acts as an application gateway in such situations where email messages are transmitted. A firewall-enabled mail gateway can transmit or discard messages based on the header fields, as well as on message size or even based on words in the message itself. Most firewalls include logging and reporting functions with a GUI (graphical user interface) for administration of the functionality on the firewall. Firewalls may include automatic alarms set to go off at given attack thresholds.

SNIFFERS

What is a sniffer and how is it used? A sniffer is a program for network analysis that monitors flow and analyzes network traffic. A sniffer detects bottlenecks and problems and works to keep traffic flowing efficiently. Since a sniffer can capture data that is being transmitted, it can be used by hackers to capture sensitive data, such as passwords and credit cards that are sent "in the clear." The network router reads data packets and determines the network destination of the data. The first step is to decide whether the destination is within the router's own network or whether the data needs to be passed further along on the Internet. A router with a sniffer on it may read data in a package along with the source address and the destination address. Routers from such vendors as Cisco and Bay Networks offer encryption on the router as a useful security measure so that data isn't sent "in the clear."

LAB 6.3 EXERCISES

6.3.1 UNDERSTAND THE FUNCTIONALITY OF A FIREWALL

a) If you are an outsider, what is your perspective on an organization's firewall?

_____

_____

b) If you are an employee of the organization, what is your perspective on that organization's firewall?

_____

_____

c) If you are the network administrator for an organization, what is your perspective on the organization's firewall then?

_____

_____

6.3.2 DISTINGUISH BETWEEN USE OF SNIFFERS BY NETWORK ADMINISTRATORS AND HACKERS

a) What is the function of a sniffer from the perspective of a network administrator?

b) What is the function of a sniffer from the perspective of a hacker?

LAB 6.3 EXERCISE ANSWERS

6.3.1 ANSWERS

a) If you are an outsider, what is your perspective on an organization's firewall?

Answer: As an outsider, you view the firewall as something that keeps you from gaining access to an organization's resources behind the firewall. Therefore, the firewall acts as a locked door to outsiders who don't have a key.

b) If you are an employee of the organization, what is your perspective on that organization's firewall?

Answer: As an employee of an organization, you view the firewall as something that protects your sensitive data and the internal resources that you use. As an employee, you may also find that a firewall controls your access to outside resources according to company policy. A company may elect to not allow access to particular Web sites such as those with pornographic content.

c) If you are the network administrator for an organization, what is your perspective on the organization's firewall then?

Answer: If you are the network administrator, you view the firewall as protection for the internal resources for which you are responsible. You also view the firewall as a window on what is happening from the outside, with logs to check on who is trying to access and possibly break into the intranet you are responsible for protecting. As network administrator, you want a firewall that offers logging and reporting capabilities as well as an easy-to-use graphical user interface for maintaining and checking the status of critical firewall features. You may want automatic alarms to alert you in case of an attempted break-in.

6.3.2 ANSWERS

a) What is the function of a sniffer from the perspective of a network administrator?

Answer: From the perspective of the network administrator, a sniffer is a useful program that can help in network analysis and administration, monitoring flow and analyzing network traffic. A network administrator can use a sniffer to detect bottlenecks and problems and thereby determine how to keep traffic flowing efficiently.

b) What is the function of a sniffer from the perspective of a hacker?

From the perspective of a hacker, a sniffer is a handy way to invade the privacy of an organization during data transmission. A hacker can use a sniffer to capture data that is being transmitted. If a hacker puts a sniffer on your line, he or she is trying to capture sensitive data, such as passwords and credit cards that are sent "in the clear." Passwords can then be used to break into an organization's intranet and use internal data resources. Credit cards can be stolen by hackers who put sniffers on the line when credit card numbers are being transmitted for payments. That is why it is good to encrypt credit card transactions rather than sending them as plain text "in the clear."

LAB 6.3 SELF-REVIEW QUESTIONS

In order to test your progress, you should be able to answer the following questions.

1) Firewalls filter all network packets and determine whether to forward the packets.

   a) _____ True
   b) _____ False

2) Sniffers can be used to capture sensitive data.

   a) _____ True
   b) _____ False

Lab 6.3: Firewalls and Sniffers

3) Firewalls are generally installed on the same system as other network servers.

   a) _____ True
   b) _____ False

4) Which of the following are true of certain firewalls? (Select all that apply.)

   a) _____ They have a GUI front-end for administration.
   b) _____ They are hardware systems.
   c) _____ They can be used as fire extinguishers in case of fire.
   d) _____ They are software systems.
   e) _____ They use the Linux (a free version of UNIX) operating system.
   f) _____ Their configuration is difficult to set up correctly.

5) How does a sniffer relate to a credit card? (Select all that apply.)

   a) _____ A sniffer can provide a digital signature for a credit card.
   b) _____ A sniffer can disrupt the encoding on the magnetic strip on a credit card.
   c) _____ A sniffer on a line may be able to capture credit card information while it is being sent.
   d) _____ Use of a credit card may lead to finding a sniffer on a line.

Quiz answers appear in the Appendix, Section 6.3.

LAB 6.4

PROXY SERVERS, VIRTUAL PRIVATE NETWORKS, AND SMARTCARDS

> **LAB OBJECTIVES**
>
> After this lab, you will be able to:
>
> ✔ Understand the Functionality of a Proxy Server
> ✔ Assess the Feasibility of a Smartcard Solution

PROXY SERVERS

What is a proxy server and how does it work? A proxy server serves as an intermediary between the workstation user and the Internet. The proxy server provides security, administrative control, and caching facilities. A proxy server is associated with, or is a component of, a gateway server, separating an intranet from the Internet or a firewall, protecting the intranet from intruders. A proxy server receives a request for Internet service from a user, for example, a Web page request. The first step is to filter the request. The proxy server, which may also be a cache server, checks the local cache of previously downloaded pages. If the server finds the requested page, it returns the cached page to the user without forwarding the request to the Internet. In this way, the proxy server acts as a client on behalf of the user. The proxy server acts in a way that is transparent to the user. If the requested page is not in cache, the proxy server uses its own IP address (rather than that of the individual workstation requesting the page) to request the page from the appropriate server on the Internet. When the appropriate page is returned, the proxy server relates the page to the original request and forwards the page to the user.

A proxy server may be combined with other server programs in a single package or there may be separate server programs, which reside on the same or different systems. The proxy server may reside on the firewall server. Alternatively, the proxy server may reside on a separate server and forward requests through the firewall. The cache serves all users and improves response to requests.

VPNs (VIRTUAL PRIVATE NETWORKS)

A VPN serves as a private data network that uses the public telecommunications infrastructure instead of owned or leased lines. It is much less expensive to share the public infrastructure rather than to install and maintain a private network. You can get the same capabilities at a lower cost with added flexibility and expansion capacity. The important factor to consider is privacy. Therefore, tunneling protocols and security procedures are instituted to provide privacy protection.

In the same way as the telephone companies provide secure shared resources for voice transmissions, extranets or wide-area intranets operating as VPNs can provide secure shared resources for data transmission. In order to protect sensitive data, the data is encrypted before sending it through the public network and then decrypted at the receiving end. In addition, both the originating and the receiving network addresses are encrypted. Microsoft, 3COM, and others have proposed a standard tunneling protocol, PPTP (Point-to-Point Tunneling Protocol).

PPTP is a protocol that allows corporations to extend their own corporate network through private "tunnels" over the public Internet. Effectively, a corporation uses a wide-area network as a single large local area network. A company no longer needs to lease its own lines for wide-area communication but can securely use the public networks. This kind of interconnection is what constitutes a VPN.

PPTP and Layer 2 Forwarding, proposed by Cisco Systems, are among the most likely proposals as the basis for a new Internet Engineering Task Force (IETF) standard. With PPTP, which is an extension of the Internet's Point-to-Point Protocol (PPP), any user of a PC with PPP client support is able to use an Internet service provider (ISP) to connect securely to a server elsewhere in the user's company.

SMARTCARDS

A smartcard is a plastic card similar in size to a credit card. A smartcard has an embedded microchip that can be loaded with data, used for telephone calling, electronic cash payments, and other applications, and then periodically "recharged" for additional use. Applications for smartcards include the ability to:

- Dial a connection on a mobile telephone and be charged on a per-call basis
- Establish your identity when logging on to an Internet access provider or to an online bank

Lab 6.4: Proxy Servers, Virtual Private Networks, and Smartcards

- Pay for parking at parking meters or to get on subways, trains, or buses
- Give hospitals or doctors personal data without filling out a form
- Make small purchases at electronic stores on the Web
- Buy gasoline at a gasoline station

A smartcard contains more information than a magnetic stripe card. In addition, a smartcard can be programmed for different applications. Some cards contain programming and data to support multiple applications and some are updated to add new applications after they are issued. Smartcards can be designed to be inserted into a slot and read by a special reader or to be read at a distance, such as at a toll booth. Cards can be designed for one-time use or to be reused.

An industry standard interface between programming and PC hardware in a smartcard has been defined by the PC/SC Working Group, representing Microsoft, IBM, Bull, Schlumberger, and other interested companies. Another standard is called OpenCard. There are currently two leading smartcard operating systems: JavaCard and MultiOS.

With more than a billion smartcards currently in use, smartcards are frequently seen in Europe. However, the United States has been slow to adopt smartcards. Computer manufacturers are developing keyboards that include smartcard slots that can be read like bank credit cards. The companies currently involved in developing hardware to make smartcards and devices to read them are Bull, Gemplus, and Schlumberger.

LAB 6.4 EXERCISES

6.4.1 UNDERSTAND THE FUNCTIONALITY OF A PROXY SERVER

The network administrator installed a free version of a proxy server at a start-up Web software company. At the same time, one of the network administrators at an established mainframe vendor purchased and installed proxy server software on the corporate network.

    a) Why do you think the network administrator at the start-up installed the free proxy server software?

_____

_____

170 Lab 6.4: Proxy Servers, Virtual Private Networks, and Smartcards

b) Why do you think the network administrator at the established company purchased and installed the proxy server software on the corporate network?

___

___

6.4.2 ASSESS THE FEASIBILITY OF A SMARTCARD SOLUTION

A hospital administrator decided to provide smartcards for use by hospital staff. Her plan was to combine three functions on one card: (1) card key for entrance to the building, (2) authorization card to gain access to the hospital records system on the intranet, and (3) personal identification card for access to wards and examining rooms.

The hospital administrator then proposed putting each patient's complete medical record on a personal smartcard that the patient would keep in his or her possession and bring to the physician's office or hospital for treatment.

a) Assess the feasibility of using a smart card for each of these purposes.

___

___

LAB 6.4 EXERCISE ANSWERS

6.4.1 ANSWERS

The network administrator installed a free version of a proxy server at a start-up Web software company. At the same time, one of the network administrators at an established mainframe vendor purchased and installed proxy server software on the corporate network.

a) Why do you think the network administrator at the start-up installed the free proxy server software?

Lab 6.4: Proxy Servers, Virtual Private Networks, and Smartcards **171**

Answer: The network administrator at the start-up chose to install a proxy server to improve security and protect the software under development on the intranet from intruders. A proxy server serves as an intermediary between the workstation user and the Internet. The proxy server provides security, administrative control, and caching facilities. A proxy server is associated with, or is a component of, a gateway server, separating an intranet from the Internet or a firewall, protecting the intranet from intruders.

b) Why do you think the network administrator at the established company purchased and installed the proxy server software on the corporate network?

Answer: Proxy servers request a Web page on behalf of a workstation user. If the requested page is still in the cache, it is retrieved from the cache. The caching server passes the page back to the requestor via the proxy server. Installing a proxy server at the established company helped improve bandwidth by caching frequently requested pages instead of fetching them from the Web multiple times.

6.4.2 ANSWER

A hospital administrator decided to provide smartcards for use by hospital staff. Her plan was to combine three functions on one card: (1) card key for entrance to the building, (2) authorization card to gain access to the hospital records system on the intranet, and (3) personal identification card for access to wards and examining rooms.

The hospital administrator then proposed putting each patient's complete medical record on a personal smart card that the patient would keep in his or her possession and bring to the physician's office or hospital for treatment.

a) Assess the feasibility of using a smart card for each of these purposes.

Answer: A smartcard makes sense as a card key to gain entrance to the hospital building. The card provides physical security for the building and the patients. In the same way, the smartcard makes sense as a personal identification card to allow hospital staff access to wards and examining rooms.

There is some question about using the smartcard to authorize access to the hospital records system on the intranet. It would be good to supplement the security provided by the card with some type of personal identification such as a thumbprint (such a facility is available on some computer systems with smartcard readers), since it is easy for a card to be lost or stolen. The other issue with using a smartcard to access the hospital records system is that systems in hospitals are often in areas where there are a fair number of people walking or standing nearby. A physician or nurse may be called away

LAB 6.4

while entering or checking patient data or may simply forget to log off the system. Therefore, it is important for the hospital records system to include a feature that automatically logs out a user after a short period of inactivity.

While some European countries have started using smartcards to store patient records in pilot projects, patients in the United States often regard this approach as an invasion of personal privacy. The other issue that has been raised about putting all patient records on a smartcard is the update process every time that a patient is seen. With nationalized health services in many European nations, a patient has one identification number throughout the healthcare system. However, at this point in the United States, patients have different patient identification numbers and are treated at different locations, each of which may have its own paper-based or electronic medical records system. By introducing a patient record smartcard into her hospital, the hospital administrator would most likely meet with objections on the basis of privacy concerns, cost of updating the information on the card, and difficulties in use outside the hospital itself.

LAB 6.4 SELF-REVIEW QUESTIONS

In order to test your progress, you should be able to answer the following questions.

1) Proxy servers provide _____. (Select all that apply.)

   a) _____ Security
   b) _____ Caching facilities
   c) _____ Speed improvement
   d) _____ Administrative control

2) VPNs use private telecommunications infrastructure.

   a) _____ True
   b) _____ False

3) The sending and receiving network addresses are encrypted in data sent over a VPN.

   a) _____ True
   b) _____ False

Lab 6.4: Proxy Servers, Virtual Private Networks, and Smartcards

4) PPTP provides the following functionality.

    a) _____ Ability to use ISP for connection
    b) _____ Secure tunneling facility
    c) _____ Smartcard
    d) _____ Both a and c
    e) _____ Both a and b
    f) _____ Both b and c

5) Encryption is used in which of the following technologies? (Select all that apply.)

    a) _____ VPN
    b) _____ Caching server
    c) _____ Proxy server
    d) _____ PPTP

Quiz answers appear in the Appendix, Section 6.4.

CHAPTER 6

TEST YOUR THINKING

Review what you have learned about public key encryption. Now, you will have the opportunity to actually use public key encryption to protect your email communication.

1) Download and install a PGP (Pretty Good Privacy) package from the Internet (www.pgp.com and www.download.com). Create a public and private key for yourself. Ask a colleague or friend to do the same. Swap public keys with each other (see software documentation for assistance).
   Encrypt an email message with your friend's public key.
   Send him or her the message.
   Have your colleague or friend decode the message.
   Have your colleague or friend send you an encoded message.
   Decrypt the coded message with your private key.

2) Set up an encrypted email conversation with some one else via the Internet.
   Swap public keys.
   Sign your emails with your key so that the other person knows who you are.

3) Go to an online e-commerce store, for example, Amazon.com. Place an item in your shopping cart. Go to the "checkout area" to fill in your credit card information. You do not need to enter any information. In your Web browser open up the security information window (see software documentation for assistance).
   Are you communicating with the server over a secure encrypted connection?
   If yes, what type of encryption are you using?
   If no, would you continue with your purchase?
   Who issued the encryption certificate?

CHAPTER 7

WEB SERVER SUPPORT

The Web server is a vital organ in the corpus of an institution and like all organs should be kept healthy, fit, and fat-free. The Webmaster is the physician, fitness trainer, and therapist assigned to keep it so.

—Anonymous

CHAPTER OBJECTIVES

In this chapter, you will learn about:

- Web Server Evaluation Issues — Page 177
- Web Site Service Models — Page 187
- Supporting Multiple Servers — Page 193
- Server Security Issues — Page 200
- Document Root Taxonomies — Page 214
- Access Authorization, Security, and Privacy — Page 221
- Searching and Indexing Issues — Page 228

For most Web surfers, a good site is judged by the quality and presentation of the content it provides. And that's the way it should be, since when a reader/user becomes involved with what is happening on the server side, it's usually for unpleasant reasons—broken links, interactions that don't work, poor response, and so on. The Web page designers get all the glory, but the maintainers of a Web server are actually the ones that make it all happen.

Chapter 7: Web Server Support

In the following labs, we will discuss a number of issues that face a Webmaster on the system side. All of these issues and the technologies that support them support a common goal of providing to the readers/users of an organizational Web site the best possible service and support. The scope of these issues and technologies is a strong indication of how complex a task Web server support has become.

LAB 7.1

WEB SERVER EVALUATION ISSUES

> **LAB OBJECTIVES**
>
> After this lab, you will be able to:
>
> ✓ Understand the Basic Concepts of Web Hosting

SERVER IMPLEMENTATION STRATEGIES

It is easy for an organization to decide to get on the Web. It is far more difficult for an organization to decide *how* to get on the Web. This decision should be based on factors centered on the role of the Web site in the organizational strategy and the level of support and resources the organization can realistically devote to its maintenance.

We will discuss three commonly used server implementation strategies:

- Hosting services—where the Web server is supported remotely, usually at the organization's Internet Service Provider (ISP)
- Turnkey solutions or server appliances—self-contained hardware and software packages maintained locally, that is, at the organization's physical location
- Dedicated server support—the fully configurable hardware and software solution either maintained locally or co-located

An important thing to remember when deciding which strategy to adopt is the impact that strategy will have on users/readers. Your audience *will not know* which strategy you have adopted since the end results are the same. Your audience *will know* if they are not receiving the Web service (speed, reliability, etc.) that they expect or that you have promised.

HOSTING SERVICES

Most major Internet Service Providers (ISPs) offer their customers a broad range of Web server hosting services. For such customers, these Web Service Providers (WSPs) are the easiest, most convenient, and fastest method of obtaining Web presence. The price of these services depends on the depth of the service provided, which varies widely and is often the result of competition between ISPs.

For an organization, the strength in contracting a hosting service is that server support and maintenance is off-loaded to that service and the organization can devote its resources to content development. Such services are most suitable for individuals, small businesses, and organizations that do not have strong technical expertise.

Typically, price is no longer an issue as the cost of Internet connectivity has dropped to the point that most every company can afford it. If the company cannot afford a dedicated Internet connection because it is in an outlying area (for example), then having access to the Web server only when the company has dialed up (or otherwise made the connection to the Internet) is not really a good choice in today's world of the Internet because it equates to a "Closed" sign on your front door.

One advantage might be the price. You choice of ISPs is limited to those serving your particular area. However, your choice of WSPs is virtually unlimited. I know at least one domain that is "physically" located in Germany, where the ISP is. In Germany, Internet connections are substantially more expensive than in the United States. However, this Web server is a virtual host on a server in the United States. Visitors do not see the difference. They simply input the URL into their browser and are brought to the site.

The disadvantage of splitting the functionality like this is that you no longer have a single point of contact should you need support. Typically, once the system is running, not much support is required, but having two organizations to deal with for support is still something worth considering.

Most hosting services offer 24 × 7 (24 hours per day, 7 days per week) support with the assurance that your Web site will be available to the fullest extent possible. Table 7.1 lists some of the other common services offered by WSPs. Many of

Table 7.1 ■ Services Offered by WSPs

Domain Name Service (DNS)	Negotiated quantity of disk space
High-speed Internet connectivity via various methods (e.g., ISDN, DSL, T1, etc.)	Technical support
File archiving and retrieval	Negotiated quantity of throughput (e.g., 1 GB per day)
Registration with major search engines (e.g., Yahoo, Lycos, etc.)	Web server logfile management and analysis
Service libraries of common Web page functions and services (e.g., page counters, shopping cart, etc.)	Streaming media support
Indexing of Web pages to support local searching	Support of a database interface
Software library maintenance and support (e.g., servers, programming language compilers, etc.)	FTP, Telnet, email services
Virtual hosting	Secure connection support(e.g., SSL)
Access authorization control	Design/programming tools and support (e.g., support of Microsoft FrontPage)

these services may be negotiable and are valuable points to be considered in a WSP evaluation.

TURNKEY SOLUTIONS

A drawback of Web hosting services is that they *are* remote. That means that your organization is depending on someone else to keep your Web server going. It means that you have to telephone someone else in the event of problems. It means that your data and information is in the care of someone other than yourself.

Server appliances or turnkey systems provide a solution that offers an organization greater control of Web service than that provided by a WSP. At the same time, they still require a minimum of technical expertise.

Server appliances are self-contained hardware and software products designed to provide an organization with Web service. They are referred to as "appliances" because of the ease of use and simplicity of setup that they provide. You simply plug the appliance into the network and into a power source, and you're on the Web.

Server appliances are designed for both small offices and large organizations. They are designed to require little or no maintenance and for use by nontechnical staff. Server configuration is usually accomplished using a Web browser/client and an easily understandable GUI interface. The software used by the appliance is typically open standard (e.g., Linux operating system or Apache Web server), so that there are no licensing issues.

DEDICATED SERVER SUPPORT

An organizational decision for a dedicated Web server represents a major commitment. It requires a well-defined organizational Web strategy and major support for hardware, software, and staff resources.

The complexity of dedicated server support does not permit it to be as easily quantified as the other strategies we have discussed in this lab. In fact, all of the issues contained in *The Advanced Website Architecture Series* are directed towards the design, support, and maintenance of a dedicated organization Web server.

SERVER EVALUATION CASE STUDY

The selection of Web server software is a major decision that must be made if an organization decides to support a dedicated Web server. This decision must be firmly rooted in the organization's overall Web strategy.

The following case study illustrates how an organization approached the decision of which server software to use. Moreover, it illustrates a well-thought-out and methodical approach for identifying those factors that should contribute to that decision.

BACKGROUND

The organization conducting this server software evaluation was seeking to replace existing software. It was running the CERN server software on a UNIX platform. The decision to replace the CERN software was motivated by the fact that support and maintenance of the software was being discontinued. Given the organization's existing technical expertise in UNIX, it was decided that the new server software would also be used on a UNIX platform.

Lab 7.1: Web Server Evaluation Issues

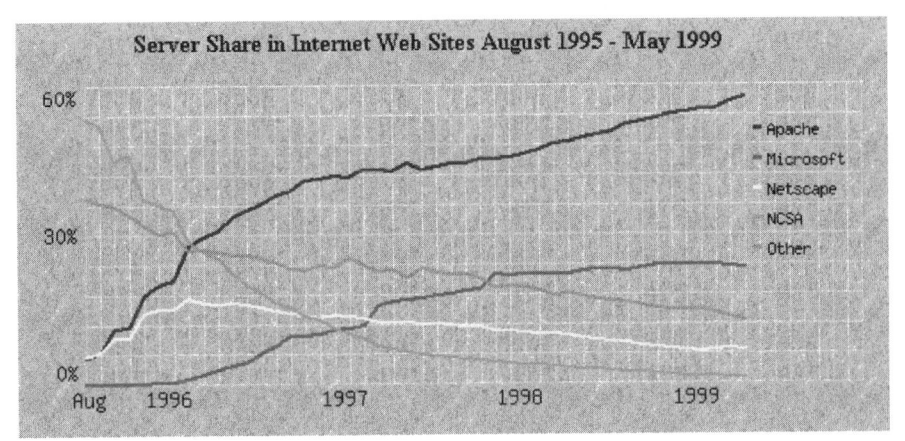

Figure 7.1 ■ Web Server Software Being Used between August 1995 and May 1999.

Market share is of questionable importance in a software decision. However, for the organization in question, market share was perceived as an indication of a user community that could possibly provide assistance and help in the support of a server. Figure 7.1 (from http://www.netcraft.com) was an indicator of server market share at the time of this evaluation.

Based upon this information, the organization decided to choose between the Apache server software and that available from Netscape Corporation. The criteria they used for the decision we will leave as an exercise.

A small committee was organized by the organization to identify those technical features that were critical and that the CERN server provided. Desirable features for the replacement server were also identified. This committee was composed of Web users and technical support staff. The availability of the identified features in each of the software packages being considered was then determined.

The resulting information is shown in Table 7.2. "Yes" in one of the table cells indicates that the server software provides the specified requirement natively or in conjunction with another application.

The requirements used in this table are obviously those of specific interest to the organization conducting this evaluation. No attempt was made to prioritize or weight these requirements although this could easily be added to this evaluation model.

Table 7.2 ■ Comparison of Server Software Features

Requirement	Who Requested	Available with Apache?	Available with Netscape?
Must support currently implemented security model	All	Yes	Yes
Must work with cgi wrapper program	All	Yes	Yes
Must be able to map part of URL space onto a CGI script and have the remainder of the URL path passed as an argument to the script	Users	Yes	Yes
Secure Socket Layer (SSL) support (e.g., for secure password transmission)	All	Yes	Yes
Supports definable limits on resources used by CGI scripts	Staff	Yes	Yes
Should allow users to set up password-protected documents without requiring administrators to change the rules file	Users	Yes	Yes
Must be able to start from /etc/rc.local when machine is rebooted	Staff	Yes	Yes
Supports the Microsoft FrontPage Extensions	All	Yes	Yes
Can run the currently used Web-based conferencing system	Users	Yes	Unknown
Supports personal directories	Users	Yes	Yes
Allows for the definition of customized error messages	All	Yes	Yes
Currently supported access authorization models must be easily migrated	Staff	Yes	Yes
Server can be easily cloned for test server and/or other servers	Staff	Yes	Yes
Provides support for Java servlets	Users	Yes	No
Automatic broken link reporting	Staff	Probably Not	Yes
Supports server-side includes	All	Yes	Yes
Search engine included	Staff	No	Yes

Lab 7.1: Web Server Evaluation Issues

The technical evaluation presented in this table was then used in conjunction with pricing and availability considerations to recommend which server software should be adopted.

LAB 7.1 EXERCISES

7.1.1 UNDERSTAND THE BASIC CONCEPTS OF WEB HOSTING

a) Discuss the difference between an Internet Service Provider (ISP) and a Web Services Provider (WSP) and when you would choose one over the other. Include a discussion of whether it is necessary that your ISP also provides Web services.

b) Discuss the advantages and disadvantages of turnkey solutions.

c) Providing Web services is no longer just having a server that delivers Web pages. Discuss what criteria would be used in the decision-making process.

LAB 7.1 EXERCISE ANSWERS

7.1.1 ANSWERS

a) Discuss the difference between an Internet Service Provider (ISP) and a Web Services Provider (WSP) and when you would choose one over the other. Include a discussion of whether it is necessary that your ISP also provides Web services.

Answer: An ISP just provides you a connection to the Internet. Depending on the ISP and the price you are willing to pay, that can be limited to simply a telephone number you dial to reach a server, which is then connected to the Internet. This is the typical case for most people (i.e., not businesses). Generally, the support is limited to basic configuration issues and may or may not be 24 × 7, depending on the provider. At the high end of the scale, an ISP might provide all of the hardware and do all of the configuration and your location and all you really need to do is hook your network to the ISP's equipment. In some cases, the ISP will even do that for you.

A WSP provides a Web server on which you place your pages. This can be anything from a subdirectory of the WSP's main server (e.g., www.web-provider.com/~user/) to a virtual host using your own domain name (which is on the same physical server as other domains) to dedicated machines just for your pages.

A WSP does not necessarily need to provide your connection to the Internet. There are a number of reasons why you might want to split the responsibility like this; for example, the cost of a 24 × 7 Internet connection might be too high.

b) Discuss the advantages and disadvantages of turnkey solutions.

Answer: The biggest advantage of a turnkey solution is the speed at which it can be in place as compared to developing the site on your own. Consider the difference between a fast-food restaurant and one with five stars. How long does it take to get your order? How much choice do you have over what side dishes you get?

Using server appliances is definitely a trade-off since their convenience also presents some drawbacks. These systems may or may not be scalable, so as your Web site grows or becomes more complex, you may "outgrow" your appliance. Likewise, most appliances do not allow hardware upgrades, such as larger hard drives, for increasing data volume. On the other hand, most server appliances are reasonably priced and can quickly recover in service the cost of the initial investment.

In addition to cost, factors that should influence the evaluation of server appliances include

- *Processor used*
- *RAM/storage capacity*
- *Maximum number of users supported*
- *Setup/backup utilities provided*

- *Server operating system*
- *Client operating systems supported*
- *Speed of network connection*

At the time of this writing, some of the major players in the Web server appliance field were Cobalt Networks, eSoft, and Whistle Communications.

c) Providing Web services is no longer just having a server that delivers Web pages. Discuss what criteria would be used in the decision-making process.

Answer: The criteria will depend on your company. Since smaller sites that just provide information about their company are less likely targets than large sites, such as Amazon.com, which sell goods over the Internet, you may be less concerned with security (although you should always be concerned to some degree).

Logically, you also need to consider the features the server provides. The more money you pay, the more control you have over what server is implemented by your WSP, so you can pretty much tell them what you want. However, if you can only afford a virtual host on an existing server, it is unlikely that you will have much to say about which server is implemented. Therefore, you might need to make a choice between features and price (which is usually the case).

LAB 7.1 SELF-REVIEW QUESTIONS

In order to test your progress, you should be able to answer the following questions.

1) For security reasons, an ISP only provides Internet access and a WSP only provides the Web server.

   a) _____ True
   b) _____ False

2) All WSPs provide 24 × 7 support.

   a) _____ True
   b) _____ False

3) A dedicated server typically provides the great level of control over the system in terms of both installed software and configuration.

   a) _____ True
   b) _____ False

4) Which is typically not a decision criteria when decided on a specific turnkey solution?

a) _____ Processor used
b) _____ RAM/storage capacity
c) _____ Maximum number of users supported
d) _____ Internet Service Provider
e) _____ Setup/backup utilities provided

Quiz answers appear in the Appendix, Section 7.1.

LAB 7.2

WEB SITE SERVICE MODELS

> **LAB OBJECTIVES**
>
> After this lab, you will be able to:
> - Understand the Basic Web Site Architectures

COMMON WEB SITE ARCHITECTURES

Selection of Web server hardware and software is no longer sufficient in the architecture of an organizational Web site. It is now necessary for the Web site administrator to determine the best Web site architecture or topology that will ensure the desired level of performance.

In this lab, we will discuss the most commonly used of these architectures.

SINGLE SERVER

The single server architecture suggests that only the network lies between a reader/user and the organizational Web server. The simplicity of this model automatically indicates its inherent problems:

- Availability and performance under high traffic conditions
- A single point of failure—if the server is unavailable, the organization is off the Web
- Security issues—vulnerability to attack

DNS ROUND ROBIN

The single server model can quickly reach its limits of scalability as traffic to the organizational Web site increases. The next logical step is often a distributed server architecture. In such an architecture, HTTP requests are distributed over a "farm" of servers. The content of each server is mirrored so that each server is functionally identical to another. We say functionally identical, since it would be possible for servers in the farm to be operating on different computer platforms and/or using different server software. The method quite often used for this architecture is *DNS Round Robin,* using a configuration similar to that in Figure 7.2.

DNS Round Robin uses a combination of the DNS server, routers, and switches to linearly distribute requests to the server "farm." In the diagram, server A gets the first request, server B the second, and server C the third. The linear rotation then begins again.

DISTRIBUTED LOAD-BALANCED SERVERS

The basic concept of a *distributed load-balanced architecture* is that HTTP requests are distributed to the servers in a "farm" not in a linear rotation (such as in the DNS Round Robin architecture), but rather according to the load (activity) of the servers. In this model, no one server in the "farm" responds to the majority of requests. "Load balancing" implies that every attempt is made to keep all servers equally busy and that a new HTTP request is sent to the server that is least busy. Figure 7.3 depicts a typical load-balanced server architecture.

Load balancing is accomplished using specialized software in the bridge. The bridge then appears as one "virtual" server to the requesting browsers/clients. All Internet traffic is directed toward a virtual IP address (virtual server) via DNS. Those requests are then distributed over a series of real IP addresses on servers (real servers). The definition of a virtual IP address is an address that is in DNS and most likely has a domain name. A real IP address is physically located on a real server behind the bridge.

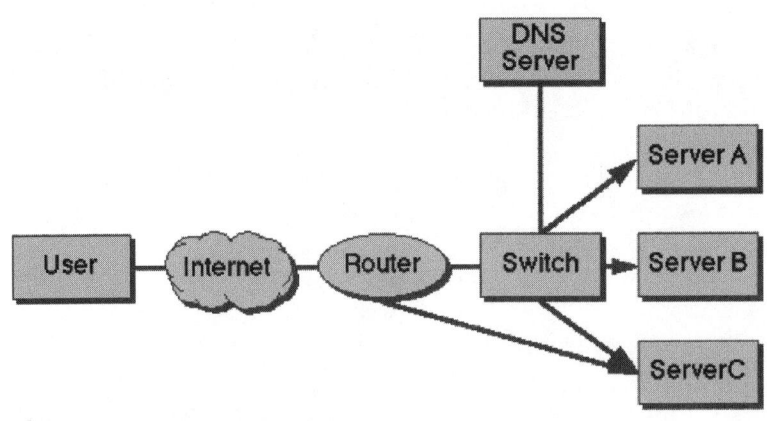

Figure 7.2 ■ **DNS Round Robin.**

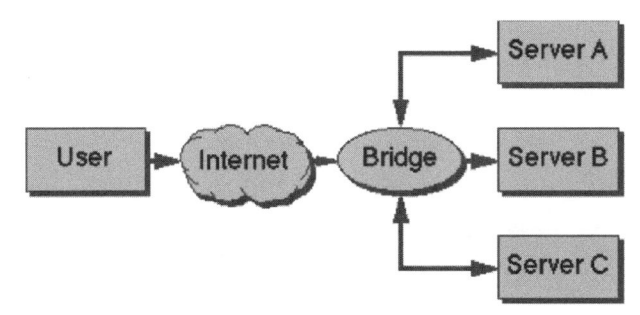

Figure 7.3 ■ **Load-Balanced Server Architecture.**

PROXY SERVERS

Proxy, cache, and *mirror* are techniques used for improving Web performance and security. These techniques aid at reducing the latency of access to Web documents, the network bandwidth required for document transfers, the demand on servers with very popular documents, and the security of electronic services.

A proxy server is a special type of Web server. It is able to act as both a server and a client. Figure 7.4 illustrates a common proxy server implementation.

A proxy acts as an agent, representing the server (or servers) to the user/client and the user/client to the server. A proxy accepts requests from users/clients and forwards those requests to one or more Web servers. Once a proxy receives responses from remote servers, it passes those responses to the users/clients. Originally, proxies were designed to provide access to the Web for users on private networks, who could only access the Internet through a firewall.

Proxy servers can do more than merely relay HTTP responses. Web proxies can be configured to cache relayed responses, thus becoming a caching proxy. Caching can be a key issue to good performance in systems such as the Web.

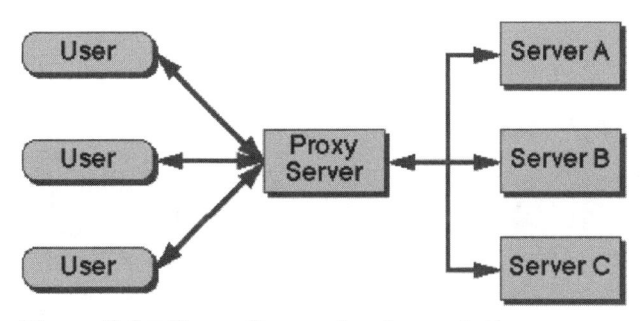

Figure 7.4 ■ **Proxy Server Implementation.**

Lab 7.2: Web Site Service Models

The basic idea in caching is simple: store frequently requested documents into local files or proxies for future use so that it will not be necessary to download the documents the next time they are requested.

LAB 7.2 EXERCISES

7.2.1 UNDERSTAND THE BASIC WEB SITE ARCHITECTURES

Discuss the advantages and disadvantages of each of the following.

    a) A single server

    b) DNS Round Robin

    c) Distributed load balancing

    d) A caching proxy server

LAB 7.2 EXERCISE ANSWERS

7.2.1 ANSWERS

Discuss the advantages and disadvantages of each of the following.

    a) A single server

    Answer: The primary advantage of a single server is the cost. All of the other methods require multiple physical servers and since the hardware is generally the most expensive component, this naturally increases the costs considerably. One major disadvantage is scalability. It is extremely difficult to move from this model to something else without a great deal of reconfiguration.

b) DNS Round Robin

Answer: The DNS Round Robin architecture can be an effective solution for distributed server systems as long as its server management shortcomings are realized. This method treats all servers as equals and does not attempt to determine server load or availability. Because of the variance in the time of a browser/client's connection and the amount of content being retrieved, load variance swings dramatically. In a four-server configuration with "normal" Internet content and traffic, one of the servers will receive 75% of the traffic, and at that point that server might fail.

This scenario illustrates another major weakness of the DNS Round Robin architecture. If a server fails, that server will continue to receive requests, and browsers/clients will receive a "server not available" message. Maintenance of servers creates another difficulty. Each of the Web servers maintains a unique IP address, so if the Web server administrator needs to take a server "off line" for maintenance, such as an operating system or application upgrade, it can take up to two days for the server's IP address to change in DNS and "percolate" throughout the Internet. In the meantime, readers/users are requesting information from a server that is not there.

c) Distributed load balancing

Answer: A distributed load-balanced architecture allows Web site administrators to incrementally increase the capacity of the Web site and easily add, remove, and reallocate servers to accommodate surges in traffic. The key disadvantage is the cost. Extra software is required to determine the current load on each of the servers and choose the one that is least busy.

d) A caching proxy server

Answer: Caching minimizes access time by bringing information closer to the users/readers who need it. Thus, caching improves access speed and cuts down on network traffic since documents often get returned from a nearby cache rather than from a faraway server. It also reduces server load and increases document availability by replicating documents among many servers.

Caching has many advantages, but it also introduces its own unique problems. For example, how can one keep a document in the cache and still be sure that document is current? What documents should be cached and for how long?

Another problem is security. If any content is use-specific (i.e., only accessible with a specific password), how do you keep others from accessing it?

Lab 7.2 Self-Review Questions

In order to test your progress, you should be able to answer the following questions.

1) A single-server Web architecture is the cheapest initially, but hardest to upgrade.

   a) _____ True
   b) _____ False

2) A load-balancing architecture "balances" the load by storing frequently used files on a single server.

   a) _____ True
   b) _____ False

3) A problem with DNS Round Robin is that the load is not evenly distributed across the available servers.

   a) _____ True
   b) _____ False

4) Which of the following is not a problem with a single-server architecture?

   a) _____ Availability and performance under high traffic conditions
   b) _____ A single point of failure—if the server is unavailable, the organization is off the Web
   c) _____ Administration is more difficult in order to ensure proper configuration
   d) _____ Security issues—vulnerability to attack

5) Which of the following is not an advantage of proxy servers?

   a) _____ The ability to provide frequently accessed pages more quickly
   b) _____ The ability to provide an additional level of security
   c) _____ The ability to match requirements for load-balancing DNS
   d) _____ The ability to distribute the load among multiple servers

Quiz answers appear in the Appendix, Section 7.2.

LAB 7.3

SUPPORTING MULTIPLE SERVERS

> **LAB OBJECTIVES**
>
> After this lab, you will be able to:
> - Choose an Appropriate Web Server Configuration

In discussing multiple servers, it is important to distinguish between the hardware and software definitions of a server. In the descriptions of client-server models, it can be confusing whether the server being described refers to hardware (e.g., a computer) or a server software application. An IP name (e.g., info.blatz.com) typically refers to a single machine/computer that has that address on the Internet. Multiple server applications/processes can be executing simultaneously on that machine. The concept of port numbers (e.g., info.blatz.com:80 or info.blatz.com:8080) provides a mechanism for a client to uniquely identify the process on that machine to which communications should be directed.

For most organizations, computer cycles are a precious commodity. Computers should be kept as busy as possible in order to optimize the investment they represent. However, any attempt to keep computers busy should have minimal impact on the services they provide.

Depending upon the Web server load, capacity, or applications supported, a Web server administrator should consider running multiple server applications on the same hardware that supports the Web server application. Possibilities include real servers of various types, hardware virtual Web servers, and software virtual Web servers.

HARDWARE VIRTUAL SERVERS

A *hardware virtual server* is a server configuration whereby one server process responds to multiple IP addresses. That is, multiple IP addresses are "virtually" assigned to the same physical machine. It is important to understand that this means that the IP addresses resolve to the same machine IP name.

For example, in Figure 7.5, the machine hosting the Web server can be accessed by clients addressing 134.79.12.34, 120.63.67.12, or 116.32.56.87. That is, these three addresses all resolve to the same server name (e.g., www.blatz.com). In other words, the following four URLs are logically (though maybe not functionally) synonymous:

1. http://134.79.12.34/
2. http://120.63.67.12/
3. http://116.32.56.87/
4. http://www.blatz.com/

In order to accomplish this configuration, separate DNS entries are required for each IP address associating them with the same physical machine. In this architecture, there is typically only a single Web server process with a single configuration file.

HARDWARE

Virtual servers can be used to provide different configurations of Web service based on IP address while only running a single Web server application. For example, the Web server could be configured such that requests coming from par-

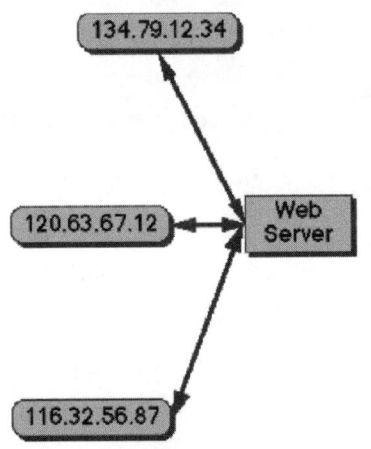

Figure 7.5 ■ A Hardware Virtual Server Configuration.

ticular addresses access unique document spaces not available to requests coming from other addresses. Similarly, all addresses might share other document spaces.

In Lab 7.1, we discussed hosting services as a strategy whereby an organization could establish a "Web presence." We indicated that users/readers of such sites are unable to tell whether a hosting service, Web appliance, or dedicated Web server is being used. Since a WSP is being used, how can the organizational URL avoid including the name or address of the Internet Service Provider (ISP)?

SOFTWARE VIRTUAL SERVERS

If you were the Web strategist for the Blatz Corporation, then you would want your corporate Web site to be addressed as http://www.blatz.com/ rather than http://116.84.22.11/ (an IP address that is not very usable or recognizable) or http://www.hosting.com/blatz/ (where www.hosting.com is the name of your ISP). This would not be possible using a hardware virtual server. *Software virtual server* architecture does make this configuration possible by allowing multiple server names (virtual software servers) to resolve to a single IP address.

For example, in Figure 7.6, the IP names www.blatz.com and www.boo.com both resolve to the same IP address of the ISP hosting Web server machine. This requires a DNS (Domain Name Server) entry and the necessary configuration of the Web server to identify the name of the virtual host.

As Figure 7.6 illustrates, the document space/directory on the host machine has been partitioned for each software virtual server name. Therefore, when the client request has been made to www.boo.com, the Web server will only access content defined for that server address. Using this technique, a WSP is able to accommodate any number of "virtual" servers.

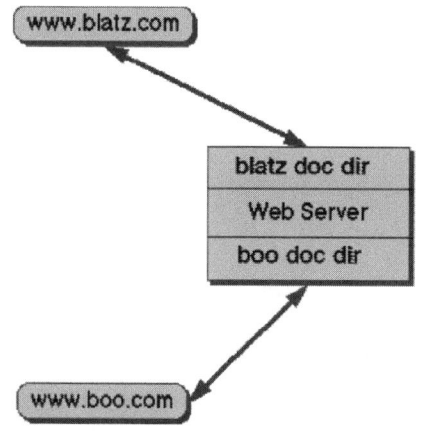

Figure 7.6 ■ **A Software Virtual Server Configuration.**

LAB 7.3 EXERCISES

7.3.1 CHOOSE AN APPROPRIATE WEB SERVER CONFIGURATION

a) Discuss what kinds of server applications would be good candidates to include on a single server. What might not be good choices?

___

___

b) Discuss what kinds of problems could occur with multiple server applications on a single physical server. How would you address these problems?

___

___

LAB 7.3 EXERCISE ANSWERS

7.3.1 ANSWERS

a) Discuss what kinds of server applications would be good candidates to include on a single server. What might not be good choices?

Answer: What servers you run on what machines depends on your circumstances and the applications. One thing to consider is what data and what files need to be shared. For example, if files need to be accessed from both FTP and HTTP, then you might want to consider having both on the same physical machine.

Some applications that might all belong on the same server are:

- *A secure Web server*
- *An indexing server*
- *An FTP server*
- *A directory server*

Lab 7.3: Supporting Multiple Servers 197

Questionable candidates include:

- A mail (SMTP) server
- A news (NNTP) server
- A Domain Name server (DNS)

These servers typically warrant their own computers due the heavy traffic usually associated with them.

In Figure 7.7, we see

- A production Web server running on port 80 (the default)
- A test Web server running on port 8080
- A secure Web server running on port 443 (the default)
- An FTP server running on port 21 (the default)
- A search server to provide local Web site indexing and searching running at an unspecified port
- A directory server running at an unspecified port

There seems no doubt that this computer/server has the potential for being kept very busy!

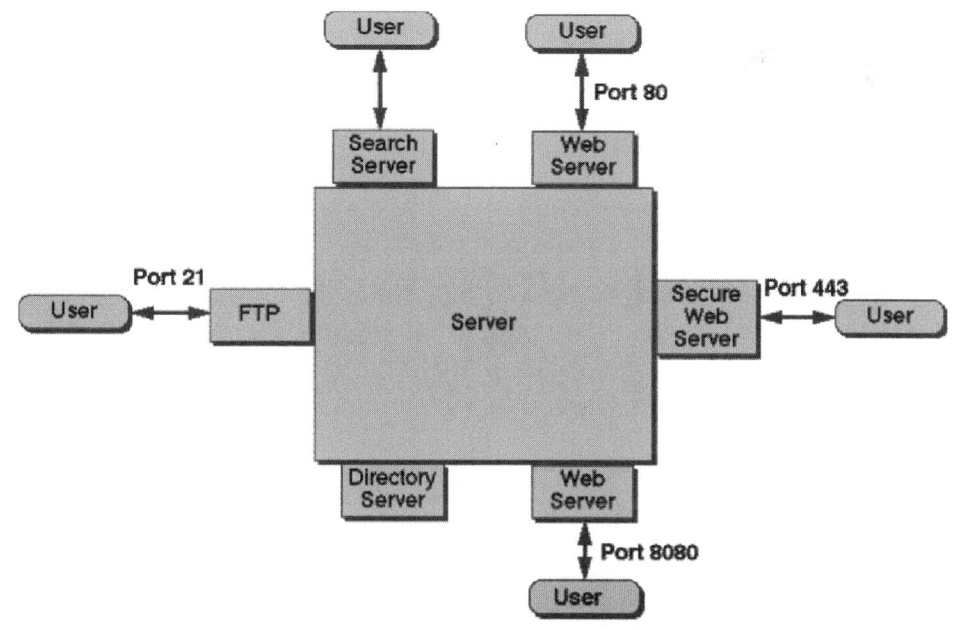

Figure 7.7 ■ **A Single Hardware Server Sharing Multiple Server Applications.**

Lab 7.3: Supporting Multiple Servers

b) Discuss what kinds of problems could occur with multiple server applications on a single physical server. How would you address these problems?

Answer: A decision to run multiple servers is not without certain drawbacks and perils. For example, unusual activity on any of the server applications due to factors such as high traffic or "runaway" processes could jeopardize the performance of the other servers or the computer itself. In addition, there is always contention for resources; for example, the FTP and Web servers contend for the same disk space or file system; a security violation (e.g., break-in) at any of the server applications could put the other applications at risk.

There are useful strategies that can address these drawbacks. For example,

- *Run the separate server applications in "padded cells." This means that the applications are kept genuinely separate with control access to system resources and no shared file space. Someone "breaking into" an application would be confined to its "padded cell."*

- *System monitoring of server status—A system-wide application could regularly check the "health" of the servers to ensure that there are no "runaway" processes or that the server is still functioning.*

- *Limited services—Security issues can be addressed by carefully selecting server services provided (e.g., no anonymous FTP).*

- *Scheduling services—Determining whether all servers should be always running; for example, is it necessary that the search engine indexer be running all the time? It could be scheduled to run during nonpeak periods.*

LAB 7.3 SELF-REVIEW QUESTIONS

In order to test your progress, you should be able to answer the following questions.

1) The index server should be running constantly to ensure pages are up to date and to limit the potential for "hogging" the system resources by doing everything at once.

   a) _____ True
   b) _____ False

2) What is the method by which multiple IP addresses are assigned to a single physical machine?

   a) _____ Hardware virtual hosts
   b) _____ Software virtual hosts
   c) _____ Load-balancing DNS
   d) _____ Virtual IP distribution

Lab 7.3: Supporting Multiple Servers

3) What advantage do software virtual hosts have over hardware virtual hosts?
   a) _____ If the server for one host stops, it does not affect the other servers.
   b) _____ A "break in" doesn't affect the security of the other servers.
   c) _____ If a server hogs a system resource, it has no effect on the servers.
   d) _____ Only a single IP address is required.

4) Which of the following is not a way of keeping multiple servers from completely preventing the others from running correctly?
   a) _____ Running the separate server applications in "padded cells"
   b) _____ System monitoring of server status
   c) _____ Running each server on a separate IP address
   d) _____ Scheduling non-essential services to run at nonpeak times

Quiz answers appear in the Appendix, Section 7.3.

LAB 7.4

SERVER SECURITY ISSUES

> *Public Web servers continue to be attractive targets for individuals or groups seeking to steal information or software, commit sabotage, embarrass organizations, promote a political agenda, or prove their competence....The same features that make the Web so attractive also make it so vulnerable.*
>
> —Unknown

> *A security incident is defined to be any adverse event in an information system or network, its data, or availability. Adverse events include compromises of integrity, denial of service, compromises of confidentiality, or damage to part of the system. Examples of incidents include: the insertion of malicious code (e.g., viruses, Trojan horses, or backdoors) unauthorized scans or probes, successful or unsuccessful intrusions, and insider attacks.*
>
> —U.S. Department of Energy

LAB OBJECTIVES

After this lab, you will be able to:

✔ Understand Basic Security Risks
✔ Implement Appropriate Security Measures

A Web site administrator needs to be a worrier! He or she needs to worry whether the organization's site content is accurate. Adinistrators need to worry whether their Web sites present the desired public image. Web server availability should always be on their minds, since unavailability may cost their organizations readers or customers. Addressing such worries may not always be under Web administrators' control—they are usually the content providers; server failure may come as a result of factors beyond their control.

Server security should also be a source of worry. However, server security is a worry that Web site administrators can address head-on. Understanding the different ways in which a Web site can be compromised and developing strategies for each of them is a critical component of site administration and management.

The areas most at risk are

- Password files—Gaining access to lists of usernames and passwords then gives the intruder free rein for ongoing and future attacks.
- Organizational data—Sensitive organizational data such as planning data, test data, or payroll information is often the target of espionage, both external and internal to an organization.
- Customer data—Commerce Web sites should realize that access to customer data, such as credit card numbers, could prove to be a bonanza for an intruder.
- Applications software—Intruders may be interested in gaining access to and downloading licensed, original, or sensitive software.

As Figure 7.8 illustrates, server system security is only one part of the security/privacy issues that a Web site administrator must face.

POTENTIAL SECURITY AREAS

The Web is a jungle. Web site administrators should always worry that the Huns are at the gates trying to break in. Once in, these intruders are capable of many actions.

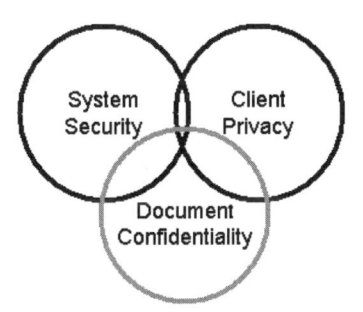

Figure 7.8 ■ **Security/Privacy Issues Faced by Web Administrators.**

The most common are

- Theft of data, files, or software
- Unauthorized use of computer resources
- Denial-of-service attacks
- Deletion and/or replacement of content
- Installation of unauthorized resources

DENIAL-OF-SERVICE ATTACKS

A common occurrence is the so-called "denial of service attacks," implying any actions whose goal is to impact server performance or access. Such attacks are not always the result of a server intrusion. For example, a robot application that swamps a Web server with HTTP requests might cause that server to fail or be otherwise slow or inattentive to other users. That robot is then denying service to that server.

Likewise, an application installed by an intruder on a server could impact system availability to the point that the server is unable to respond to user/reader requests as desired. That intruder and application are then "denying service" to the server.

DELETION AND/OR REPLACEMENT OF CONTENT

Recently there have been well-publicized Web server attacks whose goal was simply to embarrass the hosting organization. In such attacks, the intruder simply replaces existing Web site content with revised content reflecting its goal. To the user/reader of the Web site, all operations appear normal except that the intruder's content is shown rather than that desired by the organization.

Figure 7.9 shows the result of a recent, well-known attack on the U.S. Department of Justice Web site.

What is so insidious about an attack of this type (aside from the content) is that the intruder used existing file names and references such that the first indication of the attack came not from any internal server checking, but rather from users/readers responding to the content.

This example serves to illustrate that a Web server intruder has the permission to add, delete, or replace content on a server given their access to the server configuration files.

INSTALLATION OF UNAUTHORIZED RESOURCES

Similar to the issues of deletion and/or replacement of content and unauthorized use of resources, Web site intruders have also been known to install unauthorized resources on Web server systems. In addition to issues such as system perfor-

Figure 7.9 ■ Replacement of Content on the U.S. Dept. of Justice Web Site.

mance impact, such installations may present other problems. One such problem is often software licensing. If an intruder were to install licensed software on your Web server, then you automatically become responsible for the license (or lack thereof). As far as the software vendor may be concerned, your server is running illegal, unlicensed software. Aside from the obvious embarrassment this might cause your organization, there are obviously legal implications as well.

Similarly, in another well-publicized incident several years ago, an intruder installed an FTP server on the Web host of a U.S. National Laboratory. This FTP server was then used to distribute pornographic materials.

GOOD SECURITY PRACTICES

There are numerous policies and practices that can be adopted to address these and other potential security issues. It is highly unlikely that all of these policies and practices are relevant to all Web sites. It is, however, the responsibility of the Web site administrator to determine what security threats potentially may affect his or her site and then choose those policies and practices that address those threats.

FIREWALLS

Firewalls are among the most common strategies for addressing Web server security threats. There are hardware and software implementations of firewalls, which can be placed in a wide variety of network configurations.

In the simplest configuration, the Web server is placed behind a network firewall. That firewall is then configured to filter out all network requests to the server except those for the required services.

LIMITING SERVER SERVICES

In Lab 7.3, we discussed the issue of multiple services on a Web server. It was indicated in that lab that additional services always introduce potential security concerns. The Web server administrator must therefore make the trade-off decision between maximizing the utilization of the Web server computer versus the possible introduction of "security holes."

SERVER MAINTENANCE AND ADMINISTRATION

A well-maintained and well-administered system is vital to system security. You need to be aware of how the system is configured and what behavior is "normal" for the system. The administrator must also be aware of any changes that need to be made (hardware or software) to increase the security.

To the Web site administrator, the logfile provides evidence of intruder accesses or attempted accesses. It also provides a strong indication whether implemented security measures (e.g., restricted access to Web content) are actually working as desired.

To the potential intruder, the logfile can provide information such as user and machine domain names and addresses, clues as to the server's file system taxonomy (this topic will be discussed in the next lab), browser and server software and version level being used, and so on. In Figure 7.8, we illustrated the role of client privacy in an overall description of security issues. Protection of logfile data is one effort in an attempt to protect such privacy.

For example, consider the following logfile entries:

> http://www.wpi.edu/~ack/women_of_internet.html
> file:\\SHARE1\ADMIN\ARB\STOCKS_TO_SELL_SHORT.HTM
> http://bigstore.com/cgi-bin/order&product=H4219&ccno=4128002258329347

In the first entry, an intruder can recognize a domain name (wpi.edu), a username (ack) and speculate that the user is a woman. The second entry points to a local file that (judging by its name) likely contains sensitive information. The third entry is the result of a poorly written CGI script that contains user credit card information!

Strategies that address logfile security issues include the following:

- If logfiles must be stored on the Web server machine, then they should be encrypted; otherwise consider storing the logfiles on a different machine or even a different file system.
- Web server logfiles should never be visible via the Web except when using an administrative Web interface.
- Logfiles should be analyzed frequently to detect suspicious activity; logfile analysis programs will indicate the IP address or name of frequent or heavy requesters and what they are attempting to access.
- Ample disk space should always be available for logfiles; do not allow "denial of service" attacks to inflate the size of logfiles to the point of filling a disk and perhaps resulting in server failure.

PROGRAMS AND SCRIPTS

As you can see in the example above, passing the credit card number like that is an obvious security hole. Poorly written or designed server-side scripts and programs can easily introduce security vulnerabilities to a Web server. It is therefore the responsibility of the Web administrator to closely scrutinize any scripts and programs that are to run on the Web server.

At a very minimum, an organization should

- Adopt a general policy regarding the authoring and testing (especially for security concerns) of CGI scripts and other server-side applications.
- Remove all unnecessary scripts and programs from the default server script directory (usually called /cgi-bin).
- Consider server configurations that isolate CGI script or other processes, forcing them to run in "padded cells"; in such configurations the possibility of compromises resulting from poorly written scripts is minimized.
- Carefully examine any applications or services that require the installation of a script or scripts that use server APIs; examples of such applications are HTML editors and publishing systems.

SECURITY TOOLS

Security tools can be extremely useful in a Web site administrator's defensive strategy against intruders. Such tools are commercially available or can be written in house. Many general systems tools can also be used for Web server support.

A suitable "Web security toolbox" might include

- "Tripwire" or "trap" programs that detect intrusions
- Macros or scripts that periodically check the integrity of critical files; such programs could use checksums to detect whether critical files have been modified
- Programs that periodically make HTTP requests to the Web server in order to determine its availability
- Scanning programs that check for known server vulnerabilities

SERVER MAINTENANCE

The server configuration file and the server software are the "heart and soul" of Web server operation. It is therefore critical to keep these two elements in their best possible condition.

Since an intruder can determine which server software is being used, then he or she is also aware of the default architecture of the server configuration file. A *security exploit* is a bug or misconfiguration on a server that can be used by an intruder to gain unauthorized access to that server or to a network to which it is connected. Therefore, if known exploits exist in a server default configuration, then the intruder might use that knowledge to his or her advantage. It is therefore a good policy to consider the following:

- Removing and replacing the "default" document tree that is defined by the server software
- Isolating the Web document root from the "real" file system if possible ("virtual file paths" are discussed in Lab 7.5)
- Regular backup of the configuration file in the event that the active version is compromised or modified
- Disabling
  - Automatic directory listings that can provide file system information
  - Home directories that may contain "exploitable" scripts or unauthorized information
  - Server-side includes with the #EXEC option
  - CGI script execution from arbitrary directories

A Web site administrator must also stay one step ahead of intruders in the maintenance of server software. It should be remembered that potential intruders often have access to the same server patch level information and bug reports that you have. The failure of an administrator to respond quickly to bug reports and apply the appropriate fixes is an open invitation to intruders to exploit the reported bug. Administrators should keep up with the CERT (http://www.cert.org) advisories and regularly read the security newsgroups.

> The hacker newsgroups can also provide valuable and interesting clues as to currently available intruder tools, tricks, and strategies. Hackers love to brag about sites they have compromised and their future plans and goals. They are also often willing to trade information and tools with their colleagues.

Among the advantages of maintaining a Web server mirror is the ability of an organization to quickly restore Web service after the compromise of the production server. If that mirror resides behind a firewall and/or runs at a nonstandard port, then potential intruders are less likely to be aware of its existence and therefore compromise it.

IN THE EVENT OF AN INTRUSION

To a Web site administrator, an intrusion is comparable to a home burglary—a feeling of violation. In the event of an intrusion it is important to remember not to overreact, but instead to respond methodically and carefully in order to restore desired service to your users/readers. Even before attempting to "repair" the damage done you should

- Shut down the server to avoid user/reader impact and continued access by the intruder.
- Explain to your reader/user community why service is temporarily unavailable; this explanation could be accomplished via email if possible.
- Back up all server configurations in order to obtain an accurate picture of the compromised system; this backup can prove valuable for analysis as well as for potential evidence in the prosecution of the intruder.
- Report the intrusion to the appropriate authorities (e.g., CERT, law enforcement, etc.).
- Minimize any public announcement of the intrusion; this action is not to avoid embarrassment, but rather to deprive the intruder of attention (which may be exactly what he or she wants) and to discourage any further intrusion attempts.

Lab 7.4: Server Security Issues

The Web site (or a mirror) should be restored only when the intrusion mechanism and the intrusion circumstance (what the intruder did) have been identified and corrected. When the Web site is restored, you should expect additional intrusion attempts either from the original intruder or his or her colleagues, so additional scrutiny should be exercised.

LAB 7.4 EXERCISES

7.4.1 UNDERSTAND BASIC SECURITY RISKS

a) At first you might think there is nothing on a Web server to steal. However, theft is not just limited to money and other things we normally consider valuable. Discuss what kinds of things might be targets for theft from a Web server.

___

___

b) Theft from a computer is more than just stealing files. A computer has other resources that people might want to use improperly. Discuss what kinds of things might be targets for this kind of theft from a Web server.

___

___

c) Theft of files or resources is not the end of it. There are people in the world who want to leave their mark on the world like a dog on a tree. How might a malicious user cause damage to your system?

___

___

7.4.2 IMPLEMENT APPROPRIATE SECURITY MEASURES

a) A firewall is one of the primary means of preventing improper access to your system. Discuss where and how you might set up a firewall.

_____

_____

b) The fewer doors a systems has, the fewer places an intruder can gain access. Discuss ways to limit access to the system.

_____

_____

c) Even though an intruder gains access to the system, the scope of privileges might be limited (at least at first). Using information gained from the system itself, the intruder might find out about other security holes. Discuss what steps an administrator might take to limit access to important information.

_____

_____

LAB 7.4 EXERCISE ANSWERS

7.4.1 ANSWERS

a) At first you might think there is nothing on a Web server to steal. However, theft is not just limited to money and other things we normally consider valuable. Discuss what kinds of things might be targets for theft from a Web server.

Answer: Theft of organizational resources and/or data is the most common result of Web server attack. For most attacks of this type, the Web server is only the intruder's "entry point" to the organizational computer system, not the primary subject of the intruder's attention. Since the Web server often has access to the organizational file system, an intruder then gains access to the file system as well.

b) Theft from a computer is more than just stealing files. A computer has other resources that people might want to use improperly. Discuss what kinds of things might be targets for this kind of theft from a Web server.

Answer: Server intruders are not always malicious—they may just want to have fun! Large organizational computer systems may be ideal playgrounds for some intruders. Such systems often provide access to application programs, language compilers, and other resources otherwise unavailable to the intruder.

If you are running a site where you need to become a member (paying or not) to gain access to certain areas, it defeats the purpose of membership if someone can gain improper access to your system.

While intrusions of this type may appear to be harmless, Web site administrators cannot afford to be altruistic. Such intrusions can impact system performance or legitimate access to system resources. Such intrusions can often turn malicious if ignored.

c) Theft of files or resources is not the end of it. There are people in the world who want to leave their mark on the world like a dog on a tree. How might a malicious user cause damage to your system?

Answer: The most obvious way a user can cause damage is to destroy or alter system files, potentially opening up more doors into your system. In addition, some people go to the extreme of preventing anyone else from accessing the system at all.

7.4.2 ANSWERS

a) A firewall is one of the primary means of preventing improper access to your system. Discuss where and how you might set up a firewall.

Answer: In the simplest configuration, a firewall is placed between the Internet and the Web server. That firewall is then configured to filter out all network requests to the server except those for the required services, for example, port 80 (the default Web server port) and port 443 (the default secure Web server port). The firewall can also be configured to filter out HTTP requests except for those to specific Web servers. Both of these strategies enforce a policy of strict control over server management, thereby ensuring that non-authorized servers cannot present a security opportunity to a potential intruder.

More extensive use of firewalls is employed to define organizational intranets and extranets. Both configurations directly address the security issue of access to sensitive organizational data. The firewall and the "classic" intranet are configured as in Figure 7.10.

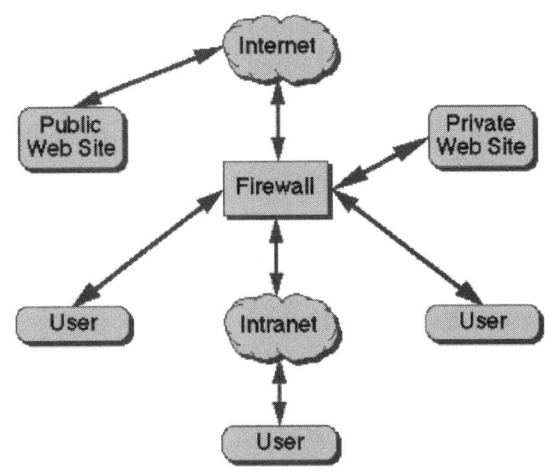

Figure 7.10 ■ **Classic Internet Configuration.**

b) The fewer doors a system has, the fewer places an intruder can gain access. Discuss ways to limit access to the system.

Answer: In general, it is recommended that all unneeded, noncritical services be removed from the Web server host. Exceptions include an FTP server (preferably not supporting anonymous access) that shares the Web server document space and a secure login capability that can be used for server configuration and maintenance.

It figures that the more accessible a Web server is to support and maintenance, the more accessible it is to potential intruders as well. An intruder who gains access to Web administration services can obviously then configure the server in any desired way. Several strategies that address this issue are

- *Disallowing all remote administration unless with a one-time password or via an encrypted link; limiting or disallowing Telnet access from any "untrusted" site*

- *Limiting the number of persons who are allowed administrator or root level access to the Web server*

- *If the Web server has a specialized administrative interface (e.g., a Web-based interface), protect that interface by limiting when it executes.*

c) Even though an intruder gains access to the system, the scope of privileges might be limited (at least at first). Using information gained from the system itself, the intruder might find out about other security holes. Discuss what steps an administrator might take to limit access to important information.

Answer: For obviously different reasons, the Web server logfile is a great asset to the Web site administrator and a potential intruder. Given its value, the logfile should include an accurate record of all Web server activity and be protected as closely as any other organizational data.

Using scripts to collect or present information is common on Web sites. However, if improperly written, they can open up the system to all sorts of security problems. This includes improper access to the system itself, but also improper access to sensitive information.

Also, it extremely important that the system be properly administered. This includes keeping the server up to date in terms of software patches (especially those related to security), as well as monitoring the system to detect intrusion as soon as possible.

Part of this administration is knowing how and when to react. Simply knowing that your system has been compromised is not enough. You need to take the necessary steps to determine what damage was caused, as well as determine if the intruder has left any back doors open.

LAB 7.4 SELF-REVIEW QUESTIONS

In order to test your progress, you should be able to answer the following questions.

1) If the server is properly configured, the administrator can "set it and forget it."

   a) _____ True
   b) _____ False

2) Although apparently innocuous at first, system logfiles can provide a wealth of information to an intruder.

   a) _____ True
   b) _____ False

3) Since it is running in the context of the Web server, which normally runs as the user "nobody," CGI script cannot be compromised to gain access to the system.

   a) _____ True
   b) _____ False

4) Despite common belief, HTTP is not a "one-way" protocol; it also allows the client to send information to the server.

   a) _____ True
   b) _____ False

5) What is the first step when a break-in is detected?

    a) _____ Notify CERT and law enforcement agencies.
    b) _____ Shut down or disconnect the server to prevent continued access by the intruder.
    c) _____ Restore the system from backups to decrease down time.
    d) _____ Notify users of the server's being unavailable.

Quiz answers appear in the Appendix, Section 7.4.

LAB 7.5

DOCUMENT ROOT TAXONOMIES

> **LAB OBJECTIVES**
>
> After this lab, you will be able to:
>
> ✔ Design Appropriate Document Root Taxonomies

Taxonomy is defined as "the systematic arrangement of entities into groups or categories according to established criteria."

Methods such as Web Engineering, Information Architecture, and Information Mapping are useful for defining logical Web document structures. The goal of these methods is to illustrate relationships between the pages and documents in a Web site such that readers/users can readily get the information they need and navigate easily and logically between those pages. These relationships can be considered to define a page or document taxonomy.

This concept of page or document taxonomy can be useful because the configuration of a Web server requires one or more document directories from which users request content. Well-designed (or poorly designed) page and file taxonomies affect all areas of Web site usage and administration.

Usability studies such as those described by Jakob Neilsen also incorporate techniques for defining the logical relationships between pages. One of the most popular of these techniques is the *card-sorting method*. In this method users are given cards upon which are written ideas and/or concepts. These ideas represent nodes in a hypertext system. Users are then asked to arrange these cards according to the relationships they perceive between the concepts. This is not a quiz in that there are no correct answers. The results of the exercise provide the Web site designer(s) with usability information.

HIERARCHICAL FILE TAXONOMIES

In order to make the information available to the server, the information must either be contained in file on the file system or contained within a database. With a file system, the structure is mapped on a hierarchical file system. Since most file systems are, in fact, inherently hierarchical, this action can be implemented on most computer platforms. The directories and subdirectories of the file system correspond to the levels of the hierarchical logical structure. Hierarchical navigation within a file system is very well understood and easily described. (In fact, this navigation is implied in Web URLs.) Likewise, methods for rearranging hierarchical structures are well defined.

The uppermost directory in this file system could be thought of as one of the document directories defined for a Web server.

Our structure has now taken on the characteristics of the file system upon which it is mapped. For example, the "Home" node has been replaced by the directory "root" node (/). Also, the longer concept names in the logical structure have been replaced by short, descriptive file and directory names.

It is recommended that careful consideration be given in mapping the concepts to names in a file structure such as this one.

- Names should be short, precise, and descriptive.
- Care should be used with mixed case names (if they are used at all).
- Names may imply content as well as usage.
- Use special server file names, e.g., index.html, home.html, and so on, as required.

As was said earlier, a path through this hierarchy closely resembles the path appearing in a URL. For example, consider a path "/admin/who/photo/joe.jpg," which identifies the path to an individual's (Joe's) photograph.

There are definite pros to carefully designed and implemented page/file taxonomy:

- It accurately reflects the document/site structure.
- It facilitates document space maintenance.
- It facilitates Web server configuration file maintenance.

- It contributes to reader/user learnability and predictability of the Web site.
- It aids in Web site indexing.
- It facilitates the author use of "relative" URLs because file and directory relationships are well defined.

As with typical hierarchies, structures that are "too deep" (e.g., have too many levels) should be avoided. Such structures would yield paths/URLs that are too long and therefore hard to remember or recall correctly. Also, some search engine indexers stop at specific levels of hierarchies, making "lower" subdirectories and pages less likely to be found in a search.

REAL AND VIRTUAL FILE PATHS

As we discussed earlier in this lab, the URL http://www.blatz.com/products/info implies a file path "/products/info" under the www.blatz.com server document root. However, this path can be either *real* or *virtual*. A "real file path" means that the path within the URL is the true path within the server document directory. In our earlier example, "/admin/who/photo/joe.jpg" is a real path since it actually exists in the file system.

All server configurations support the definition of "virtual file paths." A "virtual file path" looks like a "real file path," but does not exist as a real path in the file system. The server maps this virtual path upon a real file path. For example, the virtual path "/admin/who/joe.jpg" might actually be an alias or synonym for the real path "/admin/who/photo/joe.jpg."

LAB 7.5 EXERCISES

7.5.1 DESIGN APPROPRIATE DOCUMENT ROOT TAXONOMIES

a) Consider the type of information available on different commercial or company Web sites. Using Nielsen's card-sorting method, develop a diagram for the more important types of information available on these Web sites.

b) Taking the diagram developed in the previous exercise, map the structure to the corresponding file system (i.e., directory) structure.

c) Consider the discussion in previous labs. Discuss the advantages and disadvantages of having a virtual structure that does not exactly mirror the physical structure.

LAB 7.5 EXERCISE ANSWERS

7.5.1 ANSWERS

a) Consider the type of information available on different commercial or company Web sites. Using Nielsen's card-sorting method, develop a diagram for the more important types of information available on these Web sites.

Answer: In Figure 7.11, cards common to familiar Web site elements have been presented to a user who has then described a logical structure.

In Figure 7.12, the results of the card-sorting exercise have been described as a hierarchical structure. The "search" node has been removed from the results since it is an operation (not really a concept) that can be applied to many of the other nodes. Otherwise, the logical relationships between the nodes are unchanged.

b) Taking the diagram developed in the previous exercise, map the structure to the corresponding file system (i.e., directory) structure.

Answer: In the implementation of a Web site, the logical structure must be mapped upon a physical structure (Figure 7.13). This physical structure is typically a file system or database system.

c) Consider the discussion in previous labs. Discuss the advantages and disadvantages of having a virtual structure that does not exactly mirror the physical structure.

Lab 7.5: Document Root Taxonomies

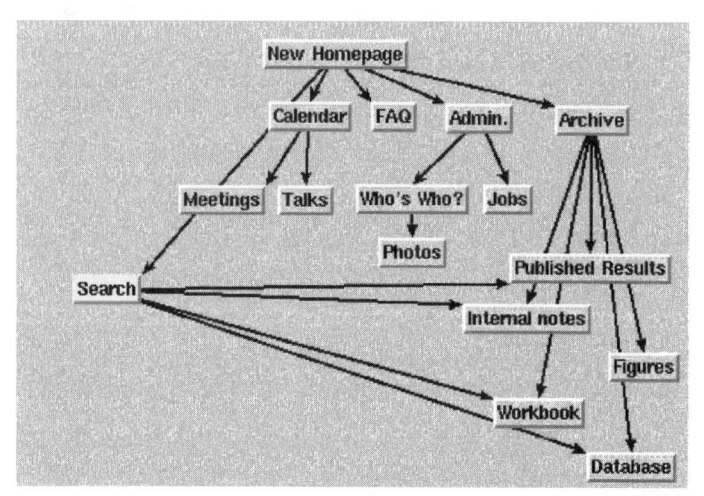

Figure 7.11 ■ **Sample Result of Card-Sorting Exercise.**

Answer: There are some very good reasons for using virtual file paths, such as security, URL length reduction, and multiple file system support. One major drawback is that a restructuring of the way the information is presented requires more work because the administrator must first determine how the new virtual structure and the existing physical structure interact.

From a security perspective, virtual file paths reduce the amount of information that a potential server intruder/hacker has about the underlying file system. Virtual file paths would not allow such an intruder to accurately build a picture of the paths in or the structure of the file system. The lack of such information might limit the success of an attack on the Web server.

Earlier in this lab, we discussed the drawbacks of long URLs resulting from "too deep" hierarchical file structures. The concept of virtual file paths would allow long file paths to remain intact (important if they best describe the document structure), but replace references to them with "shorter" virtual paths. The server is then responsible for the translation of the shorter path/URL to its longer real equivalent.

One of the cleverest uses of virtual file paths is in the support of multiple file systems or storage devices. As such, a server's "apparent document directory" might be in reality multiple directories on multiple devices. For example, suppose we have the virtual paths "/info/people" and "/info/addresses." It would appear that "people" and "addresses" are subdirectories of "info" within the same file system. However, "/info/people" might actually map to the real path "C:\info\people" and "/info/addresses" to the real path "Z:\info\addresses" where "C" and "Z" are different storage devices.

Virtual file paths are what make the software virtual servers discussed in Lab 7.3 possible. In this capacity they allow portions of the "real" server document hierarchy/tree to

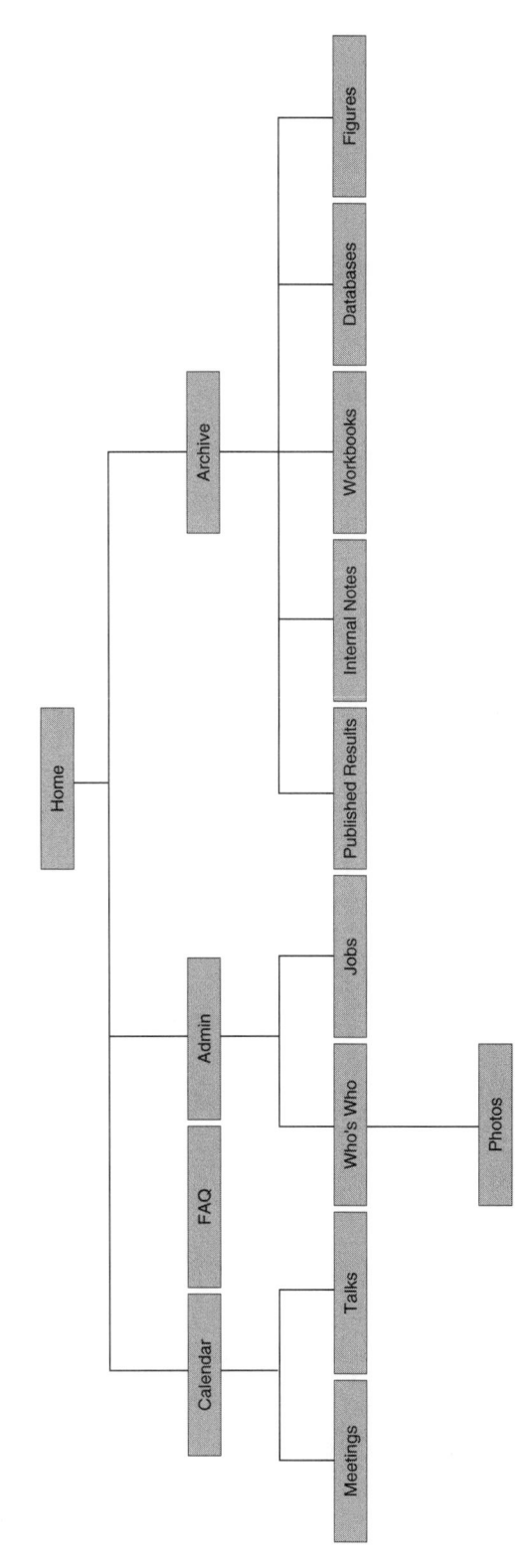

Figure 7.12 ■ **Results of Card-Sorting Exercise Mapped to Hierarchical Structure.**

Lab 7.5: Document Root Taxonomies

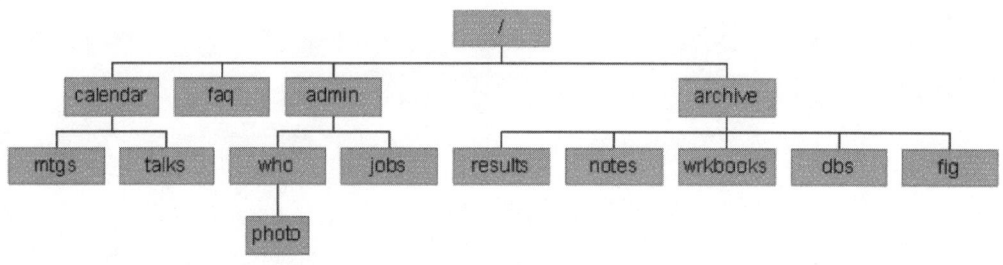

Figure 7.13 ■ **Results of Card-Sorting Exercise Mapped to Hierarchical File System.**

operate as independent document directories. This method is frequently used by ISPs to map multiple hosted servers to the same document space.

LAB 7.5 SELF-REVIEW QUESTIONS

In order to test your progress, you should be able to answer the following questions.

1) Virtual paths allow the logical structure of the Web site to differ from that of the physical structure.

   a) _____ True
   b) _____ False

2) Virtual paths are only possible with software virtual servers and not with hardware virtual servers.

   a) _____ True
   b) _____ False

3) Which of the following is not generally a consideration when developing the virtual path to logical path mappings?

   a) _____ Names should be short, precise, and descriptive
   b) _____ Care should be used with mixed case names (if they are used at all)
   c) _____ Names may imply content as well as usage
   d) _____ Care should be used to ensure that multiple virtual paths to not map to a single physical path

4) Which is not a benefit of a too carefully designed and implemented taxonomy?

   a) _____ It accurately reflects the document/site structure.
   b) _____ It facilitates document space maintenance.
   c) _____ It facilitates Web server configuration file maintenance.
   d) _____ It facilitates system configuration file maintenance.

Quiz answers appear in Appendix A, Section 7.5.

LAB 7.6

ACCESS AUTHORIZATION, SECURITY, AND PRIVACY

A Web server can potentially serve any document that its file system has access to. Therefore, limiting file system access and setting file permissions correctly will address many, if not most, access authorization, security, and privacy issues.

—Anonymous

LAB OBJECTIVES

After this lab, you will be able to:

✔ Understand Basic Security Configuration

In Lab 7.4, Server Security Issues, we illustrated the linked relationship between security, privacy, and confidentiality. In this lab we will discuss access authorization, security, and privacy as they most directly apply to the document confidentiality component of this relationship. The access authorization methods discussed operate independently, but hopefully in conjunction with, those provided by the server's underlying file system. In general, they provide a further refinement of access rules to the documents defined within the server's document directories; that is, given the full body of documents that a server can provide, what additional limitations on access might also be applied?

RESTRICTING ACCESS

In general, access to documents can be restricted by the Web server according to client/browser IP address or host/domain name, user groups, or user names. Likewise, access can be restricted by a firewall or proxy server globally, locally, or according to any component of the HTTP request. "Globally"? "Locally"? Just what do these terms mean? Does "globally" mean for the entire world or for the entire server? Does "locally" mean just for traffic meant for the firewall? Finally, directory and file access rules can be defined in the server configuration file or by the directory/file owner (with most servers).

SERVER ACCESS

The following example illustrates the definition of users and groups in the configuration file of the CERN server software. These users and groups would then be used by the server to restrict or allow access to specific documents or directories.

```
authors: john, james
trusted: authors, jim
slac_people: @134.79.*.*
hackers: marca@141.142.*.*, sanders@153.39.*.*,
     (luotonen, timbl, hallam)@128.141.*.*,
     cailliau@(128.141.201.162, 128.141.248.119)
cern_hackers: hackers@128.141.*.*
```

In this example, the group "authors" is composed of the users john and james. The group "trusted" is composed of john, james, and jim. The group "slac_people" is composed of all users using browsers/clients executing on machines in the 134.79.*.* domain. The group "hackers" associates particular users and domains and the group "cern_hackers" is a subset of "hackers" identified by their IP address.

In the next example, groups and passwords are associated with particular files and directories.

```
Protection PROT-NAME {
    UserId marcus
    GroupId nogroup
    AuthType Basic
    ServerId OurCollaboration
    PasswordFile /WWW/Admin/passwd
    GroupFile /WWW/Admin/group
    GetMask group, user, group@address, ... }
Protect /private/URL/* PROT-NAME
Protect /another/private/* PROT-NAME
```

In this example, *PROT-NAME* is the name of a uniquely defined protection scheme. Relevant components of this scheme include links to a password file and a file where groups, such as in the earlier example, are defined.

The final two lines of this example are the most significant because they define the directories to which this protection scheme is to be applied. Therefore, access to any file within the /private/URL directory to only allowed if the user, group, and address qualifications defined in the *PROT-NAME* scheme are satisfied by the requesting browser/client.

While the syntax of these specifications may be peculiar to the configuration file of the CERN server, all server applications support similar functionality.

It can be easily seen how a well-defined file taxonomy (such as discussed in Lab 7.5) can aid in the identification and protection of directories and subdirectories. Specific nodes within that taxonomy would specifically contain file and directories for which restricted access is relevant.

There are well-known security limitations to the username/IP address/hostname methods demonstrated in these examples. For example,

- Usernames and hostnames can be spoofed (i.e., modified or faked).
- IP addresses can be spoofed.
- CGI scripts can ignore access restrictions since file checking against the configuration file does not occur prior to script execution.
- Documents can be intercepted en route (between the browser/client and the server) and header information (upon which access rules may apply) can be modified.

FILE AND DIRECTORY ACCESS

While access control in server configuration is easily accomplished and well defined, it requires the intervention of the Web server administrator. This limitation places an additional bureaucratic burden upon a document author who wishes to limit access to his or her work. In addition, Web server administrators often limit changes to server configuration files in an attempt to keep the files simple and maintainable. Added to this is the fact that a server must be restarted in order to implement changes in configuration that results in a short period of server unavailability.

Most major Web server software support mechanisms allow access control at the directory level in addition to via server configuration rules. The most commonly implemented mechanism uses the ".htaccess" file. ".htaccess" files are recognized by popular server software such as Apache and the Netscape Enterprise servers.

In particular, ".htaccess"

- Allows authors to control directory access.
- Involves no Web administrator intervention.
- Resides in the directory to be controlled.

The name ".htaccess" stems from the UNIX naming convention whereby filenames starting with a period (".") are system files that ordinarily do not appear in directory listing. Despite this convention, the use of ".htaccess" is not limited to servers running on UNIX platforms.

Although the ".htaccess" file has a different format than the CERN configuration file, it provides the basic features. The ".htaccess" file is a text/ASCII file containing specific directives defining the desired access rules. The most common of these directives are:

- **<limit...>**—starts the list of limitations. Limitations can be on GET, POST, and PUT, either individually or as a group.
- **</limit>**—end of limitations.
- **order deny, allow**—allow a directory to allow or disallow its access based on where a user/reader to trying to gain access from.
- **deny from**—the domain name to be denied (keyword all).
- **allow from**—the domain name to be allowed (keyword all).
- **AuthUserFile**—the location and name of the file where password information will reside.
- **AuthGroupFile**—the location and name of the file where the groups and group members are defined (use /dev/null if no groups).
- **AuthName**—the title of the password prompt.
- **AuthType**—basic.
- **require**—used to ensure that one or more of the three criteria—user, group, or valid-user—are met prior to access.
- **satisfy**—states that any match criterion is acceptable (keywords: any/all; default:all).

ACCESS AUTHORIZATION POLICIES

The methods discussed in this lab are examples of how issues of document access, privacy, and confidentiality may be addressed at the server and directory levels. The implementation of these methods is an issue that needs to be addressed in the design of an organizational Web site. The Web site administrator must help to specify and enforce access authorization policies applicable to the organization in order to ensure that such methods are used appropriately.

Policies regarding the use of password authentication should be closely addressed. It should be noted that in the absence of secure channels (e.g., SSL), all passwords travel across the network as clear text. That means that they are subject to interception and compromise. Users accessing Web documents in this manner must be encouraged (or forced) *not* to use their login passwords as authentication passwords due to security considerations.

LAB 7.6 EXERCISES

7.6.1 UNDERSTAND BASIC SECURITY CONFIGURATION

a) Create a .htaccess directive to limit GET and POST with the following characteristics:

- Order of evaluation is deny then allow
- Access from all machines is denied at first
- Access is then allowed only from machines in the stanford.edu domain.

b) Create another .htaccess directive to limit only GET with the following characteristics using the following directives:

- AuthUserFile
- AuthGroupFile
- AuthName
- AuthType

LAB 7.6 EXERCISE ANSWERS

7.6.1 ANSWERS

a) Create a .htaccess directive to limit GET and POST with the following characteristics:
- Order of evaluation is deny then allow
- Access from all machines is denied at first
- Access is then allowed only from machines in the stanford.edu domain.

Lab 7.6: Access Authorization, Security, and Privacy

Answer: Here is one possible solution:

```
<limit GET POST>
order deny, allow
deny from all
allow from .stanford.edu
</limit>
```

As you can see, this directs that all files in the directory containing the .htaccess file are only accessible by readers/clients making requests from machines with ".stanford.edu" host names. Access is controlled only by host name; there is no username/password authentication.

b) Create another .htaccess directive to limit only GET with the following characteristics using the following directives:
- AuthUserFile
- AuthGroupFile
- AuthName
- AuthType

Answer: Here is one possible solution:

```
AuthUserFile /closed/.htpasswd
AuthGroupFile /dev/null
AuthName ByPassword
AuthType Basic
<limit GET>
require user bebo
</limit>
```

This example illustrates how specific users are allowed to access files after password authentication. The AuthUserFile directive identifies the appropriate password file to be used in user authentication. The remainder of the file indicates that HTTP GET requests should only be granted to user "bebo" (and no other users) after password authentication. Notice that there are no IP address or host name limitations in this ".htaccess" file, so user "bebo" can access the files from any client anywhere in the world.

The ".htaccess" file can also work in conjunction with a ".htgroup" file, which allows the definition of user groups. In the following ".htgroup" file

```
the-group: bebo cailliau
```

a group named "the-group" is defined consisting of users "bebo" and "cailliau." This group might then be used as such

```
AuthUserFile /u/sf/bebo/.data/.htpasswd
AuthGroupFile /u/sf/bebo/.data/.htgroup
AuthName grouptest
AuthType Basic
```

```
<limit GET POST PUT>
require group the-group
</limit>
```

The AuthGroupFile directive points to the location of the ".htgroup" file. Files in a directory containing this ".htaccess" file would only be available to HTTP GET, POST, and PUT requests coming from users "bebo" and "cailliau."

LAB 7.6 SELF-REVIEW QUESTIONS

In order to test your progress, you should be able to answer the following questions.

1) The ".htaccess" file is a good choice for directory level control as it is available on most Web servers.

   a) _____ True
   b) _____ False

2) The ".htaccess" file has the advantage over the CERN-type configuration is that it can limit access based on both client IP address/hostname *and* the resource being accessed.

   a) _____ True
   b) _____ False

3) In general, access to documents can be typically restricted by the Web server according to all but which of the following?

   a) _____ Client/browser IP address or domain name
   b) _____ Client Operating System
   c) _____ User groups
   d) _____ User names

4) The ".htaccess" file provides which of the following?

   a) _____ Allows authors to control directory access
   b) _____ Configuration without Web administrator intervention
   c) _____ The ".htaccess" file resides in the directory to be controlled
   d) _____ All of the above

Quiz answers appear in the Appendix, Section 7.6.

LAB 7.7

SEARCHING AND INDEXING ISSUES

> *The Internet's potential can only be realized if users can find exactly what they want quickly, accurately, and with little effort. The development of tools which support the finding of relevant material within a few mouse clicks and key strokes is becoming increasingly critical, given the unprecedented rate at which the Web is growing and the rising number of novice users.*
>
> —Pollock & Hockley, British Telecom Labs

LAB OBJECTIVES

After this lab, you will be able to:

✔ Understand Searching and Indexing Issues

There are fundamentally two types of Web users—the "surfers" and the "searchers." But what is the real difference between the two? "Surfing" is browsing—following hypertext links that an author has decided are relevant. "Searching" is a user attempting to find what he or she wants or needs. Web sites have to be designed to accommodate both searchers and surfers.

Of major importance is the question "what does a search button on a page tell a user?" It must be clear whether the search is of the Internet or an intranet, of a database, or of something else (such as searching a file or a page using a facility such as "find" or "grep").

In this lab we will focus only on the issues of the technologies that support searching of the Internet/Web or an intranet. The syntax of composing a search query is often dependent upon the tools (i.e., search engines) a searcher uses and will not be addressed.

ROBOTS, SPIDERS, AND INDEXERS

When a user enters a search query using his or her favorite search engine, that query obviously does not trigger a search of the entire Web. It's clear that not even the most patient of users would be willing to wait for such an action to complete. Instead, the user's query prompts a search in a database that has been specifically built and maintained to accommodate Web searches. The information in such a database has been collected by what is commonly called a robot, a spider, or an indexer. For the sake of discussion, we will use these terms interchangeably.

A *robot* is a computer program that automatically traverses a Web's hypertext structure by retrieving a page/document and recursively retrieving all pages/documents that are referenced by links. Some robots can be configured to follow the directory structure of a Web site's document directory instead of following links. This latter method insures that all pages in the document directory are visited even if there are no hypertext links pointing to them. Information collected by the robot during these traversals is stored in a database. Obviously, a major difference between robots is the types of information they collect. This issue will be discussed later.

A *search engine*, therefore, is a program that accepts a search query from a reader/user and then searches through a database produced by a robot. In the context of the Web, the term "search engine" is most often used to search databases of HTML (or other Web-supported formats) pages and documents.

TYPES OF SEARCH ENGINES

Search engines can be placed into five distinct classifications depending upon how they respond to queries and the source of the database that they search. These five classifications are:

- "True" search engines
- Mega-indexes
- Simultaneous (parallel) mega-indexes
- Subject directories (or portals)
- Robotic specialized search engines

"TRUE" SEARCH ENGINES

"True" search engines are technically known as "robotic Internet search engines." They are designed to operate according to the general model of indexing and searching described earlier. They attempt to provide search capability to as large a portion of the Web (selected randomly) as possible. Recent studies indicate that even the best of the indexers that support such engines are only able to cover approximately 16 percent of the estimated number of Web pages available to them.

MEGA-INDEXES

Mega-indexes (also sometimes known as *meta-indexes*) are search engines that do not support their own index database. Instead, they put candidate Web sites (possibly suitable for indexing) through a selection process before actually indexing them. They may also be "linked" to other robotic search engines. Examples of mega-indexes are Magellan and NetSearch.

SIMULTANEOUS (PARALLEL) MEGA-INDEXES

Simultaneous (parallel) mega-indexes (also sometimes known as *multi-threaded meta-indexes*) access robotic search engines in parallel (simulatneously) and present their results in a consolidated single package. Examples of this concept include MetaCrawler and (to some extent) Yahoo!.

SUBJECT DIRECTORIES/PORTALS

Subject directories or portals attempt to facilitate user interface by dividing the contents of their indexed site's database into categories. In theory, this allows users of the search facility to forego problems which may be encountered in formulating a good (or efficient) search request. There is an obvious issue of defining these categories so that they are descriptive and manageable. The best example of a subject directory index is Yahoo!. It is successful in this category by using a manually maintained database, instead of completely relying on robotic indexing.

ROBOTIC SPECIALIZED SEARCH ENGINES

Robotic specialized search engines are used to target specific content areas, content types, or content providers to be indexed. For example, an indexing robot could be configured to index only content that relates to legal issues. Such a site would facilitate Web searching by attorneys. The building of a searchable graphics or musical library would be an example of specialization by content type. An indexer which indexes only the Usenet newsgroups would be an example of specialization by provider.

CO-EXISTING WITH WEB ROBOTS

Search engine robots are application programs that follow links on Web sites, gathering data for search engine index databases. These databases are what is actually searched when a reader/user enters a search request at a search engine Web site. These applications are considered *robots* rather than programs because they operate independently. That is, they have not been programmed to look for specific content or pages. Other names that are frequently used for these programs are *spider* or *crawler* (because they follow links on the Web), *worm, wanderer,* and *gatherer.* Web-wide search engines use robots because they are accessing the pages remotely, just as a reader/user browsing a Web site would view the pages in his or her client/browser.

All of these Web robots behave in essentially the same way, so designing links for one robot to index will likely improve your compatibility with the other robots as well. Designing for searchability or robot indexing should therefore be considered a part of the page/document authoring process.

Most Web content providers welcome the opportunity for their pages to be indexed. This ensures that readers/users both internal and external to their organization can more easily find their work. An organization doing business on the Web hopes that the searchability of its content will bring new customers to their Web site.

THE FOUR LAWS OF WEB ROBOTICS

The *four laws of Web robotics* attempt to quantify suitable Web robot behavior that benefits both the designer of a Web robot and a Web site administrator. They suggest ways that Web sites and Web robots can peacefully co-exist with one another. Specifically, these laws are:

- A Web robot must identify itself.
- A Web robot must obey exclusion standards and respect the wishes reflected by a Web site.
- A Web robot must not "hog" resources, potentially impacting the availability of a Web site being indexed.
- A Web robot must report errors.

ROBOT IDENTIFICATION

Web robots should identify themselves when they request a page from a Web server. The Web HTTP communications protocol includes some information in the HTTP *header,* including information about the capabilities of the client (a Web browser or robot program), what type of information the request is for, as well as other information. One of these header fields is `User-Agent`, which stores the name of the *client* (the program requesting the information) and whether it is a browser or a robot. If the server monitor or logfile stores this information, the Web server administrator can see what the robot has done. For example, the following logfile entry

```
c4.googlebot.com--- [15/Aug/1999:03:07:29 -0700] "GET /
addconference.html HTTP/1.0" 200 9652 "-" "Googlebot/1.0
(googlebot@googlebot.com http://googlebot.com/)" GET /
addconference.html--"HTTP/1.0"
```

indicates that version 1.0 of the "Googlebot" robot running on c4.googlebot.com indexed a file named addconference.html. Additional information, including a URL for the robot and a contact email address, are also given.

Similar information can also be provided in the HTTP `From` or `Referrer` fields. A Web robot application compliant with this law of Web robotics should include such header information when it generates HTTP requests.

EXCLUSION STANDARDS

If a Web site administrator really wants to, he or she can completely block site access to a particular Web robot. This can be done using the access authorization capabilities available in all server software. Such an action is unlikely to benefit either of the parties concerned—the organization controlling the Web robot usually wants to have a comprehensive index database and the Web site administrator wants his or her Web site to be searchable. However, it is often the case that a Web site contains some content that the administrator wishes not to be indexed. There can be many reasons for such a wish—the decision is that of the administrator—but the second law of Web robotics dictates that such wishes should be respected.

The *de facto* standard for specifying exclusion rules is the "robots.txt" file. This file is placed at the top of the Web server document directory and should be the first file read by the Web robot. Instructions within the "robots.txt" file are intended to indicate which paths are allowed (or disallowed) in the Web robot's indexing of the Web site.

The syntax of the "robots.txt" file is deliberately simple:

- The *user-agent* directive identifies the Web robot application to which the rule applies; this Web robot identification is the same as that found in the HTTP header.

- The *disallow* directive specifies a URL path that should not be followed by the robot application.

POLITE INDEXING

The third law of Web Robotics suggests that "well-behaved" robots should not "hog" server resources. Since a robot makes HTTP requests, its impact on server operation is comparable to typical user requests. However, since robots are automated processes, a high rate of incoming requests could potentially "flood" the server, resulting effectively in a "denial of service" attack.

There are numerous ways that a "polite" indexer can behave. For example, if possible, site indexing should occur only at opportune times for the server when the indexing process is least likely to have a detrimental effect. This timing could be determined through communication with the server administrator or as simply as considering the server location and time zone.

Indexers should only index content that is needed and/or appropriate. Rarely is the indexing of an entire Web site necessary. The HTTP HEAD request allows indexers to retrieve only Web page HEAD information thus reducing the amount of information provided by the indexed server. To avoid indexer denial of service attacks, most robot software can be "throttled," thereby controlling the rate at which it generates requests.

Web robots and Web sites exist in a symbiotic relationship. They both need and want one another. Careful consideration of their interactions can make that relationship beneficial to both parties.

ERROR REPORTING

Logically the indexing process should be as efficient as possible. It benefits neither the "indexer" (robot) or the "indexee" (the site being indexed) to process requests leading to missing Web pages and other broken links. Not only do such requests waste processing power on both ends of the client-server interaction, but they clutter logfiles with error messages.

The Web indexer/robot should report errors encountered during the indexing process. Once again, this reporting as a part of the Web robot–site relationship will generally help a Web site to identify and address the problems which led to the errors and make future indexing a smoother process.

Lab 7.7 Exercises

7.7.1 Understand Searching and Indexing Issues

a) Using the four laws of Web robots discussed in the text, discuss the impact that uncontrolled robots could have on your system.

b) The two directives in the robot.txt file (user-agent and disallow) are always followed by a semicolon. Create an entry that disallows access for all robots to the directory /www/info/.

c) Assume there is a robot that announces itself as "harvest." Create an entry that disallows access for this robot to the directory /www/info/.

Lab 7.7 Exercise Answers

7.7.1 Answers

a) Using the four laws of Web robots discussed in the text, discuss the impact that uncontrolled robots could have on your system.

Answer: A Web site administrator must be considerate of the desires of the authors, but must also be aware of the impact that Web robots can have on the operation of a Web server. For example, Web robots are not "real" readers/users—they visit the site only to index document content and do not attempt to visit limited portions of a Web site (i.e., one or two pages), but rather as much of a Web site as is possible or as much as they have been instructed.

Many organizations use Web robots, so a Web site is capable of being indexed by multiple robots, both commercial and private, at any time of the day and night. Since Web robots are automated processes, they are capable of generating requests to a Web server much more rapidly then a human reader/user.

The last point is perhaps the most critical to a Web site administrator since it reflects the operational impact that Web robots can have upon Web servers. Some organizations might find that the majority of their server traffic results from robot indexing. Indexing at inopportune times (such as during peak business hours) can seriously affect server performance and response. Simultaneous indexing by multiple Web robots is capable of causing a Web server to fail.

b) The two directives in the robots.txt file (user-agent and disallow) are always followed by a semicolon. Create an entry that disallows access for all robots to the directory /www/info/.

Answer: A "robots.txt" might containing the following lines:

```
User-agent: *
Disallow: /www/info/
```

c) Assume there is a robot that announces itself as "harvest." Create an entry that disallows access for this robot to the directory /www/info/.

Answer: In this case, the "robots.txt" might containing the following lines:

```
User-agent: harvest
Disallow: /www/info/
```

The extreme case

```
User-agent: *
Disallow: /
```

directs all Web robots to "go away" and index no content on the Web site.

As was said earlier, the primary reasons for specifying exclusion rules or rejecting Web robots are because

- The indexing of specific content is not desired or appropriate.
- The indexing of certain content is likely to impact Web server performance.

For these reasons, "robots.txt" files often specify that Web robots should not execute server-side (CGI) scripts. The reason for this is obvious—many scripts expect a reader/user interaction that the robot is unable to provide, often resulting in undesirable or unpredictable results. The following lines reflect such a specification

```
User-agent: *
Disallow: /cgi-bin/
```

Lab 7.7 Self-Review Questions

In order to test your progress, you should be able to answer the following questions.

1) The most important aspect of robots is that they are capable of generating requests far more rapidly then a human reader/user and can overburden a server.

   a) _____ True
   b) _____ False

2) The four laws of Web robotics are not enforced by any facility on your server, but are rules of *expected* behavior.

   a) _____ True
   b) _____ False

3) The file used to limit a robots behavior is:

   a) _____ robots.cfg
   b) _____ robots.inf
   c) _____ robots.txt
   d) _____ robots.rc

4) All but which of the following is a type of search engine?
   a) _____ "True" search engines
   b) _____ Mega-indexes and simultaneous (parallel) mega-indexes
   c) _____ Subject directories (or portals)
   d) _____ Encyclopedic indexes
   e) _____ Robotic specialized search engines

Quiz answers appear in the Appendix, Section 7.7.

CHAPTER 7

TEST YOUR THINKING

1) Looking at Figure 7.1, you see that Apache server software is used on more than twice as many servers as the next competitor. This provides a paradox because the Apache Web server is basically free and comes from a group of developers spread out over the Internet, and businesses tend to want software from a company they can call to get support (or even blame) when something goes wrong. In addition, the price of the server software is always such an insignificant part of the total price that it is rarely a consideration. Because ISPs and WSPs are obviously "risking" their business on this free software, we seem to have a paradox. Why is this?

2) Visit the various search engines such as Yahoo!, Alta Vista, Lycos, and so forth. Examine what kind of search mechanisms they provide. Search for information on a number of varied subjects and see what pages are returned.

3) Search the Web for an number of different ISPs and WSPs (not necessarily in your area). Investigate the services they offer compared to each other and in light of what your company needs.

CHAPTER 8

THE WEB PROGRAMMING AND SCRIPTING ENVIRONMENT

Polished brass will pass upon more people than rough gold.
—Chesterfield

CHAPTER OBJECTIVES

In this chapter, you will learn about:

- Reasons Why Developers Write Server-Side Script   Page 240
- 3-Tiered Web Application Design   Page 245

One of the most amazing things about the Internet (and about the World Wide Web in particular) is the platform agnosticism between client and server. The details of the underlying operating system, computer hardware, or network configuration don't matter one bit, as long as both client and server conform to a standard set of protocols. For that reason, there has been a recent explosion of options for Web servers, browsers, programming languages, and scripting technologies. In this chapter, we classify Web technologies into two functional categories (server-side and client-side) and then again into three conceptual layers (presentation layer, business logic, and persistence layer). By learning to identify the right tool for the right job, you will be able to select the technologies that will best suit your deployment requirements, your development environment, and your projected scalability needs.

LAB 8.1

REASONS WHY DEVELOPERS WRITE SERVER-SIDE SCRIPT

> **LAB OBJECTIVES**
>
> After this lab, you will be able to:
>
> ✔ Discuss the Problems of Writing Client-Side Code
> ✔ Explain the "Lowest Common Denominator" Solution

Back in the "good old days" of software development (before the Web existed, but not so far back as punch cards), there were a few programming languages to choose from, and there were a few compilers for each language. Once you had selected a language and a compiler, all that was left was to write code that compiled. You had complete control over your development environment.

Writing code for the Web has always been a little different. The development pace is rapid, the number of Web standards is literally exploding, and nobody has the time to keep on top of all the various standards being debated, implemented, and deprecated. Even worse, browser support for these standards often varies widely. Each Web browser implements the various Web standards in a slightly different way. Client-side code that works fine in Internet Explorer and Opera might crash Netscape and be completely useless in Lynx (or any other text-based browser).

The problem with writing client-side code quickly became apparent: The developer has virtually no control over the execution environment. True, good developers can make educated guesses about which browsers are most likely to access their pages, but there is always some uncertainty. Trying to write code that works in all major browsers is like trying to write code that will compile in several different compilers at once (if readers are not familiar with the joys of trying to compile code on multiple platforms, they may consider themselves extremely lucky).

Faced with a variety of incompatible browser "enhancements" and incomplete support for Web standards, one of the more prevalent (albeit disheartening) techniques of development is to write code that only uses the subset of HTML, CSS, JavaScript, and DHTML functionality that is consistently supported by the major browsers (the "lowest common denominator"). Just as prime-time television is dumbed down to appeal to the widest possible audience, compatibility on the World Wide Web often means hobbling the code to avoid breaking the oldest, least advanced browser still in wide usage. This "compromise" of practicality over functionality left many Web developers dissatisfied at least in part because it means neglecting new and exciting features that older browsers are not designed to handle.

Responding to this developer discontent, Sun made a lot of noise promoting Java, which was supposed to provide a "write once, run anywhere" approach to cross-platform coding. In practice—so the joke goes—it often worked out to be more of a "write once, debug everywhere" approach for the developer, because Java virtual machine implementations also varied somewhat from platform to platform (and from browser to browser).

About the same time that Java was appearing on the scene, CGI scripts were becoming increasingly advanced (they had been around years before Java, of course). These scripts were pieces of code that ran on the Web server, not on the user's browser. By running code on a server, in a controlled environment, the whole question of cross-browser compatibility became moot. As long as the Web server returns nothing but HTML to the client, the Web application developer doesn't have to worry about cross-browser quirks at all. One can almost picture Web developers breathing a sigh of relief as they began writing code in a server-side environment they could control, after struggling to produce client-side code that had to work in a variety of browser environments out of their control.

LAB 8.1 EXERCISES

8.1.1 DISCUSS THE PROBLEMS OF WRITING CLIENT-SIDE CODE

a) Which major browser do you think supports more than 75% of all client-side JavaScript features?

b) When can you depend on client-side scripting for mission-critical logic?

c) Suppose there is a form on the page, and that form needs to be checked for mistakes (letters in number boxes, blank fields, invalid dates, etc.) before the information can be entered in the database. Do you want to write client-side or server-side code to do that error checking? Why?

8.1.2 EXPLAIN THE "LOWEST COMMON DENOMINATOR" SOLUTION

Imagine that you're working on a Web site for a client. He wants to make sure that anyone with Internet access can get full functionality out of his Web site. In fact, he'll be viewing your work via a dialup connection and AOL.

a) What design limitations are you under?

b) How much functionality do you think you can build in?

LAB 8.1 EXERCISE ANSWERS

8.1.1 ANSWERS

a) Which major browser do you think supports more than 75% of all client-side JavaScript features?

Answer: Sorry. This was a trick question. No one has written a browser that supports anywhere near 75% of all the features and functionality defined in JavaScript. Stay on the beaten path and you'll be okay, but if you go wandering off into some of the darker corners of JavaScript, you may rapidly find yourself running into subtle bugs caused by quirky or incomplete browser support.

b) When can you depend on client-side scripting for mission-critical logic?

Answer: Never. If there is a feature of your publicly accessible Web site that is absolutely critical—that your site cannot work without—under no circumstances should you rely on client-side routines to perform that logic.

As a side note to that answer, there are times, especially when developing Web applications for a company's internal use, when the developer is in a position to standardize the browser configuration for an application. If you know that all of the visitors to your page will be using Browser X with JavaScript enabled, than you can feel confident in making the most of the client-side code supported by Browser X. When writing Web pages for general Internet use, however, you can make no such assumptions.

c) Suppose there are forms on the page, and those forms need to be checked for mistakes (letters in number boxes, blank fields, invalid dates, etc.) before the information can be entered in the database. Do you want to write client-side or server-side code to do that error checking? Why?

Answer: You want to do server side checking at the bare minimum. There are times when it's nice to have a client-side box pop up informing the user of an error before the form is submitted, but don't rely exclusively on JavaScript error checking. The reason? Users are allowed to turn off JavaScript from within their browsers, and they often do.

Whenever you insert any information into a database, it's a good idea to error-check the data before adding it. We will touch on this topic again in Chapter 10 on security issues, but it bears repeating. Speaking from experience, it is incredibly embarrassing to have your database-driven application crash due to relational inconsistencies after someone turned off JavaScript in his or her browser and submitted an incomplete form that bypassed your intricately written JavaScript error-checking routines, inserting bad data into your database.

8.1.2 ANSWERS

a) What design limitations are you under?

Answer: You are under some serious design restrictions. Avoid any unnecessary client-side code and try to stick to straight HTML. Also remember to keep the graphics light: Web developers (designers especially) often forget the pain of a dial-up connection.

b) How much functionality do you think you can build in?

Answer: A surprising amount, provided you build most, if not all of all the application's functionality into server-side code. Rumor has it that amazon.com is completely functional through a 2.0 browser. That means that Amazon uses nothing more advanced than HTML tables on the client side. It's completely possible to build a functional dynamic Web site that is compatible with all 3.0 browsers. You will just need to avoid adding functionality through client-side scripting.

It used to be that writing for the lowest common denominator meant that everything on the site had to work properly in a 3.0 browser. More recently, however, it is not considered unreasonable to build sites for browsers comparable to (or better than) Internet Explorer or Netscape 4.0.

LAB 8.1 SELF-REVIEW QUESTIONS

In order to test your progress, you should be able to answer the following questions.

1) As long as a Web server returns nothing but HTML to a client, the Web application developer doesn't have to worry about cross-browser quirks at all.

   a) _____ True
   b) _____ False

2) Both Netscape Navigator and Internet Explorer, versions 5.0 and higher, support more than 75% of all client-side JavaScript features.

   a) _____ True
   b) _____ False

3) Even the very best developers can make educated guesses about which browsers are most likely to access their pages, but there is always some uncertainty.

   a) _____ True
   b) _____ False

Quiz answers appear in the Appendix, Section 8.2.

LAB 8.2

3-TIERED WEB APPLICATION DESIGN

> **LAB OBJECTIVES**
>
> After this lab, you will be able to:
> - Understand and Explain the Presentation Layer
> - Understand and Explain the Business Logic Layer
> - Understand and Explain the Persistence Layer

When you start coding Web applications more advanced than pages that know when to say "good morning" and when to say "good afternoon," you will rapidly discover that scripting languages are relatively simple and extremely flexible. So flexible, in fact, that there aren't any clear guidelines for how code should be written. Sure, the syntax is straightforward, but actually organizing a single page can get to be a chore. Getting five pages to talk to each other can be a jumbled mess. And getting twenty or thirty different pages to all work together to form one cohesive Web application can be a nightmare . . . unless you impose some artificial structure onto the process.

Most Web design is broken down into three layers, or tiers. You may have heard it referred to as 3-tiered Web design or possibly even N-tiered application design ("N-tiered" means that the application can be broken down into an arbitrarily large number of conceptual pieces, with the possibility that each piece could reside on its own machine). The three tiers are as follows: the presentation layer, the business logic layer, and the persistence layer.

The presentation layer is the front end of the site. The look and feel of the site is within the domain of presentation. The user interface also falls into the presentation layer, as does personalization code. In fact, pretty much anything the user interacts with, clicks on, or reads from is within the presentation layer.

The technologies underlying the presentation layer are Web scripting languages. These languages are all interpreted languages; they are parsed by the Web server (or by a program integrated with the Web server) when the Web page is accessed.

The business logic layer is the "mind" of the application. It does all the error checking, all the form field validation, and all of the . . . well, all of the business logic. If you need to calculate sales tax, then that code belongs in the business logic layer. If you need to send an email to the warehouse when a package is to be drop shipped to an address other than the customer's billing address, then all that logic belongs in the business logic layer.

Because interpreted languages (and, by extension, most Web scripting languages) are interpreted at run-time, they are notoriously slow at performing some types of processing (string comparisons in particular). These are tasks better left to compiled, server-side objects. If you need to perform a large number of repetitive operations as part of your business logic, you might want to consider creating a compiled object to handle the processing.

Finally, there is the persistence layer. After performing all your calculations, you will probably want someplace to store some information. At this point the reader may be inclined to say, "Just stick it in a database already!" or "Just write it to a text file!" As simple an idea as this is, it's always a good idea to abstract the job of storing and retrieving your information. In the event that you need to change databases, for example, you can change your persistence layer code without affecting your business logic. Some scripting languages will make it easy to abstract the database interactions. There are many specialized database solutions in the world today, and many have proprietary enhancements. Choosing an ODBC-compliant database server can ease the pain of transitioning from one database to another.

LAB 8.2 EXERCISES

8.2.1 UNDERSTAND AND EXPLAIN THE PRESENTATION LAYER

    a) Can you identify any scripting technologies that lend themselves to use in the presentation layer?

Lab 8.2: 3-Tiered Web Application Design

b) Imagine that you've just spent three months developing a Web site for a client who likes lime green. Against all your better judgment, you've written a complete site in lime green. Two days before the site is due to launch, the client has a change of heart and wants the site to be purple instead. What do you do and why?

8.2.2 UNDERSTAND AND EXPLAIN THE BUSINESS LOGIC LAYER

a) You need to parse a list of phone numbers and extract the area code from within the parentheses. Is this operation best done by script or by a compiled object? Why?

b) You need to take product information from the database, format the price so it appears in the format "$00.00," and display it on the product catalog page. Is this operation best done by script or by a compiled object? Why?

c) Can you identify any technologies that can be used to create compiled server-side objects?

d) Can you identify any technologies that could be used for interpreted (non-compiled, i.e., scripted) business logic?

8.2.3 UNDERSTAND AND EXPLAIN THE PERSISTENCE LAYER

Often a database will support an ODBC (Open Database Connectivity) interface as well as a native interface. The native interface often provides faster access and more features than the databases ODBC interface.

a) Why would anyone want to use ODBC when a database supports faster native drivers with more features?

LAB 8.2 EXERCISE ANSWERS

8.2.1 ANSWERS

a) Can you identify any scripting technologies that lend themselves to use in the persistence layer?

Answer: HTML, DHTML, CSS, JavaScript, Cold Fusion, ASP, PHP, SSI, and even APIs.

b) Imagine that you've just spent three months developing a Web site for a client who likes lime green. Against all your better judgment, you've written the complete site in lime green. Two days before the site is due to launch, the client has a change of heart and wants the site to be purple instead. What do you do and why?

Answer: If you answered "cry," then you've probably been in this situation before. If you suggested running a global search-and-replace on the Web site directory, changing all occurrences of "#00FF00" to "#993399," then you're getting warmer. If you suggested abstracting the site's color process into a server-side include file or variable, then you're on the right track. By replacing the literal string "#00FF00" with a server-side variable, we can change the whole site's colors as often as we like, painlessly. Alternatively, we could use multiple stylesheets, or a single stylesheet and client-side JavaScript to accomplish the same goal, tailoring the entire site to each individual user's preferences. Either way, everything can appear in the user's favorite color scheme, whether that is black and white, reds and blues, or forest green on kelly green.

The persistence layer can be an extremely versatile tool. Don't just think of it as the layer that does colors and formatting, but remember that it can be as dynamic as the content you're serving. You can pass dynamic content to Java Applets, to Macromedia

Flash or Shockwave movies, to XML (eXtensible Markup Language, the emerging standard for information transfer), to WML (Wireless Markup Language, a standard for cell phone Web browsers), a text-to-speech engine, or you can render some good old-fashioned HTML. The possibilities are nearly limitless.

8.2.2 ANSWERS

a) You need to parse a list of phone numbers and extract the area code from within the parentheses. Is this operation best done by script or by a compiled object? Why?

Answer: Using a compiled script is preferable in situations like this. Implementing processor-intensive or repetitious tasks with compiled objects can substantially increase the speed of the operations performed. Scripts can be 10 to 100 times slower than pre-compiled objects, especially when it comes to repetitive loops and string manipulation.

If your aim is to build a solution that will scale from humble beginnings to taking ridiculous numbers of hits per day, it's a good idea to separate the business logic into compiled objects from the beginning.

b) You need to take product information from the database, format the price so it appears in the format "$00.00," and display it on the product catalog page. Is this operation best done by script or by a compiled object? Why?

Answer: This is more easily done with an interpreted script than by a compiled object. Combining presentation and business logic is fairly common, since there are rarely clear lines drawn between a client's requirements for functionality and requirements for appearance.

Scripting the business logic in the page (or into an included file) is generally quicker than compiling server-side objects. It's also great for proof of concept Web sites. There is a caveat, however: Try to avoid mixing display code with business logic. It can be extremely time-consuming to change the page's appearance when the display logic is nestled among the business logic.

c) Can you identify any technologies that can be used to create compiled-server side objects?

Answer: Server-side compiled components can be made with any of your favorite programming languages: Java, C, C++, Visual Basic, VJ++, Pascal, or most anything else. You can build standalone executables, or build yourself some Java Beans or DLLs (on Windows boxes), or you might choose to architect a COM, DCOM, or CORBA solution.

d) Can you identify any technologies that could be used for noncompiled business logic?

Answer: Cold Fusion (which runs under the Cold Fusion Server), ASP (Active Server Pages, which run under Microsoft's Internet Information Server), JSP (Java Server Pages), or PHP (a recursive acronym which stands for "PHP Hypertext Preprocessor").

We will learn more about these technologies in the next chapter.

8.2.3 ANSWERS

a) Why would anyone want to use ODBC when a database supports faster native drivers with more features?

Answer: Writing a Web application that is coded to a database's native driver is fine, assuming there will never come a time when you need to switch to another database server. It is extremely painful to switch from one db to another when there is a substantial amount of code in place in a proprietary—and now useless—format.

LAB 8.2 SELF-REVIEW QUESTIONS

In order to test your progress, you should be able to answer the following questions.

1) Name the three tiers of application design.

    a) _____ Web portal, co-branding, e-commerce
    b) _____ Presentation, venture capital, perseverance
    c) _____ Presentation, business, persistence
    d) _____ Perpetrate, design, polish

2) The graphical look-and-feel aspects of the Web site belongs to which tier?

    a) _____ Presentation
    b) _____ Business
    c) _____ Persistence

3) In which tier should you calculate sales tax for an order?

    a) _____ Presentation
    b) _____ Business
    c) _____ Persistence

Lab 8.2: 3-Tiered Web Application Design 251

4) Which tier is most closely tied to the database?

   a) _____ Presentation
   b) _____ Business
   c) _____ Persistence

5) Which tier would retrieve a list of names from a corporate roster, order them according to seniority, and print out their names in descending size order? Check all that apply.

   a) _____ Presentation
   b) _____ Business
   c) _____ Persistence

Quiz answers appear in the Appendix, Section 8.2.

CHAPTER 8

TEST YOUR THINKING

1) If you are currently planning a Web application, examine your application's structure and functionality in terms of the presentation layer, business logic, and persistence layer. If you don't currently have a Web application plan lying around, pick something simple—like an online bookstore—and follow along.
   What is your target browser?
   Do you anticipate needing to use any client-side code?
   How do customers navigate the site?
   Do you need to provide your customers with dynamic content?
   Do you need to get information from your visitors? Detailed information?
   How much information will you need to store?
   What is the most processor-intensive part of your application?
   What is the most Web server-intensive?
2) By examining the URL and URL parameters of a Web site, you can usually deduce how a site provides dynamic content. Active Server Pages have an ".asp" extension, while Java Server Pages end in ".jsp." Cold Fusion pages end in ".cfm." Pages written in CGI generally have a ".cgi" extension. Go onto the Internet and see what server-side programming techniques some of the major sites are using.
   a) Go to live.altavista.com and read any news story on the site. Can you tell, just from the URL, what kind of server-side code the site is running? Does that tell you what operating system the Web server is running?
   b) Now check out www.microsoft.com. Click a few links. See if you can identify the server-side technology used to provide content there.
   c) Surf on to www.casio.com. Do the file extensions there give you any hints as to what technology that site is built with?
   d) Now visit the San Diego Zoo at www.sandiegozoo.org. How does it provide dynamic content?
   e) To see some really cryptic-looking URLs, go to Kelley Blue Book Web site at www.kbb.com. Click any link and look at the incomprehensible jumble of letters that makes up the page's URL. Now look more closely. Can you spot the one piece of information that gives away what technology Kelley uses?
   f) Finally, try to develop an appreciation for well-designed content presentation on the Web. Learn from other people's good design.

CHAPTER 9

PROGRAMMING AND SCRIPTING IN A CLIENT-SERVER SYSTEM

When choosing between two evils, I always like to try the one I've never tried before.

—Mae West

CHAPTER OBJECTIVES

In this chapter, you will learn about:

- Server-side Programming — Page 254
- Client-side Programming — Page 261
- Combining Client-Side and Server-Side Scripting — Page 269

So far we've seen some arguments for server-side scripting over client-side scripting and useful ways to classify code according to function, but now we're going to dig deeper into the guts of what you can—and can't—do with server-side and client-side programming tools. Following that, we'll take a brief look at ways to bridge the gap between server-side and client-side.

LAB 9.1

SERVER-SIDE PROGRAMMING

> **LAB OBJECTIVES**
>
> After this lab, you will be able to:
> - Identify Key Technologies for Processing Server-Side Code
> - List Advantages and Disadvantages of Server-Side Code

There are currently a ridiculous number of Web servers out on the Internet right now running an astounding variety of operating systems and a plethora of Web servers, each designed and configured a little differently from the others, all being bombarded constantly with a barrage of standardized requests from a dozen or so browsers running on a handful of operating systems. With that said, the following discussion of server-side scripting should apply (at least in part) to your particular situation.

There is currently no shortage of server-side programming interfaces that can generate and send HTML through the Web server. Some rely on compiled objects, but the majority are based on a scripting language model. Scripting languages differ from compiled programming languages in subtle yet important ways:

- Scripting languages do not need to be compiled before they can be run.
- Scripting languages are parsed at run-time by an interpreter.
- Scripting languages almost always run more slowly than compiled code.

The end goal is, of course, to include dynamically created content into a Web page. There are various technologies designed to achieve this goal: SSI, CGI, APIs, and SSS. Don't worry about acronyms overload; we will go through each acronym individually.

You can use Server-Side Includes (SSIs) to replace specially formatted HTML comments with dynamic content just before the Web page is sent to the Web server. SSI will allow you to replace SSI tags with dynamic content, but it will not allow you to return anything other than HTML to the browser (it can't return an image or a movie, for example).

CGI is not a programming language in itself, but rather a standardized gateway through which server-side code can interface with a Web server (thus the name, Common Gateway Interface). These server-side scripts can create a Web page dynamically (headers and all) and then output that page through a Web server to the client. CGI scripts can be written in a programming language like C, C++, Perl, or in virtually any other language that can write to a standard output. The CGI script dynamically writes the text of the Web page to the Web server, which sends it on to the client. Because CGI scripts aren't limited to outputting dynamic content, CGI scripting is more powerful than SSI and much better suited to handling form processing. This requires some processing overhead, however, since each CGI request creates a separate process, in a separate memory space, before handling the request. Because anyone who knows a programming language can write a CGI script, CGI is—and continues to be—very popular.

Now, when the nice folks who write Web servers for a living noticed that developers were finding ways to generate dynamic content using stand-alone CGI applications, they got worried. It wouldn't be long before CGI scripts sent their output straight to the client, bypassing their Web servers altogether. So they put their heads together and each came up with a proprietary Application Programming Interface (API) that their Web servers could support. They knew that once developers started to write code for Web servers, it pretty much guaranteed the Web server company a customer for life, since changing Web servers means that an organization also has to rewrite all the code written for their old Web server's API. The cloud has a silver lining, of course: These APIs are tightly integrated with the Web server, so they run faster and scale better than CGI scripts. Consequently, they also offer the programmer more detailed control over the application's processes and threads.

The Whole Truth About Web Server APIs

API programming has a serious portability problem. There are a few Web servers that run on multiple platforms (Apache is one), but choosing to develop a Web application in an API means that you will be married to one particular Web server for the long haul, unless you're prepared to rewrite the application when you change to another server. That said, if you have a Web server that you're not planning on changing any time soon and you are in the market for a server-side programming solution, then you might consider coding for your Web server's API.

Server-side scripting languages fall somewhere between CGI scripts and API programming. These scripting languages are either interpreted by a stand-alone application that interfaces with the Web server or by the Web server itself. Just like Server-Side Includes, the code is embedded in the Web page itself, and the page is processed before being sent to the client. Unlike SSI, more can happen than just replacing tags with dynamic content. These interpreted languages are capable of database access, as well as all of the fundamentals of programming (if-then-else logic, loops, assignment, output, etc.). Languages in this class include Active Server Pages (ASP), Java Server Pages (JSP), Cold Fusion Markup Language (CFML), and PHP. In addition to providing server-side logic, server-side scripting languages can also be used to interface with compiled objects (which can provide functionality and performance that the scripting language alone can't match).

LAB 9.1 EXERCISES

9.1.1 IDENTIFY KEY TECHNOLOGIES FOR PROCESSING SERVER-SIDE CODE

You are building a Web site that is intended to bring together large numbers of junk food fans with junk food message boards and junk food ads. You hope for millions of hits per day (and are counting on scaling that high before your IPO).

a) What are the advantages and disadvantages of building a site using CGI scripts?

b) What are the advantages and disadvantages of building a site using Server-Side Includes?

c) What are the advantages and disadvantages of building a site using an API?

d) What are the advantages and disadvantages of building a site using a server-side scripting language like ASP, Cold Fusion, or PHP?

9.1.2 LIST ADVANTAGES AND DISADVANTAGES OF SERVER-SIDE CODE

a) What kinds of processing can you do with server-side code?

b) What are some advantages to running code on the Web server?

c) What are some of the disadvantages to running code on the Web server?

LAB 9.1 EXERCISE ANSWERS

9.1.1 ANSWERS

You are building a Web site that is intended to bring together large numbers of junk food fans with junk food message boards and junk food ads. You hope for millions of hits per day (and are counting on scaling that high before your IPO).

a) What are the advantages and disadvantages of building a site using CGI scripts?

Answer: CGI scripts will certainly handle the job of creating online message boards and targeted ads. Scaling to millions of hits per day, however, may give you performance problems. CGI scripts don't always scale well under heavy use.

b) What are the advantages and disadvantages of building a site using Server-Side Includes?

Answer: Server-Side Includes are completely wrong for this project. You could probably come up with a really clever way to display message board content dynamically, but you will need to use some other technology to take the user's messages and save them to a database.

c) What are the advantages and disadvantages of building a site using an API?

Answer: Just make sure, before you begin, that you won't need to change Web servers partway through the project. If there's a chance you will need to upgrade to a new Web server that will handle a higher load than your current choice, then it would be prudent not to develop your current Web server's API.

d) What are the advantages and disadvantages of building a site using a server-side scripting language like ASP, Cold Fusion, or PHP?

Answer: Advantages include rapid prototyping and easy database access. Potential disadvantages are fairly few, though interpreted languages aren't the fastest, so you may need to add hardware to successfully scale up to handle millions of hits per day.

9.1.2 ANSWERS

a) What kinds of processing can you do with server-side code?

Answer: You can format information in different ways, perform business logic, call compiled objects, run queries against databases, display query results, validate user input, and store user input. One of the most common input-validation tasks you will face is checking to see if the user has left a required field blank. That is done server-side by checking the length of the form field.

There is, of course, a caveat to even this seemingly simple process. Macintosh computers running some versions of Internet Explorer have a pesky habit of passing a space instead of an empty string when submitting a form. So a server-side check to verify that a field has, in fact, been left blank, will need to strip the leading and trailing spaces from the field's value before checking the length. Even server-side code is not completely immune from the browser variation that plagues client-side code.

b) What are some advantages to running code on the Web server?

Answer: Unlike client-side code, server-side code is executed on the server, in a carefully controlled environment. You gain a lot of stability and confidence in such an environment. You can also run processor-intensive applications on the server without having to worry about the limitations of the user's computer.

c) What are some of the disadvantages to running code on the Web server?

Answer: There are several potential disadvantages. First, the demand on the CPU to parse and execute server-side scripts is much greater than just running a Web server. Intensive script processing can impact the performance of the Web server.

Second, the communication lag between client and server can be a problem. Each request for information requires a trip from client to server and back again, in addition to whatever processing time is required at the server. Server-side code simply cannot respond as quickly to user input as client-side code can. Internet connections are getting faster all the time, but executing processes on remote computers is still no match for running code locally.

The exception to this, of course, is that your machine may not have the memory to search an index of a billion or so Web pages, while there are certainly servers out on the net that can receive your request, process a massive amount of information, and return a result in the blink of an eye. There is logic that is suited for client-side calculation, and then there is processing that is best left to a remote server. It's up to you to tell the difference.

LAB 9.1 SELF-REVIEW QUESTIONS

In order to test your progress, you should be able to answer the following questions.

1) Which of the following can only return html files?
   a) _____ SSI
   b) _____ CGI
   c) _____ API
   d) _____ SSS

2) Which of the following lets you program in any language you choose?
   a) _____ SSI
   b) _____ CGI
   c) _____ API
   d) _____ SSS

3) Which of the following describes a way for a program to access the Web server?
   a) _____ SSI
   b) _____ CGI
   c) _____ API
   d) _____ SSS

Lab 9.1: Server-Side Programming

4) Active Server Pages (ASP) written in VBScript are only understood by Microsoft's Internet information server. Which of the following describes ASP?

   a) _____ SSI
   b) _____ CGI
   c) _____ API
   d) _____ SSS

5) Can you error-check a form with server-side code?

   a) _____ Yes, but only after you submit it.
   b) _____ Yes, but only before you submit it.
   c) _____ No, that has to be done client-side.

   Quiz answers appear in the Appendix, Section 9.1.

LAB 9.2

CLIENT-SIDE PROGRAMMING

> **LAB OBJECTIVES**
>
> After this lab, you will be able to:
>
> ✔ Write Simple Client-Side JavaScript
> ✔ Perform Basic Client-Side Form Validation

There are a myriad of client-side programming technologies that are designed to enhance the browsing experience (Java applets, ActiveX, Shockwave, Flash, and various other plug-ins). Of these, Java was the first to attempt to fill the need for a single, portable, universally compatible client-side programming technology. JavaScript is the subset of Java (though "subset" may not be strong enough a word) that is directly interpreted by the browser. Despite the lingering echoes of Sun's call for complete cross-browser compatibility, multiple flavors of JavaScript and a variety of JavaScript implementations emerged rapidly. Here's a quick etymology of the assorted variations on JavaScript:

- JavaScript is an interpreted, Java-based scripting language developed jointly by Sun and Netscape.
- Jscript is Microsoft's version of JavaScript. "Enhanced" with various proprietary features, it has drawn the ire of Netscape, Sun, and the U.S. Justice Department.
- ECMAScript is a relatively new attempt to create a standardized, client-side, interpreted scripting language.
- VBScript is another interpreted scripting language from Microsoft, nearly identical in functionality to JavaScript, but based on a subset of Visual Basic syntax and functionality (and only supported by Microsoft Web browsers).

When we visit a Web site and download and run client-side code, we are quite literally executing someone else's arbitrary code on his or her own machine. Executing malicious or untrusted code on any machine in any way constitutes a serious security risk, so strict security measures exist to keep client-side code from crashing the user's system, reading or writing files on the user's hard drive, launching programs, or accessing system resources. This security model is called the "sandbox" model: Client-side code is given a little electronic box that it is allowed to play in, and it is not allowed outside that box for any reason.

The necessarily restrictive nature of this sandbox does have side effects: It severely curtails the amount of functionality one can build into a client-side script. This security precaution has limited the usefulness of client-side code, but it should be noted that it has also limited the amount of trouble that malicious client-side code can cause.

> **The Whole Truth About ECMAScript**
>
> ECMAScript is named after the organization that is in the process of standardizing the syntax: the ECMA (formerly named the "European Computer Manufacturers Association," but now simply called "ECMA"). ECMAScript has evolved over time (the final version is ECMAScript-262) to specify exactly how a well-behaved client-side programming language should work (the final version is closely related to JavaScript 1.1). Unfortunately for developers, the ECMAScript standard specifies the syntax of the language but not the browser's underlying Document Object Model (DOM), thus limiting the potential usefulness of ECMAScript as a standardized client-side language.

Given the limitations that are imposed on client-side scripts for security reasons, what can we actually do with them? A surprising amount. JavaScript has dominion over anything that relates directly to the browser, forms on the page, the current page itself, or other pages in the frameset. Of all the possibilities offered by this wide playground, client-side form validation is one of the most useful things JavaScript can do.

■ FOR EXAMPLE

- We can verify that required form fields have not been left blank.
- We can verify that numeric form fields do not contain letters, spaces, dashes, or symbols.
- We can verify that an email address contains an "@" sign.
- We can verify that a zip code has at least five digits.

Lab 9.2: Client-Side Programming **263**

Client-side code can do all of these things without taking the time to post the form to the server, check it, and send back a response.

LAB 9.2 EXERCISES

9.2.1 WRITE SIMPLE CLIENT-SIDE JAVASCRIPT

Save the following as an HTML file and open it in your browser:

```
<html>
 <script language="JavaScript">
  alert("Welcome to my site!");
 </script>
 <body>Hi.</body>
</html>
```

a) What happens when you load the page? Why?

_____

_____

Now change the page slightly by making your greeting into a function:

```
<html>
 <script language="JavaScript">
  function Greeting() {
   alert("Welcome to my site!");
  }
 </script>
 <body>Hi.</body>
</html>
```

b) What happens when you load the page? Why?

_____

_____

Now change the code again by adding an onLoad event to the body tag:

```
<html>
 <script language="JavaScript">
  function Greeting() {
   alert("Welcome to my site!");
  }
 </script>
```

```
<body onLoad="Greeting();">Hi.</body>
</html>
```

c) What happens when you load the page? Why?

9.2.2 Perform Basic Client-Side Form Validation

Save the following as an HTML file and open it in your browser:

```
<html>
 <script language="JavaScript">
  function formValidate() {
   if(document.forms[0].emailAddress.value.length > 0) {
    return true;
   }else{
    alert("please enter an email address");
    return false;
   }
  }
 </script>
 <form onSubmit="return formValidate();">
  email address: <input type="text" name="emailAddress">
  <input type="submit" name="submit" value="submit">
 </form>
</html>
```

a) What happens when you submit the page without filling in the text box? Why?

Now change the script block to read as follows:

```
<script language="JavaScript">
 function formValidate() {
  if(document.forms[0].emailAddress.value.length < 6) {
   alert("please enter a valid email address");
   return false;
  }
```

```
    if (document.forms[0].emailAddress.value.search("@") ==
    -1){
     alert("please enter a valid email address");
     return false;
    }
    return true;
   }
  </script>
```

   b) What happens when you submit the page without entering a valid email address? How are we identifying a valid email address?

   c) What are some reasons to choose client-side over server-side form validation?

   d) In addition to the forms on the page, what attributes of the user's browser would you like to access?

LAB 9.2 EXERCISE ANSWERS

9.2.1 ANSWERS

   a) What happens when you load the page? Why?

     Answer: A message box pops up, cordially welcoming your visitor to your Web page.

   b) What happens when you load the page? Why?

     Answer: Nothing happens this time. No pop-up message box appears. Why doesn't it appear? Because the code that used to run when the page was loaded—the code that called the alert box—is now wrapped up in a function that is never called.

c) What happens when you load the page? Why?

Answer: Your message box appears correctly again. The body tag's onLoad event fires after the entire page is loaded. Any code specified in that onLoad event will be run as soon as all the form elements have been drawn and everything is ready to go.

Simply including client-side code at the top of the page (as we did in exercise a) is no guarantee that the rest of the page will be completely loaded. If your code refers to an object further down the page, and that object hasn't finished loading yet (perhaps your visitor is using a 28.8 modem), then the user will receive a JavaScript error. To ensure the entire page is loaded before you start running any client-side code, it is good form to include any client-side initialization code in a function that is called by the onLoad event of the body tag.

9.2.2 ANSWERS

a) What happens when you submit the page without filling in the text box? Why?

Answer: You will receive a message box informing you that you need to enter an email address. The form will not be submitted until you enter at least one character into the box.

Returning false to the onSubmit event of the form prevents the form from submitting. Similarly, you can return false to a standard <a> tag to prevent a link from being followed until some condition has been met. That code would look something like this:

```
<a href="wherever.htm" onClick="return motherMayI();">
```

b) What happens when you submit the page without entering a valid email address? How are we identifying a valid email address?

Answer: If you don't enter a valid email address, you will receive a message box informing you that you need to enter a valid email address. In this context, a valid email address must be longer then five letters (the shortest conceivably valid email address being "A@B.US") and must contain the "@" sign.

c) What are some reasons to choose client-side over server-side form validation?

Answer: Using client-side form validation means not making your user wait for the page to post to the server, execute there, pass the result back through the Web server, and then find out that he or she forgot to fill in a form field. It is almost always quicker than server-side form validation.

Server-side validation can also be especially infuriating when there are form upload fields involved, because those cannot hold their value from one post to the next. All other html form fields can have their values repopulated except for <input type="file">. So if you have a form that requires a user to upload more than two files at one time, it stands to reason that the user will prefer client-side error-checking to server-side checking, which could force the user to reenter those files if a mistake was made.

d) In addition to the forms on the page, what attributes of the user's browser would you like to access? In other words, what has been left in the sandbox for us to play with?

Answer: There are many useful attributes of the browser that can be accessed with client-side code. Here's a partial list:

- *The document the user is viewing: A simple document.location assignment will take the user's browser to another page (assuming he or she has JavaScript enabled). In addition, you can use JavaScript to access multiple frames within a frameset, setting and getting variables in those other pages.*

- *Cascading Stylesheet properties: JavaScript has complete access to all CSS properties and you can achieve some eye-catching effects by manipulating them (this is the essence of DHTML).*

- *Windows: You can create new ones with complete control over size, position, and the existence (or not) of toolbars, scrollbars, etc.*

- *Window position: This writable attribute can be used to "shake" the entire browser window, simulating an earthquake or some other impact (example code is available at http://javascript.Internet.com/bgeffects/shake-screen.html).*

- *The Browser itself: JavaScript can return information about your user's browser type, version, and installed plug-ins (useful for redirecting your visitor to a site optimized for his or her browser).*

- *Cookies: JavaScript can set and read cookies off the user's computer (assuming the user has JavaScript enabled and hasn't disabled cookies).*

LAB 9.2 SELF-REVIEW QUESTIONS

In order to test your progress, you should be able to answer the following questions.

1) The sandbox security model prevents client-side code from accessing anything outside the browser window (and some elements within the browser as well), which:

    a) _____ Increases the overall security of client-side code.
    b) _____ Reduces the overall security of client-side code.
    c) _____ Reduces the overall functionality of client-side code.
    d) _____ Increases the overall functionality of client-side code.
    e) _____ Means other code can't play with JavaScript's toys without its permission.

Lab 9.2: Client-Side Programming

2) If an onSubmit function returns "true," the form will

   a) _____ Submit properly.
   b) _____ Not submit at all.
   c) _____ Pop up an error message of your choice.
   d) _____ Do whatever the onTrue event says to do.

3) Which of the following items can JavaScript not access?

   a) _____ document.opener
   b) _____ document.bgColor
   c) _____ document.forms[0].superSecretInformation.value
   d) _____ documents on your hard drive

4) Which of the following is not a drawback of client-side code?

   a) _____ It can be disabled by the user.
   b) _____ It responds faster to user input.
   c) _____ It may not work in every browser.
   d) _____ It is limited to performing only safe actions.

Quiz answers appear in the Appendix, Section 9.2.

LAB 9.3

COMBINING CLIENT-SIDE AND SERVER-SIDE SCRIPTING

LAB OBJECTIVES
After this lab, you will be able to:
- Combine Server-Side and Client-Side Logic
- Explain How Cookies Are Both Client- and Server-Side Objects

There are quite a few areas where either server-side code or client-side code has a distinct advantage. Client-side code can access form variables before a form has been submitted, while server-side code can only access form variables after the form is submitted. Server-side code has access to database queries, while client-side code cannot run queries at all. The obvious conclusion is to not choose between using one or using the other, but to use both. Combining server-side code with client-side logic can provide a powerful (and highly functional) browsing environment for visitors to your site (or for users of your Web application, if you prefer to think of them that way).

Form validation has been the ongoing example, so it may pay to revisit the process. We have seen drawbacks to doing validation on either side, but doing it in both places is by far the most functional approach. The quick responses from client-side checking are great, but we can't rely exclusively on client-side checking before inserting information into the database. Consequently, we can implement our slick client-side checking, but also add an additional level of last-chance data validation on the server-side before we do any database inserts. This provides a base level of required functionality while simultaneously providing an additional level of desirable functionality. A Web site designed to use JavaScript for handy but not mission-critical uses is said to degrade gracefully.

Server-side scripting can also be combined more closely with client-side code. For example, a server-side script can write JavaScript into a Web page, dynamically adding variables and parameters. These values may be the results of a query or of some other process that JavaScript itself may not be able to execute. If the idea of writing code that writes code makes your head spin, don't worry: It's just like writing regular code, only doubly so. In any case, using server-side code to write client-side code is a relatively painless way to get the best of both worlds.

There are also times when the two areas overlap. Form validation is a typical gray area that can be done by client-side code, server-side code, or by both. Cookies are a similar gray area. Client-side code can set (and read) cookies, and most server-side languages support cookies as well (exactly how that is done depends on the language). Setting and reading cookies more or less simultaneously at both ends is not a good programming practice: It is very easy get into what is called a "race condition," where the programmer ends up hoping the server-side code gets a cookie set before some client-side code checks its value, or vice versa. Cookies have fairly limited uses—a problem compounded by the fact that users can choose to not accept them—but it deserves to be noted that client-side and server-side code can share data via cookies.

LAB 9.3 EXERCISES

9.3.1 COMBINE SERVER-SIDE AND CLIENT-SIDE LOGIC

Passing variables and values from server-side code to client-side code is one of the challenges to combining the two. Whenever one performs validation (or any processing) on a value, there needs to be a way to pass the result to code on "the other side."

    a) Name two ways to get a value from server-side logic to client-side code.

_____

_____

    b) Name two ways to get a value from client-side logic to server-side code.

_____

_____

Lab 9.3: Combining Client-Side and Server-Side Scripting

9.3.2 EXPLAIN HOW COOKIES ARE BOTH CLIENT- AND SERVER-SIDE OBJECTS

a) How do you set a cookie using client-side code?

b) How do you set a cookie using server-side code?

c) How can client-side code and server-side code use cookies to share data?

LAB 9.3 EXERCISE ANSWERS

9.3.1 ANSWERS

a) Name two ways to get a value from server-side logic to client-side code.

Answer: The easiest way to feed server-side variables to client-side code is to output the values right into the client-side code. If you needed to give some JavaScript access to values from a recordset, for example, you could write a server-side loop that looped through the recordset, declaring JavaScript variables with names and values equal to those in the server-side recordset.

Alternatively, you could use cookies to store the information, and then access the cookie's value later with client-side code.

b) Name two ways to get a value from client-side logic to server-side code.

Answer: Passing variables from client-side code to server-side code is trickier. It almost always involves sending a request to the server. You can use client-side code to generate the target URL, passing variable values in the page's URL (remember to encode them first, or unpredictable results may occur). The server-side code will be able to pull the variables out of the URL and decode them. Alternatively, you can use client-side code to set values in hidden text fields on a form. When the form is submitted, server-side code will have access to all the form fields. This is especially sneaky, since forms need not be submitted with a big gray "submit" button: They can be submitted by any client-side action (loading a page, leaving a page, clicking on something, mousing over something, etc.), and the variable values you pass won't show up in the target page's URL (assuming you submit the form with a POST command and not with a GET).

You can also use cookies to pass data from client-side to server-side.

9.3.2 ANSWERS

a) How do you set a cookie using client-side code?

Answer: It's easy. Here's an example in JavaScript:

```
function SetCookie (name,value,expires,path,domain,secure)
{
  document.cookie = name + "=" + escape (value) +
    ((expires) ? "; expires=" + expires.toGMTString() :
    "") +
    ((path) ? "; path=" + path : "") +
    ((domain) ? "; domain=" + domain : "") +
    ((secure) ? "; secure" : "");
}
```

Okay, so maybe that wasn't the easiest thing in the world, but it's easier now than ever before, thanks to a swell guy named Bill Dortch. Mr. Dortch has written a comprehensive set of cookie-related functions (setting them, getting them, and making them work across browsers and platforms). This code is freely available at http://www.hidaho.com/cookies/cookie.txt. The above function is an example of his immaculate JavaScript.

b) How do you set a cookie using server-side code?

Answer: It depends on the language.

Here's an approach in VBScript:

```
<SCRIPT language=VBScript>
    document.cookie="foo=bar; path=/; expires Mon, 01-Jan-
    2001 00:00:00 GMT"
</SCRIPT>
```

To set a cookie with Perl is even easier. You just write the cookie into a document header:

```
Content-type: text/html
Set-Cookie: foo=bar; path=/; expires=Mon, 01-Jan-2001
00:00:00 GMT
```

And here's how it's done in Cold Fusion:

```
<cfcookie name="foo" value="bar" path="/"
expires="1/1/2001">
```

c) How can client-side code and server-side code use cookies to share data?

Answer: Server-side code can set cookies that client-side code can access and vice versa. It's pretty straightforward, really.

The Whole Truth About Sharing Cookies

The concept of cookie sharing is extremely straightforward, but the actual implementation may not be. As you start working with cookies, you may discover some quirks in individual cookie implementations. Don't plan on sharing data between client-side and server-side code via cookies without allowing yourself some serious debugging time. Each server-side scripting language handles cookies a little differently. Client-side code always varies greatly in implementation details, and cookies are unfortunately no exception. Expect to find incompatibilities between cookies written on different systems and by different browsers. You may even find that your server-side code is unable to read cookies set by client-side code in some browsers but has no problem with cookies set through other browsers.

LAB 9.3 SELF-REVIEW QUESTIONS

In order to test your progress, you should be able to answer the following questions.

1) Can client-side code set server-side variables?

   a) _____ Yes, any time
   b) _____ No, never
   c) _____ Not without a trip to the server
   d) _____ Only with a cookie

2) Can server-side code set client-side variables?

   a) _____ Yes, anytime
   b) _____ No, never
   c) _____ Only before the page loads
   d) _____ Only after the page submits to the server

3) How can you set and get cookies?

    a) _____ Only with client-side code
    b) _____ Only with server-side code
    c) _____ Only with Mrs. Field's help
    d) _____ Only with the user's browser's permission

4) You have set a client-side variable with server-side code, and then you change that variable's value with client-side logic. When can your server-side code find out the variable's new value?

    a) _____ As soon as the variable's value changes
    b) _____ As soon as the client sends the variable to the server
    c) _____ As soon as the client sets a cookie
    d) _____ The server-side code will never find out

5) You want to error-check a form and would like to minimize the amount of time the user spends waiting. You do your checking:

    a) _____ Client-side
    b) _____ Server-side
    c) _____ Both client-side and server-side
    d) _____ Neither place, the database can handle the error checking

Quiz answers appear in the Appendix, Section 9.3.

CHAPTER 9

TEST YOUR THINKING

1) Select a server-side programming/scripting language that sounds interesting to you. Research and install whatever software you will need to write and run your own scripts locally. Next, perform a Web search to find pages that provide online tutorials of the language you have chosen. Skim a tutorial or two, find some code samples, read them, and run them. Understanding sample code is the fastest way to get you started writing your own code.

2) Perform another Web search, this time looking for sites that feature free cross-browser client-side code. Writing cross-browser compatible code is difficult, but it's not hard to find dedicated and talented individuals on the Web who have mastered some of the intricacies of writing cross-browser compatible JavaScript. Skim through a script or two. Note how the authors perform a browser check early on and then store information about the visitor's browser (and Document Object Model) for use later. See if you can adapt any of their code to situations you may be facing. In the interest of providing a consistent viewing experience for your visitors, it's always good form to code for multiple browsers and platforms.

   Conservatively speaking, how many different browser types do you need to check for to ensure your JavaScript's cross-browser compatibility?

   If you were going to aggressively pursue complete cross-browser compatibility for your client-side code, how many different Document Object Models would you have to account for?

3) Practice setting and retrieving cookies using whatever means you prefer.
   a) If you set a cookie with an expiration date in the past, how long will that cookie last?
   b) If you set a cookie with a path of "/admin," what limitations does that place on code that tries to access that cookie? What about a path of a path of "/"?
   c) If you set a cookie from a machine called "one.mydomain.com," how will that affect your attempts to retrieve the cookie from that machine? How will it affect your attempts to retrieve the cookie from "two.mydomain.com"? What happens if you explicitly set the cookie's domain equal to "mydomain.com"?

CHAPTER 10

PROGRAMMING AND SCRIPTING SECURITY ISSUES

An error gracefully acknowledged is a victory won.
—Caroline L. Gascoigne

CHAPTER OBJECTIVES

In this chapter, you will learn about:

- Security Tradeoffs — Page 278
- The Importance of Validating User Input — Page 283
- User versus Webmaster Scripting — Page 290

Good security is an integral part of Web development. Server uptime is a crucial part of maintaining a Web presence, and lax security is the shortest path to long server downtimes. It is no longer simply enough to write a useful Web application. There are security considerations to every piece of functionality you build into a Web application. Expecting the unexpected is essential for anyone building a publicly accessible Web site. More than anyone else, Webmasters need to be aware of what constitutes a secure application design. There is functionality that is appropriate to secure intranets, and there is functionality that is appropriate to expose to the entire world. This chapter will teach you how to tell the difference between the two.

LAB 10.1

SECURITY TRADEOFFS

> **LAB OBJECTIVES**
>
> After this lab, you will be able to:
>
> ✔ Identify Potential Security Threats
> ✔ Find a Balance Between Restrictive and Functional

There are tradeoffs to running a Web server. You are essentially inviting the entire world to come and visit your server. It's almost like inviting strangers into your home. You cannot assume, under any circumstances, that all of your visitors will behave themselves. Perhaps you stash your best wines under the bed, or maybe you hide everything that isn't nailed down. The choice is up to you. The more you let your visitors do, the happier they will be (but the more trouble they can cause). Really, you want to be sure that your visitors have a good time without being able to cause any trouble while visiting.

Opening your server to the world is both a testament to the quality of your Web application and a vote of confidence in your security precautions. There is a direct relationship between the amount of functionality you provide and the amount of security you will need to implement. The more you allow your visitor to do, the more security precautions you need to take. The converse of this is also true: Less functionality means less vulnerability to attack.

The key is finding a balance between the security you need and the functionality you want. If you can restrict a server to just performing the minimum amount of required functionality, you can minimize the risk of your server being compromised.

Lab 10.1 Exercises

10.1.1 Identify Potential Security Threats

a) Every service you run on your server creates a potential vulnerability. Name three common services and a way each can be compromised.

b) What are your server's default security settings?

10.1.2 Find a Balance Between Restrictive and Functional

More functionality means less security (the reverse is also true). With that in mind, answer the following questions:

a) How do you make a server perfectly secure?

b) How can you ensure that your visitors don't access any services other than those you specifically allow?

c) As you develop your site, it will become clear which functionality you need to implement. What are some ways you can ensure the security of the software you run?

LAB 10.1 EXERCISE ANSWERS

10.1.1 ANSWERS

a) Every service you run on your server creates a potential vulnerability. Name three common services and a way each can be compromised.

Answer: If you run a mail server on your site, then you need to make sure that users aren't using your server to send unsolicited emails ("spam") to others. If you provide FTP access to your users (or just for yourself), you need to make sure that you have left no world-writable directories unsecured by a password (the last thing you need is a gang of software pirates using your server to trade gigabytes of pirated applications). If you run a Web server, you need to ensure that the Web server can't be compromised, giving a remote attacker control of your computer (for more information about running a secure Web server, see Lab 10.2 in Web Servers, Security, and Maintenance). If you're running SENDMAIL, just be aware that you're running one of the most often-exploited pieces of code in the history of the Internet. If your server allows telnet access, you'd better make sure your telnet server is secure. If you're running a remote-access tool like PCAnywhere, VNC, Remotely Possible, or others, you had better have some kind of secondary protection (like a firewall), so the entire world isn't able to try to get control of your server.

b) What are your server's default security settings?

Answer: That depends on what operating system you run, and on what server you're running. It's probably worth noting, in the interest of security, that Microsoft Windows NT defaults new directories to "Full Control" (readable and writable) and IIS under Windows defaults new FTP site roots to "Writable."

10.1.2 ANSWERS

a) How do you make a server perfectly secure?

Answer: The most secure setup for a server is off and unplugged, alone in a bunker in Fort Knox. If you're really feeling paranoid, you can shield the entire bunker in lead and encase the computer in a concrete-filled steel drum first. This is, of course, a completely useless server. That is the tradeoff for having a completely secure server.

There is another potential tradeoff for a secure setup, of course: money. A large cash expenditure will get you a server setup that meets all sorts of government standards for secure computing. There are actually security ratings that require the presence of an armed guard in the room where the computer is being assembled. If you want more in-

formation about extreme network security, there is an excellent summary of various security books (essentially the Cliff Notes to the "rainbow series" of security specifications) available online at http://www.c4i.org/ntob.html.

b) How can you ensure that your visitors don't access any services other than those you specifically allow?

Answer: A firewall is the quickest and easiest way to ensure that your visitors can't access any parts of your server that they aren't welcome to access. Servers listen at different ports for incoming client requests. A firewall can be placed between the server and the Internet and configured to restrict inbound traffic to only those ports you want your users to be able to access. If you don't want anyone to be able to access, say, the telnet server, you can tell the firewall to ignore all traffic bound for the telnet port (port 21, if you're interested). You could also just shut down your telnet server. That's even more secure, but less useful. If you want a few trusted individuals to be able to telnet to your server, you can configure the firewall to allow those individuals to connect to any port you trust them to. That would be more functional, but—as always—less secure, because an attacker could masquerade as a trusted individual to gain access to your system.

c) As you develop your site, it will become clear which functionality you need to implement. What are some ways you can ensure the security of the software you run?

Answer: You could always write your own software. Then you'll know exactly how secure it is. Otherwise, there is a growing amount of software on the market that prides itself on being both secure and functional. You can find server software that will provide both functionality and security, but it will usually cost lots of money (unless it's free, of course). Once you choose a piece of software, you must keep an eye out for advisories concerning potential vulnerabilities in your new software. CERT (www.cert.org) is an invaluable source of security advisories. Remember: You're in trouble if the bad guys find out about your site's vulnerabilities before you do.

Practical, useful implementations of secure servers are never static. An admin who strives for complete security must constantly stay informed of developments in the security field. Security holes are constantly being found and patched in the world's most secure software. To find a secure server solution that meets your company's needs, it pays to read more than the vendor's information. Check security Web sites, mailing lists, and publications for information on limitations (and known holes) in various pieces of software. For more information on finding and using online security resources, see Lab 8.3 of Administrating Web Servers, Security, & Maintenance.

Lab 10.1 Self-Review Questions

In order to test your progress, you should be able to answer the following questions.

1) You just added a mail service to your server. Your server is now:

   a) _____ Just as functional and more secure
   b) _____ More functional but less secure
   c) _____ Less functional and more secure
   d) _____ Just as functional but less secure

2) You just installed a firewall between your server and the Internet. Your server is now:

   a) _____ Just as functional and more secure
   b) _____ More functional but less secure
   c) _____ Less functional and more secure
   d) _____ Just as functional but less secure

3) You've configured your Web server to only respond to requests on port 80 (the standard HTTP request port). Your server is now:

   a) _____ Functional enough and more secure than before
   b) _____ Functional enough but less secure than before
   c) _____ Useless

4) You discover that your server's security has been compromised. What do you do first?

   a) _____ Turn the server off before it happens again.
   b) _____ Install a firewall immediately.
   c) _____ Check the server's logs and figure out how it happened.
   d) _____ Fire the person in charge of security. It must have been an inside job.

Quiz answers appear in the Appendix, Section 10.1.

LAB 10.2

THE IMPORTANCE OF VALIDATING USER INPUT

> **LAB OBJECTIVES**
>
> After this lab, you will be able to:
>
> ✔ Examine User Input
> ✔ Prevent Users from Entering HTML
> ✔ Filter Out Malicious SQL Code

When creating an application prototype on a tight schedule, it can be easy to forget about things like error checking and input validation. Too often the focus is on functionality, rather than robustness. Robustness is key, however, when building a Web application for a production environment. Application robustness can come in many forms. For example, coding for an intranet is easier than coding a site the whole world will hit. On an intranet, you can presume that your visitors will all be relatively well behaved. Consequently, the only thing you need to worry about is input validation: making sure the user hasn't left any required fields blank, put letters into a number box, left digits out of a phone number, and so on. If the user makes an error, the application should respond with some sort of helpful error message, not with an application error. For intranets, the key is to expect the unexpected and code accordingly.

When writing an application that is to be made available to the whole world, programmers must recognize and deal with another problem: identifying and ignoring malicious input. For example, back in the early days of the World Wide Web, there were some individuals (the author included) who enjoyed visiting Web sites' guest books. When leaving a note or a signature, it was usually possible to enter an HTML tag or two as well. This author's favorite happened to be the <blink> tag. By opening a blink tag in the page's HTML, everything between the opening <blink> and the closing </html> (because there was no closing </blink> tag) would begin to blink on and off. This was simultaneously annoying, amusing, and easy. It was also harmless. Well, mostly harmless.

Internet Explorer no longer supports the <blink> tag, but there is no shortage of other text that a user can slip into your page to give you grief. Users may try to insert style tags (<H1> is notoriously big and ugly), hyperlinks (which you may or may not want to allow), client-side JavaScript (pop-up windows, alert boxes, redirects, and more), and even calls to malicious ActiveX controls. Or they may just choose to insert profanity into what is supposed to be a family-friendly Web site. In all of these cases, it is up to the programmer to filter potentially objectionable content out of the user's input before it causes a problem anywhere else.

LAB 10.2 EXERCISES

10.2.1 EXAMINE USER INPUT

a) You want to make sure a user has entered a valid number into a phone number box. What defines a valid phone number?

b) Let's suppose you want to make sure that no inappropriate language is used in a discussion board. Should you check the user's post before they submit it, when you save it, or when you display it? Why?

10.2.2 PREVENT USERS FROM ENTERING HTML

a) Where is the best place to make sure there is no malicious HTML embedded in the user input?

Lab 10.2: The Importance of Validating User Input

b) What is the easiest way to ensure that no HTML is snuck into an application like a guestbook or a threaded discussion?

c) What are some HTML tags that could be benign enough to allow into a user's posts on a message board? What are some that should definitely not be allowed?

10.2.3 FILTER OUT MALICIOUS SQL CODE

Inserting a blink tag to make an entire page blink is malicious, but does no permanent damage. Unfortunately, there are other ways a user can cripple your application with malformed (or just malicious) input. If the site has a database back end (SQL is just one option, but it's the example we'll use here) and the application generates dynamic queries on database, then the entire application is vulnerable to attack. The only databases vulnerable to this type of attack are those implementations that allow multiple SQL statements to be separated by a semicolon. If this feature is available and enabled (it may be enabled by default), some serious fireworks can ensue. Imagine that your application dynamically generates the following query based on user input:

```
SELECT * from users where username = 'bob'
```

a) Where does the string "bob" come from?

b) Pretend to be a malicious hacker for a moment. You know that you may be able to add a SQL query after the first one, and you're fairly sure that the Web application's list of users is stored in a table named "users." You also suspect that there is a field in that table called "username." Given that information, what can you type into the "username" form field to delete every user but yourself?

c) How can you protect your Web applications from attacks of this kind?

LAB 10.2 EXERCISE ANSWERS

10.2.1 ANSWERS

a) You want to make sure a user has entered a valid number into a phone number box. What defines a valid phone number?

Answer: A valid phone number should be 12 characters long, with no letters. It should have three numbers, a dash, three more numbers, a dash, and four more numbers.

Or should it? The user might enter the area code in parentheses. That would make the number 13 characters long. Or there might be periods instead of dashes. Or it might be an international number with an international dialing code (or an unusual number of digits). When validating a phone number, about the only thing you can count on is that the number probably shouldn't contain any letters.

b) Let's suppose you want to make sure that no inappropriate language is used in a discussion board. Should you check the user's post before they submit it, when you save it, or when you display it?

Answer: A client-side check for profanity would appear in the page's source code. That means that all the words you don't want your users to see would be in the source, and would also be picked up by search engines. You probably don't want a string of profanity in the source code of your Web page, so consider a server-side check, preferably one that runs before the information is inserted into the database. An insert only happens once, but the information could be retrieved numerous times. It will save processing power if you only have to check the string once, on insert.

10.2.2 ANSWERS

a) Where is the best place to make sure there is no malicious HTML embedded in the user input?

Answer: It's probably best to do this with server-side code, especially if you're trying to stop people from entering malicious code. A client-side check would be visible in the source code, and your attacker could easily see what was being blocked (and thus could figure out what wasn't being blocked). A server-side check is more secure.

b) What is the easiest way to ensure that no HTML is snuck into an application like a guestbook or a threaded discussion?

Answer: Remove all of the opening HTML brackets ("<") in the string. Better still, replace them with the escaped HTML equivalent, "<". If you just removed all "<" tags from the input string, that would mangle input like "5 < 9" and I'm sad: ":-<". Conveniently, most scripting languages have a string replace function, and Cold Fusion even has a built-in function to escape HTML for you (HTMLEditFormat). Without that opening bracket, any HTML the user enters will be visible, but not executed by the browser, protecting your site (and your viewers) from any malicious HTML.

c) What are some HTML tags that could be benign enough to allow into a user's posts on a message board? What are some that should definitely not be allowed?

Answer: <A> (anchor) tags are probably okay. Your users will appreciate the ability to include hyperlinks in their posts. You might also consider allowing formatting tags like <font>, <em> (emphasis), and <b> (bold), unless you plan on strictly enforcing your own styles and formatting. Script blocks, applets, and object tags are all definitely dangerous enough to warrant stripping them out of a user's post before displaying it.

10.2.3 ANSWERS

a) Where does the string "bob" come from?

Answer: The user enters it into a form field on a Web page. The form field might be called "username."

b) Pretend to be a malicious hacker for a moment. You know that you may be able to add a SQL query after the first one, and you're fairly sure that the Web application's list of users is stored in a table named "users." You also suspect that there is a field in that table called "username." Given that information, what can you type into the "username" form field to delete every user but yourself?

Answer: All you have to do is to enter your username as

```
bob' ; delete from users where username <> 'bob
```

If you note the use of single quotes, you can see that they will line up correctly when inserted into the query string in the very same place that the programmer expected nothing but a username. It'll only work sometimes, but it can cripple an application (and destroy a database) when it works. Make sure it doesn't work on your site.

c) How can you protect your Web applications from attacks of this kind?

Answer: First, make sure your database server does not allow multiple statements per query. Then add checks to all your inputs. Make sure that all numeric fields contain nothing but numbers. Make sure text fields don't contain any numbers. Escape out any illegal characters that could be used to control the database server, the Web server, the script interpreter, or the Web page that displays the input.

LAB 10.2 SELF-REVIEW QUESTIONS

In order to test your progress, you should be able to answer the following questions.

1) Which of the following is true of user input?

   a) _____ It is more predictable on an intranet.
   b) _____ It is more predictable on the Internet.
   c) _____ You never know what you're going to get.
   d) _____ People never make mistakes.

2) Where can you run code to validate user input?

   a) _____ Only server-side
   b) _____ Only client-side
   c) _____ Both client and server-side
   d) _____ Neither place

3) When building an intranet application, you need to be:

   a) _____ More concerned about malicious input
   b) _____ Less concerned about malicious input
   c) _____ More concerned about friendly error messages
   d) _____ Less concerned about friendly error messages

4) Which of the following should be filtered out of a discussion board post?

   a) _____ <A HREF="...">
   b) _____ <SCRIPT>
   c) _____ <B>
   d) _____ <BLINK>

5) How can you best protect your database from malicious SQL that a user might enter?

    a) _____ Make sure number fields aren't left blank.
    b) _____ Make sure text fields only contain letters.
    c) _____ Don't allow any semicolons in user input.
    d) _____ Configure your SQL server correctly.

Quiz answers appear in the Appendix, Section 10.2.

LAB 10.3

USER VERSUS WEBMASTER SCRIPTING

> **LAB OBJECTIVES**
>
> After this lab, you will be able to:
>
> ✔ Identify Web Applications That Are Both Fun and Safe
> ✔ Identify Web Applications That Are Useful but Dangerous

Some Web-based applications are large and complex, while others fit two and three to a page. There are many uses for a good Web-based application besides business (and e-business) solutions. There are freely available scripts to provide fun user interactions, there are custom scripts to allow Webmasters to monitor server statistics, and there are a whole variety of custom scripts that automate just about every computing process under the sun. Whether you are evaluating a free script, planning on buying one, or thinking of writing your own, it is important to think about the ways that running this code will impact the security of your site.

If you are a Webmaster, you will need to know what "fun" scripts you can safely allow your users to run on your server. Similarly, if you are a user who wants to add functionality to your Web page without annoying the Webmaster or server admin, then you too need to know what kinds of programs you can and cannot run. Programs that require database access to function properly generally require more of the Webmaster's attention, and programs that write to a database require even more attention.

In addition to having the power to veto user applications, the Webmaster needs to pick and choose which administrative-level programs, services, and applications can run safely on the server. This includes custom scripts that are designed to give the server administrator remote control over the server. Understandably, these programs create a more significant security concern than the user scripts. In either case, it is crucial to be able to decide what software is safe to run.

LAB 10.3 EXERCISES

10.3.1 IDENTIFY WEB APPLICATIONS THAT ARE BOTH FUN AND SAFE

a) Brainstorm some relatively harmless, relatively small server-side applications. Think of stand-alone pieces of code that you see all over the Web.

b) Which of those applications need to pull information from a database? Do any of them need to save information back to a database?

c) There are lots of different ways to provide functionality that your users can easily include on their Web pages. Not all of those ways require running server-side code. Can you name some client-side solutions that provide engaging user interaction?

10.3.2 IDENTIFY WEB APPLICATIONS THAT ARE USEFUL BUT DANGEROUS

a) As a server admin, what might you need to do to your server through a Web browser? Could you do the same from a telnet terminal or a WAP-enabled phone?

b) Exposing administrative functionality to the entire world is potentially dangerous. What are the security risks involved?

c) What are some ways you can maximize the security of Webmaster-only scripts?

LAB 10.3 EXERCISE ANSWERS

10.3.1 ANSWERS

a) Brainstorm some relatively harmless, relatively small server-side applications. Think of stand-alone pieces of code that you see all over the Web.

Answer: Guestbooks ("Please leave me a note"), personalized greetings ("Welcome back, Bob."), hit counters ("This page has been viewed 400 times"), a Magic 8-ball ("Reply hazy, ask again later"), random ads, random images, random quotes, horoscopes, fortune cookies, etc.

b) Which of those applications need to pull information from a database? Do any of them need to save information back to a database?

Answer: Guestbooks and hit counters both need to read and write to a database (or at least to a text file). A quotation or fortune-cookie type application might need to read from a database (or a text file), but shouldn't ever need to write to one.

c) There are lots of different ways to provide functionality that your users can easily include on their Web pages. Not all of those ways require running server-side code. Can you name some client-side solutions that provide engaging user interaction?

Answer: Client-side user interaction can be accomplished with applets, JavaScript, DHTML, Shockwave, Flash, Active-X controls, or even your own custom plug-in. By making it easy to add dynamic client-side elements to a Web page, a Webmaster can simultaneously impress users, as well as visitors to users' pages. In a hosting environment, this can mean the difference between being just another Web host and being a well-rounded Internet Service Provider.

10.3.2 ANSWERS

a) As a server admin, what might you need to do to your server through a Web browser? Could you do the same from a telnet terminal or a WAP-enabled phone?

Answer: Server administrators might feel a need to remotely check server uptime, performance statistics, set or reset passwords or permissions, and initiate various housekeeping processes. There may also be a need for hooks into the operating system (or scripts that can be executed by the OS) to perform network maintenance.

b) Exposing administrative functionality to the entire world is potentially dangerous. What are the security risks involved?

Answer: Worst-case scenario: An intruder gains control of your server and steals passwords, documents, and company secrets. Less than worst-case, but still really bad: someone defaces your Web site or creates and abuses FTP accounts.

Never ever expose more functionality than is required. In addition to examining what functionality you allow the entire world access to, this often means reconfiguring your Web server after installing it, because the default configuration may install administrative tools or example sites that are not safe to run in a production environment.

c) What are some ways you can maximize the security of webmaster-only scripts?

Answer: Passwords, passwords, passwords. When possible, write the code yourself, or at least check it carefully. Implement IP restrictions where feasible, so only trusted computers can access the restricted functionality. When dealing with extremely sensitive information, use encryption where appropriate.

LAB 10.3 SELF-REVIEW QUESTIONS

In order to test your progress, you should be able to answer the following questions.

1) Which of the following write to a database? Select all that apply.

   a) _____ A magic 8-ball
   b) _____ An animated .gif
   c) _____ A guestbook
   d) _____ A random quote generator

2) Which of the following requires the least attention from a webmaster?

   a) _____ A guestbook
   b) _____ A client-side applet
   c) _____ A custom Web application script
   d) _____ An application that has to run as root

Lab 10.3: User versus Webmaster Scripting

3) Which of the following poses the largest potential security threat?

   a) _____ A guestbook
   b) _____ A client-side applet
   c) _____ A custom Web application script
   d) _____ An application that has to run as root

4) Why would a Webmaster risk making server administration tools available over the Internet?

   a) _____ So hackers can break in more easily
   b) _____ So other sysadmins can copy their server configuration
   c) _____ So the Webmaster can do his or her job from anywhere in the world
   d) _____ So users can view the server's uptime statistics and memory usage

5) Which of the following will not help you create a fun client-side piece of code?

   a) _____ Applet
   b) _____ Active Server Pages
   c) _____ DHTML
   d) _____ JavaScript

Quiz answers appear in the Appendix, Section 10.3.

CHAPTER 10

TEST YOUR THINKING

1) If you have access to a Web server, try to find out what permissions the Web server is running with. What directories does it have access to? Is it allowed to write files? Can it read from files? Can it create files? Can it create files anywhere? Why is the Web server restricted to low-privilege accounts? Why not just run a Web server as root (or administrator on a Windows machine)?

2) Running additional services on a server increases the probability of security holes. This holds true for Web scripting interpreters as well.

   a) Find the Web page for the Web scripting solution you are currently running (or thinking about running). Have there been any recent updates to the application? Do you need to install any patches or hot fixes? Is there a new version coming out any time soon? Will your old code be backwards compatible with the newer version?

   b) Keep in mind that you may need to look outside of the company Web site to learn everything you need to know about your scripting solution. Try searching the Web for additional information. Are there any outstanding security issues that have not yet been addressed by the vendor? Odds are the vendor won't tell you if there are. Have there been any contests to see if hackers can break into a server running the software that you're interested in? Did anyone win the prize money in that contest?

CHAPTER 11

SCRIPTING LANGUAGE EVOLUTION

If you have built castles in the air, your work need not be lost; that is where they should be. Now put foundations under them.
—Henry David Thoreau

CHAPTER OBJECTIVES

In this chapter, you will learn about:

- ASP — Page 298
- Cold Fusion — Page 305
- PHP — Page 313
- Language Evolution — Page 323

There came a time in the early days of the Web when static content was no longer enough for programmers at the cutting edge of the Web. Data can change too quickly and information moves too fast to be captured effectively in a handcrafted, static HTML page. That's why dynamic page content has become a necessity. Plus, hooking one dynamic Web page up to a database with a million entries sure beats writing a million static pages. Your basic active server page does two things: It manipulates and displays data pulled dynamically from a database and it takes user input and inserts it into the database. Additionally, it may be responsible for handing data off to a compiled object for additional processing.

LAB 11.1

ASP

> **LAB OBJECTIVES**
>
> After this lab, you will be able to:
>
> ✓ Output Basic Variables
> ✓ Code a Basic If-Then Statement
> ✓ Code a While Loop

To understand Active Server Pages (ASP), it helps to first understand that the primary language—VBScript—is a subset of the Microsoft's Visual Basic programming language. If you are familiar with Microsoft Visual Basic, then picking up VBScript will be incredibly easy for you. In addition to VBScript, ASP pages can also be written in JScript or PerlScript.

ASP pages work on a very simple principle: Code is embedded into an HTML page between special tags. The server executes the code between the special tags before sending the result—pure HTML—to the browser. ASP pages can dynamically display data from any number of sources, but they most commonly display the results of database queries. ASP pages also excel at interfacing with COM objects, making and maintaining database connections, and formatting and displaying information. Large Web applications built solely in ASP often have scalability problems, however.

There have been multiple versions of ASP, all informally called "ASP." The last version to use VBScript was ASP 3.0 (a version widely used in production). Microsoft has just released ASP+, which is essentially ASP 4.0. A significant step up from the 3.0 product, ASP+ has more flexibility, more control, and better performance than its predecessor. ASP+ is also backwards compatible with ASP 3.0 code, but is no longer restricted to VBScript. ASP+ pages can be written in virtually any programming language, though Microsoft is pushing its newest language, C# ("see sharp"). Currently, ASP+ only runs under Windows 2000, while

ASP 3.0 is still natively supported by Microsoft's Web server, IIS (Internet Information Server). Microsoft basically gives away IIS, which makes for some stiff price competition for Cold Fusion (PHP is also free).

LAB 11.1 EXERCISES

11.1.1 OUTPUT BASIC VARIABLES

Create a file called test.asp in a subdirectory of the webroot of a Windows machine running IIS (available free from www.microsoft.com as part of the NT 4.0 Option pack). Enter the following text into the file, one question at a time, and answer the following questions:

a) Place the following in your file:

```
<%@ LANGUAGE="VBSCRIPT" %>
<html><body>
    <% Response.write("Hello, world!") %>
</body></html>
```

Open the page in a browser. What do you see? Why?

___

___

b) Now add a variable to that code:

```
<%@ LANGUAGE="VBSCRIPT" %>
<html><body>
    <% Dim hello
    hello = "Hello, world!"
    Response.write(hello)%>
</body></html>
```

Open the page in a browser. What do you see now? Why?

___

___

c) Now change that code again by misspelling "hello":

```
<%@ LANGUAGE="VBSCRIPT" %>
<html><body>
```

Lab 11.1: ASP

```
<% Dim hello
hello = "Hello, world!"
Response.write(helo)%>
</body></html>
```

Open the page in a browser. What do you see? Why?

_____

_____

d) Finally, change that code again by adding "option explicit":

```
<%@ LANGUAGE="VBSCRIPT" %>
<% option explicit %>
<html><body>
    <% Dim hello
hello = "Hello, world!"
Response.write(helo)%>
</body></html>
```

Open the page in a browser. What do you see? Why?

_____

_____

11.1.2 CODE A BASIC IF-THEN STATEMENT

If-then statements in any language rely heavily on Boolean values (true and false) and equality checking (equal to, greater than, less than, etc.). Using your intuition, predict the results of the following code:

a) What will this code print to the screen?

```
<% if true
    response.write("Truth is beauty.")
else
    response.write("Beauty is truth.")
end if %>
```

_____

_____

Lab 11.1: ASP

b) What will this code print to the screen? How is this code different from the preceding code? Which do you prefer?

```
<% if 0 %>
    The truth is out there.
<% else %>
    You can't handle the truth.
<% end if %>
```

11.1.3 CODE A WHILE LOOP

a) What is the output of the following code?

```
<% For myCounter = 1 to 5 %>
<% =myCounter %> Mississippi, %>
<% Next %>
```

b) Let's change that code slightly:

```
<% For myCounter = 2 to 8 STEP 2 %>
<%= myCounter %>,
<% Next %>
<% response.write(" who do we appreciate?") %>
```

What will this code output? Why?

c) Loops can also be done coded using the VBScript "do while … loop" instruction:

```
<% myCounter = 0
Do While myCounter < 5
response.write(myCounter & "one thousand, ")
myCounter = myCounter +1
Loop %>
```

Lab 11.1: ASP

What will this code output? Why?

_____

_____

LAB 11.1 EXERCISE ANSWERS

11.1.1 ANSWERS

a) Open the page in a browser. What do you see? Why?

Answer: You should see the words "Hello, world!" in your browser window. If you see anything other than that phrase, check your test.asp file for typos and check your IIS installation for problems.

b) Open the page in a browser. What do you see now? Why?

Answer: You should see the same thing: "Hello world!" The "Dim" operator creates (or "dimensions") a variable (VBScript variables, incidentally, are not case sensitive). Then we then assign a string to that variable (variables in VBScript are not typed by default, you can throw anything at a variable, and it will hold it for you) and output it.

If you find "response.write(myVariable)" to be too much to type every time you want to output a variable, you can use a shortened form: "<%= myVariable%>" accomplishes the same thing with less typing.

c) Now change that code again by misspelling "hello." Open the page in a browser. What do you see? Why?

Answer: You don't see anything. As you might have guessed, the interpreter isn't smart enough to figure out that "helo" is actually supposed to be "hello." ASP is a scripting language, not a spell checker. Instead, your code just ignores the error and skips over it (technically, it creates a variable names "helo" and assumes that it contains no data). This is actually sort of inconvenient, since you might want to get an error message in a situation like this.

d) Finally change that code again by adding "option explicit." Open the page in a browser. What do you see? Why?

Answer: Now you see a useful error message informing you that "helo" has not been defined. Adding "option explicit" to the top of an ASP page is good programming practice. In fact, as we saw in the previous example, it's almost required. As an added bonus, pages that include the "option explicit" call will execute faster than those that don't.

11.1.2 ANSWERS

a) What will this code print to the screen?

Answer: This code will write "Truth is beauty." to the screen. VBScript will accept true, "true", 1, and "1" as positive Boolean values, and false, "false", 0, and "0" as negative Boolean values. In this case true is true, so we execute the first part of the if statement.

b) What will this code print to the screen? How is this code different from the preceding code? Which do you prefer?

Answer: This code will write "You can't handle the truth." to the screen. Because VBScript evaluates zero as a false Boolean statement. The difference between this example and the previous one is in the VBScript brackets. The example in question a was entirely enclosed in one set of script brackets, necessitating the use of response.write calls to output our text to the Web page. In this example, we close the brackets between VBScript statements, allowing us to display HTML without having to explicitly output it. This simple shortcut can save the programmer lots of time (and substantially reduce the number of "response.write" statements needed in a page).

11.1.3 ANSWERS

a) What is the output of the following code?

Answer: Your output should look something like this: "1 Mississippi, 2 Mississippi, 3 Mississippi, 4 Mississippi, 5 Mississippi,".

For loops are best used when you need to perform a task (or series of tasks) a fixed number of times. If you are not sure how many times you will need to repeat the task, a while loop is more appropriate.

b) What will this code output?

Answer: "2, 4, 6, 8, who do we appreciate?" The "STEP" command causes the variable to increment by 2 (or by whatever value you specify) instead of the default increment of one.

c) What will this code output?

Answer: The code will output: "1 one thousand, 2 one thousand, 3 one thousand, 4 one thousand, 5 one thousand,". Note the use of a string concatenator ("&") to append the variable's value to the string "one thousand,".

VBScript has several other ways to create a loop: There is a "do until ... loop" (which is just a negative form of the "do while" loop), a "do ... loop until" (which will always run at least once because it does its conditional check after running through the loop) and a "while ... wend" loop (the least flexible of all the loops, this simple checks a Boolean condition at the beginning of the loop, and executes the loop until that condition is no longer true).

LAB 11.1 SELF-REVIEW QUESTIONS

In order to test your progress, you should be able to answer the following questions.

1) VBScript variable names are case-sensitive.

   a) _____ True
   b) _____ False

2) ASP+ requires you to use VBScript.

   a) _____ True
   b) _____ False

3) Specifying "option explicit" in your page will make ASP:

   a) _____ Correct your spelling errors
   b) _____ Ignore variables that haven't been declared
   c) _____ Complain about variables that haven't been declared
   d) _____ Run more slowly

4) Which of the following is equivalent to "<% Response.write(hello) %>"?

   a) _____ <% Document.write("hello") %>
   b) _____ <% Response.write("hello") %>
   c) _____ hello
   d) _____ <%= hello %>

Quiz answers appear in the Appendix, Section 11.1.

LAB 11.2

COLD FUSION

> **LAB OBJECTIVES**
>
> After this lab, you will be able to:
> - Output Variables
> - Code a Basic If-Then Statement
> - Code a Loop

Cold Fusion is a server-side interpreted language with a twist: It's entirely tag-based. Your server-side code will look just like regular HTML, only with the addition of some new tags. These tags are relatively easy to distinguish from standard HTML tags because they all begin with the letters "cf." When a user tries to access your Cold Fusion pages, the Cold Fusion server will parse the text file, find the CF tags, evaluate the code contained in those tags, and then write pure HTML to the user's browser. No Cold Fusion tags are ever sent to the user's browser.

Cold Fusion tags are closed exactly the same way as HTML tags: Just as every <html> has a matching </html>, almost every Cold Fusion tag has a matching closing tag.

■ FOR EXAMPLE

- The <cfoutput> tag will always have a corresponding </cfoutput> tag.
- The <cfif> tag will always have a corresponding </cfif> tag.

As the careful reader may have noticed, *almost* every tag in Cold Fusion has a closing tag. Every language, whether spoken or coded, has exceptions to the rules, and Cold Fusion is no exception.

FOR EXAMPLE

- The <cfset> tag needs no closing tag, since it acts as an assignment operator.
- The <cfabort> tag also needs no closing tag, since it unconditionally aborts server-side processing of the page. Even if there were a closing tag, it would never, ever be executed.

LAB 11.2 EXERCISES

11.2.1 OUTPUT VARIABLES

Create a file called test.cfm in a subdirectory of the Web root of a machine running Cold Fusion Server (a free demo is available from www.allaire.com). Enter the following text into the file, one question at a time, and answer the following questions:

a) Place the following in your file:

```
<html><body>
    <cfset hello = "Hello, world!">
    <cfoutput>#hello#</cfoutput>
</body></html>
```

Open the page in a browser. What do you see? Why?

_____

_____

b) Now change that code slightly by removing one line:

```
<html><body>
    <cfoutput>#hello#</cfoutput>
</body></html>
```

Open the page in a browser. What do you see now? Why?

_____

_____

c) Now change that code one more time:

```
<html><body>
    <cfoutput>hello</cfoutput>
</body></html>
```

Open the page in a browser. What do you see? Why?

d) What do you suppose you would do if you wanted to output an actual pound sign ("#") from inside a <cfoutput> block?

11.2.2 CODE A BASIC IF-THEN STATEMENT

If-then statements in any language rely heavily on Boolean values (true and false) and equality checking (equal to, greater than, less than, etc.). Cold Fusion is no exception.

a) What will this code print to the screen?

```
<cfif true>
    Truth is beauty.
<cfelse>
    Beauty is truth.
</cfif>
```

b) What will this code print to the screen?

```
<cfif 0>
    The truth is out there.
<cfelse>
    You can't handle the truth.
</cfif>
```

c) Cold Fusion has some strange mathematical operators. You use "GT" for "greater than," "LT" for "less than," and "EQ" for "equals." Again, using your intuition, what do you suppose "LTE" and "GTE" stand for?

11.2.3 CODE A LOOP

Now that you know a little about <cfset> and <cfif>, let's add in <cfloop>. To complete part a, you will need to know that cfloop can take an argument called "condition." When the condition evaluates to true, Cold Fusion stops looping through the loop and moves on to the next line of code.

a) Using <cfoutput>, <cfset>, and "LTE," print out all the integers from 1 to 100, each on its own line. The first line of code has been written for you.

```
<CFSET i = 0>
```

b) Cfloop can also take arguments called "from," "to," and "index." Try coding the same loop as in question a again. This time, do it without using <cfset> or "LTE."

c) Cfloop can also take an argument called "step." Rewrite your loop to count to 100 by fives (5, 10, 15, 20...).

LAB 11.2 EXERCISE ANSWERS

11.2.1 ANSWERS

a) Open the page in a browser. What do you see? Why?

Answer: You should see the words "Hello, world!" in your browser window. If you see anything other than that phrase, check your test.cfm file for typos, and check your Cold Fusion Server installation for problems.

The second line of code (the first line that isn't elementary HTML) sets a variable called "hello" equal to the string "Hello, world!" The <cfoutput> tags tell the CF Server that any word surrounded by pound signs (you may call it a number sign, a pound, a hash, a sharp, a hex, a crunch, a tic-tac-toe, a thump, a thud, or a splat, but we're talking about "#" here, and it will be called a "pound sign" from this point forward) is to be evaluated as a variable, and the value of that variable is to be written to the Web browser as text.

b) Now change that code slightly by removing one line. Open the page in a browser. What do you see now? Why?

Answer: You will see one of Cold Fusion's wonderfully helpful error messages.

When a word is surrounded by pound signs within a <cfoutput> tag, Cold Fusion assumes that word is a variable and attempts to evaluate it. In the event that the word is not a valid variable (and that is the case here, since we deleted the line that both created the variable and assigned it a value), Cold Fusion will stop processing the page so that it can inform you of your error. Unlike many, many programming languages, Cold Fusion was designed to provide helpful error messages when something goes wrong. It will tell you the line that the error is on, the file the error is in, and even attempt to suggest the possible cause of the error. This helpfulness is a double-edged sword, however, since the error message may give your site's users (and potential hackers) more information about your site's internal workings than you would prefer them to have. Consequently, the helpful error messages can be disabled for the production system.

c) Now change that code one more time. Open the page in a browser. What do you see? Why?

Answer: You see only the word "hello."

Since we've removed the pound signs around the nonvariable "hello," Cold Fusion no longer attempts to evaluate it as a variable; it simply outputs the string. In this case, the <cfoutput> tags are unnecessary. It is not necessary to enclose every string in an output tag. You will only need to use <cfoutput> tags around string you wish to write to the browser when you are outputting variables.

d) What do you suppose you would do if you wanted to output an actual pound sign ("#") from inside a <cfoutput> block?

Answer: This is a toughie. If you answered "escape it somehow," then you are on the right track. There are a variety of ways that programming languages escape special characters. To escape a pound sign in Cold Fusion (so it will be written to the Web browser), use two in a row. For example:

```
<cfoutput>we're #1!</cfoutput>
```

will throw an error, but

```
<cfoutput>we're ##1!</cfoutput>
```

will write the phrase to the browser correctly.

11.2.2 ANSWERS

a) What will this code print to the screen?

Answer: This code will write "Truth is beauty." to the screen. Cold Fusion will accept true, "true," and "yes" as positive Boolean values, and false, "false," and "no" as negative Boolean values. In this case true is true, so we execute the first part of the if statement.

b) What will this code print to the screen?

Answer: This code will write "You can't handle the truth." to the screen. To Cold Fusion, zero is equivalent to false." Conversely, any number other than zero (*** greater than zero?) is equivalent to true. This is especially handy for situations when you want to check to see if a string has a length greater than zero: `<cfif Len(myString)>` *will evaluate to true if there exists a variable named "myString" with a length of one or more. If the variable doesn't exist, you will receive an error.*

c) Cold Fusion has some unique equality and comparison operators. You use "GT" for "greater than," "LT" for "less than," and "EQ" for "equals." Again, using your intuition, what do you suppose "LTE" and "GTE" stand for?

Answer: LTE stands for "Less Than or Equal to."

GTE stands for "Greater Than or Equal to."

If you find these operators hard to remember, you can actually write out the phrases (i.e., "less than or equal to," and even "greater than or equal to") in your code. The choice is yours, but do try to be consistent, whichever technique you choose.

11.2.3 ANSWERS

a) Using <cfoutput>, <cfset>, and "LTE," print out all the integers from 1 to 100, each on its own line.

Answer: Your code should look something like this:

```
<CFSET i=i + 1>
<CFLOOP CONDITION="i LTE TO 100">
    <CFSET i=i + 1>
    <CFOUTPUT>#i#</CFOUTPUT>.<BR>
</CFLOOP>
```

This is a fairly straightforward loop, often called a "while loop." You may have seen something conceptually similar in some other programming language. You arbitrarily choose a variable to be the counter—or index—variable, set a condition that will terminate the loop, and increment (or decrement, if you prefer counting down) your index variable. Pretty straightforward, really.

b) Cfloop can also take arguments called "from," "to," and "index." Try coding the same loop as in question a again. This time, do it without using <cfset> or "LTE."

Answer: Your code might look something like this:

```
<CFLOOP from="0" to="100" index="i">
    <CFOUTPUT>#i#</CFOUTPUT>.<BR>
</CFLOOP>
```

c) Cfloop can also take an argument called "step." Rewrite your loop to count to 100 by fives (5, 10, 15, 20…).

Answer: Your code might look something like this:

```
<CFLOOP from="0" to="100" index="i" step="5">
    <CFOUTPUT>#i#</CFOUTPUT>.<BR>
</CFLOOP>
```

Wasn't that easy? Cold Fusion's developer-friendly style make it a natural choice for quick-and-dirty applications, rapid development, tight time frames, and cranking out prototypes of large projects. The overall performance, however, doesn't always compare favorably with compiled server-side objects. For rapid development, Cold Fusion can't be beat. In addition, Allaire has written a Cold Fusion coding environment (Cold Fusion Studio) that provides tips on all available tag attributes, so you'll never miss an obscure attribute.

LAB 11.2 SELF-REVIEW QUESTIONS

In order to test your progress, you should be able to answer the following questions.

1) Which major browsers support CFML (Cold Fusion Markup Language)?

   a) _____ Microsoft Internet Explorer
   b) _____ Netscape
   c) _____ Opera
   d) _____ None of the above

2) Which of the following will evaluate to true?

   a) _____ <cfif true>
   b) _____ <cfif 5>
   c) _____ <cfif "yes">
   d) _____ <cfif len("false")>
   e) _____ None of the above
   f) _____ All of the above

3) You want to check to see if a number is less than 100. Which of the following is correct Cold Fusion syntax?

   a) _____ LTE 100
   b) _____ GTE 100
   c) _____ LESS THAN 100
   d) _____ LT 101

4) You are setting a variable equal to another. Which of the following is correct Cold Fusion syntax?

   a) _____ <CFSET "foo" = bar>
   b) _____ <CFSET foo EQ "bar">
   c) _____ <CFSET foo = bar>
   d) _____ <CFSET foo = "bar">

Quiz answers appear in the Appendix, Section 11.2.

LAB 11.3

PHP

> **LAB OBJECTIVES**
>
> After this lab, you will be able to:
> - Output Basic Variables
> - Code a Basic If-Then Statement
> - Code a While Loop

PHP is another scripting language designed to process scripting code embedded within an HTML file before passing the resulting HTML on to the Web browser. The name "PHP" is a recursive acronym that stands for "PHP: Hypertext Preprocessor." Other famous recursive acronyms include "PINE" (PINE Is Not ELM) and Scott Adam's "TTP" (The TTP Project).

It is perhaps easiest to explain PHP by comparing it to other languages. PHP lines end in a semicolon, just like JavaScript. Like PERL, PHP variables begin with a dollar sign ("$"), but unlike PERL, variables may *only* begin with a dollar sign. PHP handles Boolean logic about the same way Cold Fusion does: zero, the null string, and "false" all evaluate to false, and pretty much everything else will evaluate to true.

There are times, however, when PHP is unique. For example, PHP is case-sensitive for variable names, but not for calls to built-in functions. PHP is also unique in that it has more object-oriented features than the other scripting languages we have examined. Variables can have a function-level scope, a class-level scope, or a global scope (scopes are a way of restricting access to variables based on how and where they are declared). In addition, PHP supports more C-like functionality than the other scripting languages mentioned here. For example, you can set a PHP variable equal to a pointer to another variable (if that doesn't mean anything to you, don't worry about it; it's not something that comes up every day) by including an ampersand in the assignment expression:

Lab 11.3: PHP

```
$varOne = &$varTwo
```

PHP is also noteworthy in that there are three different ways to say "equals," each with a different usage. If you have programmed before, this may not seem particularly exciting. But if you are only familiar with the standard algebraic uses of "equals," then this may take some getting used to. A single equals ("=") performs assignment (it assigns a value to a variable), Double equals ("==") does a basic equality test, and triple equals ("===") does a type *and* equality check.

One equals sign alone always performs assignments, so `if $five = 5` will always evaluate to true, regardless of the value of `$five`. In fact, it is almost always a mistake to use a single equals in an equality test. Two equals signs together do equality checking: `if "5" == 5` evaluates to true because the string "5" has the same value as the number 5, but `if "six" == 6` will evaluate to false, since the string "six" is not at all the same as the number 6. The third equality check—new to PHP4—is more rigorous: It examines the type of a variable as well as the value. In this case, `if "7" === 7` will return false, since the string "7" is not the same data type as the number 7.

LAB 11.3 EXERCISES

11.3.1 OUTPUT BASIC VARIABLES

Create a file called test.php in a subdirectory of the webroot of a machine running PHP Web server extensions (available free from www.zend.com). Enter the following text into the file, one question at a time, and answer the following questions:

a) Place the following in your file:

```
<html><body>
<?php echo "Hello, world!"; ?>
</body></html>
```

Open the page in a browser. What do you see? Why?

---

b) Now let's try a variation on that code:

```
<html><body>
<script language="php">
```

```
    echo "Hello, world!";
</script>
</body></html>
```

Open the page in a browser. What do you see now? Which style of coding do you prefer?

c) Now replace that code with the following:

```
<html><body>
<?php $hello = "Hello, world!"; ?>
<?php print $hello; ?>
</body></html>
```

Open the page in a browser. What do you see? Why?

d) Finally, replace that code with the following:

```
<html><body>
<?php $hello = "Hello, world!"; ?>
<?= $hello; ?>
</body></html>
```

Open the page in a browser. What do you see? Why?

e) PHP has stringent requirements for variable names. The first letter after the dollar sign has to be a letter, and the variable name cannot contain any spaces or periods. Knowing that, which of the following are not valid PHP variables?

$one, $2, $three, $_four, $5ive, $six, $$even, $eight, nine, $ten_

11.3.2 CODE A BASIC IF-THEN STATEMENT

If-then statements in any language rely heavily on Boolean values (true and false) and equality checking (equal to, greater than, less than, etc.). Predict the results of the following code:

a) If myValue is true, what will this code print to the screen? What if myValue is false?

```
<script language="php">
    if ($myValue):
        echo "Truth is beauty.";
    else:
        echo "Beauty is truth.";
    endif;
</script>
```

b) What will this code print to the screen?

```
<script language="php">
    if (0):
        echo "The truth is out there.";
    else:
        echo "You can't handle the truth.";
    endif;
</script>
```

c) PHP has a variety of equality operators to choose from: "and," "or," "xor," "&&," "||," "&," and "|," in addition to "!" (not). Why on earth would anyone need so many ways to say "and" and "or"? What could all the different variations mean?

11.3.3 CODE A WHILE LOOP

While loops in PHP function exactly the same as while loops in C. An expression (or a group of expressions) is checked at the beginning of the loop, and if the expression evaluates to true, then the block of code contained within the loop is executed.

a) What is the output of the following while loop?

```
$counter = 99
while ($counter > 0):
    print $counter . " bottles of beer on the wall.<br>";
    print $counter-- . " bottles of beer.<br>";
    print "take one down, pass it around, ";
        print $counter . " bottles of beer.<br>";
endwhile;
```

b) What is the output of the following while loop? Why?

```
$counter = 0
while ($counter > 0):
    echo "Mom, may I have more lima beans, please?";
    $counter--;
endwhile;
```

c) What is the output of this while loop? Why? How does this loop differ from the previous example?

```
$counter = 0
do (
    echo "Mom, may I have another cookie, please?";
    $counter--;
) (while ($counter > 0);
```

LAB 11.3 EXERCISE ANSWERS

11.3.1 ANSWERS

a) Open the page in a browser. What do you see? Why?

Answer: You should see the words "Hello, world!" in your browser window. If you see anything other than that phrase, check your test.php file for typos and check your PHP installation for problems.

The second line of code (the first line that isn't elementary HTML) does a simple PHP echo. That is, it writes the string you specify into the text of the Web page. Admittedly, hard-coding strings to echo isn't any faster than just writing them into the HTML by hand, but as we're about to see, the echo command is good for much more than echoing static strings.

b) Open the page in a browser. What do you see now? Which style of coding do you prefer?

Answer: You should see the same result as before. The scripting style you prefer to use is entirely up to you, unless you are coding in a team environment, in which case all team members should agree to standardize on one style (in the interests of code readability and maintainability).

c) Open the page in a browser. What do you see? Why?

Answer: Again, you see the string "Hello world!" in your browser. But this time, instead of echoing a static string to the browser, we have sent a dynamic one. This is the foundation for almost all of the dynamic things PHP is capable of performing. Once you can modify and output variables, the sky's the limit on what you can do.

d) Open the page in a browser. What do you see? Why

Answer: You see the string "Hello world!" in your browser once more. This time we used a shorthand way of outputting a variable. This method dispenses with the ungainly echo command and takes a cue from asp (where <%= hello %> is an acceptable shorthand for <% response.write(hello) %>).

e) PHP has stringent requirements for variable names. The first letter after the dollar sign has to be a letter, and the variable name cannot contain any spaces or periods. Knowing that, which of the following are not valid PHP variables?

Answer: The following are invalid variable names: $2 (starts with a number, not a letter), $_four (doesn't start with a letter either), $5ive (starts with a number), $$even (doesn't start with a letter), nine (doesn't start with a dollar sign). The rest are fine.

You may notice that "$ten_" is a valid variable name. Did that catch you? The variable name is allowed to contain underscores as long as there is a letter preceding the underscore. In addition, you may notice times when PHP changes the names of variables it doesn't create so the variable name is valid in the PHP namespace. For example, if you click on an image of type submit, the browser will automatically pass the X and Y coordinates of your click to the script that receives the form submission. If the image is named "foo," then the variable names will be foo.x and foo.y. Neither of these names is valid in PHP, however, so they will be available to your code as foo_x and foo_y. Last, be aware that the designers of PHP took international considerations into account when designing PHP. Consequently, the ASCII characters from 127 through 255 also count as valid letters. That means that "$überVariable" is valid in PHP, since "ü" (ASCII 129) is within the valid range.

11.3.2 ANSWERS

a) If myValue is true, what will this code print to the screen? What if myValue is false?

Answer: If mvValue is true, the code will write "Truth is beauty." to the screen. Otherwise, it will echo "Beauty is truth."

b) What will this code print to the screen?

Answer: This code will write "You can't handle the truth." to the screen. To PHP, zero is equivalent to false. Any number other than zero (even negative numbers) will evaluate to true. For strings, only the empty string ("") and the zero string ("0") are considered false. All other strings will evaluate to true.

c) PHP has a variety of equality operators to choose from: "and," "or," "xor," "&&," "||," "&," and "|," in addition to "!" (not). Why on earth would anyone need so many ways to say "and" and "or"? What could all the different variations mean?

Answer: PHP has many, many operators that each handle a different nuance of equality checking.

The difference between "&&" and "&" (and, by extension, between "||" and "|") is that the double operator is a "short-circuit operator." That is, if you are evaluating $A && $B, *if* $A *is false, then a short circuit operator won't bother to check the value of* $B. *Evaluating* $A & $B *will check the value of* $B *regardless of the value of* $A. *Using a* short-circuit operator is a relatively advanced programming technique that can be used to simultaneously perform an equality check and an if statement. Here's an example:

```
if $A && throwError ("A is false! Oh no!");
```

If A is true, the short circuit won't evaluate the following statement (which, in this case, is an error handler of some kind). Really, it is simply a quicker, less readable way to write:

```
if (! $A):
    throwError ("A is false! Oh no!");
endif;
```

The operators "and" and "or" short-circuit just like "&&" and "||" do. The difference between "&&" and "and" is based on precedence. As you may have learned in elementary school, 1 + 2 * 3 is equal to 7, not to 9. Evaluating the expression from left to right is an error, because multiplication takes precedence over addition. Similarly, "&&" has a higher precedence in PHP than "and." The same holds true for the relationship between "||" and "or." For the sake of clarity and readability, rules of precedence can also be modified by using parenthesis to force certain calculations to take place before others.

11.3.3 ANSWERS

a) What is the output of the following while loop?

Answer: The loops writes out (more or less) the lyrics to "99 Bottles of Beer on the Wall." It isn't sophisticated enough to handle the last case ("no bottles of beer on the wall"), but it handles the other 98 verses well enough.

It's especially important to note the location of the variable decrement ("$counter--;"). That sets counter equal to one less than it was equal to previously, but only after returning the value of the variable before subtracting one. We could code that loop slightly differently if we wanted, using a pre-decrement instead of a post-decrement to reduce the value of the variable before displaying it. Here's how:

```
$counter = 99
while ($counter > 0):
    print $counter . " bottles of beer on the wall.<br>";
    print $counter . " bottles of beer.<br>";
        print "take one down, pass it around, ";
    print --$counter . " bottles of beer.<br>";
endwhile;
```

b) What is the output of the following while loop? Why?

Answer: The loop has no output. Since $counter is equal to zero, and zero is not greater than zero, the check to see if $counter > 0 returns false before the code inside the loop—the code that would output our plea for more lima beans—ever runs.

c) What is the output of this while loop? Why? How does this loop differ from the previous example?

Answer: This loop outputs the string "Mom, may I have another cookie, please?" It does this because the loop runs once before checking the "while" condition. The previous example was a standard "while loop," while this question provides an example of a "do… while" loop. The main difference between "while" loops and "do… while" loops is in the location of the condition checking. "While" loops perform a check at the top of the loop, so there can be cases when a loop won't run at all (if the check evaluates to false before the loop is ever entered, the program execution skips right over the contents of the loop and picks up after the "endwhile" marker). In a "do… while" loop, execution is guaranteed to pass through the body of the loop at least once before evaluating the while condition.

LAB 11.3 SELF-REVIEW QUESTIONS

In order to test your progress, you should be able to answer the following questions.

1) Is PHP case-sensitive?

   a) _____ Always
   b) _____ Never
   c) _____ Only for variable names
   d) _____ Only for function calls

2) Which of the following is not a valid PHP variable name?

   a) _____ $username
   b) _____ $user_name
   c) _____ $user.name
   d) _____ $userName

3) You want to check to see if a number in a string is equal to another number. Which of the following is correct syntax?

   a) _____ $stringNumber = $otherNumber
   b) _____ $stringNumber == $otherNumber
   c) _____ $stringNumber === $otherNumber

4) How many times will a loop coded as "While (1)" execute?

   a) _____ Once
   b) _____ Forever
   c) _____ Never

5) The expression $A && $B evaluates to true. What does that tell you about $A and $B?

a) _____ $A is true and $B is false
b) _____ $A is false and $B is true
c) _____ $A is true and $B is true
d) _____ $A is false and $B is false

Quiz answers appear in the Appendix, Section 11.3.

LAB 11.4

LANGUAGE EVOLUTION

> **LAB OBJECTIVES**
>
> After this lab, you will be able to:
>
> ✔ Describe Conceptual Building Blocks
> ✔ Identify Emerging and Evolving Technologies

The near future of Web scripting languages is easy to see. Using the languages mentioned previously in this chapter is not unlike building a house using some lumber, a hammer, and some nails. It's relatively slow going, but it gets the job done. Many programmers consider this to be a step up from writing Web applications in PERL, which is more like constructing a house out of bricks. Solid, but extremely time-consuming to put together. There are programming techniques available now that make the Web design process start to feel like a prefab house: quick and easy, but not necessarily cheaper or well made. You can even buy off-the-shelf Web applications that are comparable to a trailer house that you just pull onto your property and park.

The early years of Web design taught a lot of people a lot of lessons about how best to do things that had never been done before, and many the lessons learned from early mistakes are reflected in the tools that are becoming available now. How many times do different teams of developers have to write and rewrite an online shopping cart system before someone starts to sell an off-the-shelf solution? How long before other common tasks, like order processing and fulfillment, online catalogs, Web site searching, and object-oriented data storage become the blocks we build with, instead of *if-then-else* statements and *while loops?* All of these solutions have been implemented and are available to developers. To put it metaphorically, why build a cabin out of toothpicks when you can work with logs?

The price for ready-made pieces of code is, of course, higher, and sometimes a pre-fab building block is too big, too heavy, or just won't quite fit the hole it needs to fill. In those cases, it pays to know when you can save time by developing an application yourself, instead of spending your time trying to implement someone else's solution. Time is—as they say—money, and saving time is—in the Internet world—the same as making money.

Speaking of cost, there is at least one other area in which Web-based scripting languages are improving: Some are now free. Thanks to open source movements across the world, there are free operating systems, free Web servers, and free programming and scripting languages. It's hard to believe if you aren't familiar with the open source movement, but the old "you get what you pay for" saying isn't always true: Some of the best things in life *are* free.

Farther down the road we can look forward to shortened development time, as complex tasks are definitively solved and simplified into standalone objects to plug into other code. Even as these metaphorical building blocks get larger and more sophisticated, it pays to know how to use the glue to hold them all together. And that glue will include Web scripting languages for some time to come.

LAB 11.4 EXERCISES

11.4.1 DESCRIBE CONCEPTUAL BUILDING BLOCKS

Going back to the metaphor of building blocks, imagine yourself designing a Web application like a prefabricated house, arranging blocks of functionality into a predetermined shape.

   a) Think of some functional building blocks (common Web-application tasks) that you would prefer to only write once.
   _____
   _____

   b) Can you think of some building blocks that you would rather buy than write?
   _____
   _____

Lab 11.4: Language Evolution

c) Can you think of some application functions that are probably too specific to buy off the shelf? Things you might have to write yourself?

_____

_____

11.4.2 IDENTIFY EMERGING AND EVOLVING TECHNOLOGIES

a) Brainstorm some features and functionality that you would expect to find in a cutting-edge Web programming solution.

_____

_____

b) What are some technologies that provide those features?

_____

_____

LAB 11.4 EXERCISE ANSWERS

11.4.1 ANSWERS

a) Think of some functional building blocks (common Web-application tasks) that you would prefer to only write once.

Answer: Really, any reusable piece of code can act as a building block. It may be something as basic as a dropdown menu that knows how to query a database for its contents, a page wrapper that encapsulates the look and feel of an entire application into one file, or a single data-validation module. It might be as complicated as a module that renders online content into custom XML structures, code that calculates geographic proximity based on zip codes, or an interface to a legacy system (a mainframe or possibly some manufacturing equipment).

One of the reasons people started programming computers was to save themselves from repetitive tasks. It stands to reason that when someone writes a bigger building block, he or she uses it as often as possible. Some companies choose to leverage their useful building blocks by selling them, while other companies with different goals may choose to build with theirs. Regardless of what you intend to do with your collection of building blocks, if people give you a hard time for playing with little blocks all day, you may feel free to inform them that you're actually attempting to compartmentalize the application's functions into discrete functional elements. If that fails to impress them, then feel free to fling a block or two in their general direction.

b) Can you think of some building blocks that you would rather buy than write?

Answer: Web searching, credit card validation (and debiting and crediting), and graphic manipulation are all areas where it is probably easier and cheaper to buy (or license) a ready-made product than to write your own from scratch.

There are a number of companies now who prefer to hone one particular aspect of a process instead of building an application around those processes. Rather than competing in a crowded e-business space (B2B, B2C, etc.), many companies find it preferable to control a niche market providing a single online service better than anyone else. If your application requires functionality that your development staff aren't equipped to provide, then it's a perfect time to start investigating the opportunities for licensing someone else's technology. If things work out well, a software licensing deal can quickly turn into a strategic partnership with a third party software developer. So in addition to the expertise, you get to drop the developer's name along with yours. A little extra name recognition never hurts in the Internet space.

c) Can you think of some application functions that are probably too specific to buy off-the-shelf? Things you might have to write yourself?

Answer: It can be hard to find software to create graphics other than graphs, charts, and maps. If you were running a site about dogs, you might not be able to find a ready-made database of species and pedigrees and eating habits. So you might need to make one. Furthermore, if you want morphing software so breeders can see the results of breeding a Great Dane with a Chihuahua before actually trying it, you might need to write that yourself (unless you can adapt a more generalized morphing application to your particular needs).

It's unlikely that you will be able to find off-the-shelf components that will be able to handle custom business logic. If the application has to perform a number of specific steps, in a particular order, and all of the steps are unique to your particular situation, then odds are infinitesimally small that there is a product out there that will do what you need. Still, it never hurts to check. If the business logic is based on a methodology used by your entire industry, then the odds of finding a ready-made solution improve significantly.

11.4.2 Answers

a) Brainstorm some features and functionality that you would expect to find in a cutting-edge Web programming solution.

Answer: Ease of development is always nice to have in a programming language. When performance is an issue (and it almost always is), having a language that understands and transparently supports clustering will simplify the process of building a scalable Web solution. Easy (and optimized) database access can reduce development time significantly by relieving the programmer of the responsibility of managing database connections. It would also be nice to have an integrated search engine that can be used to search your site's content. Finally, development times could be slashed by a platform that would allow a developer to drag-and-drop multiple reusable code modules into a single framework that would allow them to seamlessly interoperate. Such a product would effectively eliminate the position of the "Web developer" as we know it.

b) What are some technologies that provide those features?

Answer: No one product offers all of the features mentioned above, but each of the following next-generation Web applications has several of those desirable and time-saving features: Allaire Spectra, Microsoft SiteServer, ASP+ (the successor to ASP 3.0), Vignette, and Zope (an extension of the PHP parsing engine).

LAB 11.4 SELF-REVIEW QUESTIONS

In order to test your progress, you should be able to answer the following questions.

1) Off-the-shelf Web application servers provide more functionality than is actually needed.

   a) _____ True
   b) _____ False
   c) _____ All of the above

2) Which of the following is least important when choosing a server-side development platform?

   a) _____ Scalability
   b) _____ Performance
   c) _____ Reliability
   d) _____ Price

3) Selecting an advanced web development platform means which of the following?

    a) _____ More time spent planning and less time spent coding
    b) _____ Less time spent planning and more time spent coding
    c) _____ No change in planning or development times

4) Licensing software solutions from other companies is:

    a) _____ Expensive
    b) _____ Easier than writing it yourself
    c) _____ Dangerous
    d) _____ Illegal

Quiz answers appear in the Appendix, Section 11.4.

CHAPTER 11

TEST YOUR THINKING

1) Pick a Web scripting language. Any language. Start experimenting with it.
   a) Try creating and outputting variables. Try setting HTML object attributes (background colors, text size, etc.) using server-side scripts.
   b) Try running database queries and looping through the result set. Take user input and save it to a database. Be sure to validate it first. Write some queries to retrieve information from the database. Output that information into a Web page.
   c) Consider setting and getting some cookie values. Try maintaining a continuous user state with session-level variables (Hint: It'll be easier if you select a language that handles states automatically).

CHAPTER 12

SUPPORTING SUPPLEMENTARY TECHNOLOGIES

> **CHAPTER OBJECTIVES**
>
> In this chapter, you will learn about:
>
> - Internet and WWW Standardization Activities — Page 333
> - Strategies for Evaluating New Technologies — Page 346
> - New Technologies to Watch — Page 355

One of the difficult technical decisions that a Web site administrator/Webmaster must make regards the evaluation of and possible adoption of a new technology. The rapid growth of the Web combined with constant development of new Web technologies and high reader/user expectations easily tempts a Web site administrator to be "on the bleeding edge." A mistake in deciding which technologies to adopt can have costly effects in terms of user perception, as well as misspent system and staff resources.

The technological demands of the Web community have stretched the limits of the computer standardization process. That process, which has worked so well at standardizing programming languages and protocols, has generally proven unable to operate at the breakneck speed demanded by Web growth. Consequently, the major Web players have independently developed their own technologies in response to user demand. Such nonstandard technologies have splintered the reader/user and authoring communities, who have found themselves unclear on which technologies were safe to adopt.

Chapter 12: Supporting Supplementary Technologies

In this chapter we will discuss the standardization process and organizations that define and help shape Web technology. The operation of these organizations can help a Web site administrator/Webmaster to decide which new technologies should be investigated, the status of the technology development, and even how to become involved in that development.

We will also discuss various strategies for evaluating new technologies. This evaluation will help to determine whether a technology is a "good fit" for an organization's Web strategy and what the potential impact of adopting that technology may be.

Finally, this chapter will identify some of the new technologies currently under development that promise to have a significant impact on the Web's future. Most of these technologies are still in the development/standardization process and have not been generally adopted by the Web community. However, in the opinion of this book's authors, they are technologies to watch and to consider for your Web site's future.

LAB 12.1

INTERNET AND WWW STANDARDIZATION ACTIVITIES

Common specifications are essential. This competition, which is a great force toward innovation, would not be happening if it were not building on a base of HTTP, URL, and HTML standards. These forces are strong. They are the forces which, by their threat to tear the web apart into fragmented incompatible pieces, force companies toward common specifications.

—Tim Berners-Lee, WWW inventor and W3C Director

LAB OBJECTIVES

After this lab, you will:

- Understand the Role of Standards and Standardization
- Know Which Organizations Impact the Development of WWW Standards
- Understand the Standardization Processes Used by These Organizations
- Understand How to Use These Organizations as an Information Resource

STANDARDS

What are standards? A formal definition states that "standards are documented agreements containing technical specifications or other precise criteria to be used consistently as rules, guidelines, or definitions of characteristics, to ensure that materials, products, processes, and services are fit for their purpose."

While everyone agrees on the importance of standards—suppose there were an unlimited number of connector types for adding your computer to a network—many are also frustrated by the time that the standardization process takes. As we said earlier, the rapid growth of the Web has placed a severe strain on the development of Web standards. An unknown source summarized the differing opinions about standards by saying, "The nice thing about standards is:

- There are so many of them to choose from;
- By the time things become standards, they're obsolete;
- Real standards are set by the market, not committees."

It is important to distinguish standards from design. In design, you choose between alternatives (say A, B, and C) in order to optimize function, performance, reliability, cost, and so on. Standardization helps you when the options are perhaps less clear and you must choose between variables such as "one," "some," "all," "undefined," "implementation-dependent," "discoverable," and so on. Your goal is, more likely, to optimize features such as flexibility, interoperability, politics, extensibility, enforced cooperation, and so on. As such, the scope of what is to be standardized often dictates who writes the standards. Therefore, standards are written by national or international standards organizations, consortia of interested or involved parties, companies, and even individuals.

STANDARDS ORGANIZATIONS

Perhaps the best-known (and largest) standards organization is *ISO*—The International Organization for Standardization. ISO is a worldwide federation of national standards bodies from some 130 countries, one from each country, that was founded in 1947. Since it is multinational, it is also nongovernmental. Its offices are located in Geneva, Switzerland.

The mission of ISO is to promote the development of standardization and related activities in the world with a view to facilitating the international exchange of goods and services, and to developing cooperation in the spheres of intellectual, scientific, technological and economic activity.
—The ISO Web site: *http://www.iso.ch/infoe/intro.htm*

> Since the name of the organization is The International Organization for Standardization, you may be wondering why it is "ISO" and not "IOS"? In reality, ISO is not an acronym, but comes instead from the Greek word *isos*, meaning "equal." This name says a great deal about the goals of the organization.

ISO's work results in international agreements that are published as International Standards. The Standard Generalized Markup Language (SGML) is defined in ISO 8879.

ANSI (the American National Standards Institute) is the U.S. representative to ISO. It was a founding member of ISO, is one of the five permanent members to the governing ISO Council, and one of the four permanent members of ISO's Technical Management Board. Therefore, one of its goals is to promote the use of U.S. standards internationally.

Examples of well-known ANSI standards are those for computer programming languages such as C and C++. Such standards are developed by committees from commercial and academic organizations and often take years to develop.

WEB STANDARDS ORGANIZATIONS

At first it might be useful to identify those areas of the Web that are most likely to be subject to (or require) standardization. They are

- Content—the data that we want to move around on the Internet/Web (e.g., HTML)
- References—how do we identify, reference, etc. the items we use on the Web (e.g., URLs)
- Protocols—how do we move Web items around the Internet (e.g., HTTP)

It is clear that these are areas within which there can be little ambiguity if the Web is to operate as expected. So, standardization (and standardization organizations) for these areas has to be a high priority.

In addition to ISO and ANSI, there are two organizations that are particularly interested in developing standards for the Web—the Internet Engineering Task Force (*IETF*) and the World Wide Web Consortium (*W3C*).

IETF

The Internet Engineering Task Force (http://www.ietf.org/) can only be described as a "loosely self-organized" group of people who make technical and other contributions to the engineering and evolution of the Internet and its technologies. As such, it is the principal body engaged in the development of new Internet standard specifications. Bear in mind that the IETF concerns itself with the *entire* Internet, not just the World Wide Web!

The Tao of IETF—A Guide for New Attendees of the Internet Engineering Task Force defines the organization's mission as including

- Identifying, and proposing solutions to, pressing operational and technical problems in the Internet.
- Specifying the development or usage of protocols and the near-term architecture to solve such technical problems for the Internet.
- Making recommendations to the Internet Engineering Steering Group (IESG) regarding the standardization of protocols and protocol usage in the Internet.
- Facilitating technology transfer from the Internet Research Task Force (IRTF) to the wider Internet community.
- Providing a forum for the exchange of information within the Internet community between vendors, users, researchers, agency contractors, and network managers.

The IETF meets three times per year. The IETF meeting is not a conference, although there are technical presentations and discussions. The IETF is not a traditional standards organization, such as ISO or ANSI, although many specifications that it produces become standards.

Perhaps most importantly, there is no membership in the IETF. Anyone may register for and attend any meeting. The closest thing there is to being an IETF member is being on the IETF or working group mailing lists.

The IETF is not as anarchical as it may appear. It is only one part of a well-defined organizational structure that also includes the Internet Society (ISOC), the Internet Advisory Board (IAB), and the Internet Engineering Steering Group (IESG).

The structure within the IETF is indicative of how it accomplishes its tasks. It is divided into eight functional areas:

- Applications
- Internet

- IP: Next Generation
- Network Management
- Operational Requirements
- Routing
- Security
- Transport and User Services

Each area has several working groups. A working group is a team of people who work under a charter to achieve a specific goal. That goal might be the creation of an informational document, the creation of a protocol specification, or the resolution of an Internet problem. Most working groups have a finite lifetime. That is, once a working group has achieved its goal, it disbands. As with the IETF in general, there is no official membership for a working group—if you join the working group's mailing list, you are a member.

The products of IETF working groups are often RFCs and Internet Drafts. The term RFC (Request for Comments) provides a historical glimpse into the manner by which the IETF used to conduct its business. RFCs are often treated as though they are standards, but this is not completely accurate. There are two special subseries within RFCs: FYIs and STDs. The For Your Information (FYI) subseries was created to document overviews and topics that are introductory. The STD RFC subseries was created to identify those RFCs that do in fact specify Internet standards.

Every RFC, including FYIs and STDs, have an RFC number by which they are indexed and by which they can be retrieved. FYIs and STDs have FYI numbers and STD numbers, respectively, in addition to RFC numbers. This makes it easier for a user, for example, to find all of the helpful, informational documents by looking for the FYIs among all the RFCs. If an FYI or STD is revised, its RFC number will change, but its FYI or STD number will remain the same for ease of reference.

Internet Drafts are working documents of the IETF, its areas, and its working groups.

Remember that the IETF concerns itself with the entire Internet, so that some Web issues may not be directly applicable. Examples of Web-related RFCs are *Hypertext Transfer Protocol—HTTP/1.1* (RFC 2616, June 1999) and *Security Extensions For HTML* (RFC 2659, August 1999). An example of an off-beat RFC is RFC 2324—*Hyper Text Coffee Pot Control Protocol (HTCPCP/1.0)*.

RFCs may be obtained via email or FTP from many RFC repositories. Many of these repositories also have Web servers. A good place to start is RFC Editor (http://www.rfc-editor.org/).

W3C

The World Wide Web Consortium (W3C)—http://www.w3.org/—was established in 1994 specifically to address the standardization of existing and future Web technologies. It has offices internationally at the Massachusetts Institute of Technology (MIT) in the United States, the *Institut National de Recherche en Informatique et en Automatique* (INRIA) in France, and Keio University in Japan. Its director is Tim Berners-Lee, the inventor of the Web.

> The W3C was modeled after the X Consortium (http://www.x.org/), the international organization established for the development of X Window technology and standards.

Like the IETF, the W3C has a specific public mission:

- Developing and maintaining a repository of information about the World Wide Web for developers and users, especially specifications about the Web.
- Developing and maintaining sample code implementations to embody and promote standards.
- Developing various prototype and sample applications to demonstrate use of new Web technology.

The W3C also participates in the annual International World Wide Web conferences sponsored by the International World Wide Web Conference Committee (IW3C2)—http://www.iw3c2.org/.

Unlike the IETF, the W3C is a membership organization with a very impressive list of members from international hardware, software, electronic, governmental, and academic organizations. Membership is not free, but the annual fee varies for nonprofit, government, and commercial organizations based on annual gross revenue. The W3C does not allow individuals to be members independent of an organizational membership.

Where the IETF is divided into functional areas, the W3C has defined domains:

- The User Interface Domain is concerned with technologies such as HTML, cascading stylesheets, etc.
- The Technology and Society Domain addresses technologies such as E-commerce, metadata, etc.

- The Architecture Domain studies technologies such as HTTP and Web characterization.
- The Web Accessibility Initiative (WAI) addresses the wide range of accessibility issues.

For members, the W3C provides a place to meet, to discuss, and to reach agreement on common specifications of interest. W3C staff help by:

- Organizing meetings
- Facilitating discussions
- Providing expert editing and writing skills
- Helping to devise a consistent plan for reaching consensus

Employees of member organizations are able to participate in Working Groups and Projects within these domain areas. Very often these working groups work in conjunction with IETF working groups addressing the same technologies.

The publications of the W3C are:

- Recommendations
- Proposed Recommendations
- Working Drafts
- Notes

A *Recommendation* is work that represents consensus within the W3C and has the Director's stamp of approval. The W3C considers that the ideas or technology specified by a Recommendation are appropriate for widespread deployment and to promote W3C's mission. A Recommendation is the closest that the W3C comes to producing a standard.

A *Proposed Recommendation* is work that represents consensus within the group that produced it and has been proposed by the Director to the W3C Advisory Committee for review. Most, but not all, Proposed Recommendations ultimately become Recommendations.

Working Drafts are documents that have been submitted for review by W3C members and/or other interested parties. These are *draft documents* and may be updated, replaced, or obsoleted by other documents at any time. It is inappropriate to use W3C working drafts as reference material or to cite them as other than "work in progress."

W3C *Notes* are documents that have been published at the Director's discretion. A Note does not represent commitment by the W3C to pursue work related to the Note.

The W3C Web site provides a constant update on the work being performed by the various working groups and announces when work results in a Recommendation or a Proposed Recommendation. Examples of recent W3C Recommendations are *Web Content Accessibility Guidelines 1.0* (May 1999) and the *Synchronized Multimedia Integration Language (SMIL) 1.0 Specification* (June 1998). As will be mentioned in a later lab, the W3C Web site is an excellent resource for learning about new technologies that will affect Web development.

OTHER ORGANIZATIONS INVOLVED WITH WEB STANDARDIZATION

It is certainly inaccurate and unfair to suggest that the W3C and the IETF are the only organizations involved in the standardization of Web technologies and that any activities other than theirs should not warrant attention.

The European Computer Manufacturers Association (ECMA)—http://www.ecma.ch—has been involved since 1961 in the standardization of key computer technologies. Of particular interest to the Web community, an ECMA committee is currently in the process of developing a standard for JavaScript/Jscript.

> The JavaScript programming/scripting language is very often (and easily) confused with the Java programming language. There are some similarities, but the two languages are significantly different in structure and potential use. JavaScript was invented by Netscape Corporation, which originally named it LiveScript. Microsoft, not wanting to bow to Netscape, named their implementation JScript. Given the current efforts at standardization, the now "politically correct" name for the language is ECMAScript.

Another organization that should be mentioned is the Web Standards Project (WSP)—http://www.webstandards.org/. The WSP describes itself as "a coalition of web developers and users." Its "mission is to stop the fragmentation of the web, by persuading browser makers that standards are in everyone's best interest. Together we can make the web accessible to everyone."

Lab 12.1 Exercises

12.1.1 Understand the Role of Standards and Standardization

The standardization process is an "alphabet soup" of acronyms that relate to various technologies. The following acronyms are important to a thorough understanding of the process or to future technologies. Look them up and identify their meanings.

a) HTTP-NG

b) IANA

c) MIME

d) NIST

e) PICS

12.1.2 KNOW WHICH ORGANIZATIONS IMPACT THE DEVELOPMENT OF WWW STANDARDS

a) Investigate the relationship, if any, between ISO, ANSI, the IETF, and the W3C.

12.1.3 UNDERSTAND THE STANDARDIZATION PROCESS USED BY THESE ORGANIZATIONS

Identify an area where the IETF and the W3C are conducting joint work. Compare the IETF documentation and that from the W3C.

a) What does each document tell you about how the respective organizations operate as standards bodies?

12.1.4 UNDERSTAND HOW TO USE THESE ORGANIZATIONS AS AN INFORMATION RESOURCE

At the time that this book was written, Microsoft and Netscape produced the two most widely used Web browsers (clients). Both Microsoft and Netscape are members of the W3C.

a) Identify some feature available in one of the browsers but not in the other that indicates an adherence to (or lack of adherence to) a specific W3C Recommendation.

Lab 12.1 Exercise Answers

12.1.1 Answers

The standardization process is an "alphabet soup" of acronyms that relate to various technologies. The following acronyms are important to a thorough understanding of the process or to future technologies. Look them up and identify their meanings.

a) HTTP-NG

   Answer: HyperText Transport Protocol—Next Generation

b) IANA

   Answer: Internet Assigned Numbers Authority

c) MIME

   Answer: Multipurpose Internet Mail Extensions

d) NIST

   Answer: National Institute of Standards and Technology

e) PICS

   Answer: Platform for Internet Content Selection

12.1.2 Answer

a) Investigate the relationship, if any, between ISO, ANSI, the IETF, and the W3C.

   Answer: ISO is an international standards organization. ANSI is the sole U.S. representative to ISO. ISO and ANSI develop standards (that are called standards). The IETF is a branch of the Internet Society. The W3C is a membership-based consortium. The IETF and the W3C develop specifications (or recommendations) that cannot accurately be called standards but are often accepted as such.

12.1.3 ANSWER

Identify an area where the IETF and the W3C are conducting joint work. Compare the IETF documentation and that from the IETF.

- a) What does each document tell you about how the respective organizations operate as a standards body?

    Answer: Development of HTTP (the HyperText Transport Protocol) is a technology with which both the IETF and W3C are involved.

    W3C documentation on the HTTP effort can be found at http://www.w3.org/Protocols/.

    IETF documentation of the HTTP effort can be found at http://www.ietf.org/rfc/rfc2616.txt.

    By looking at the membership of the working groups, the level of cooperation between the two groups can readily be seen.

12.1.4 ANSWER

At the time that this book was written, Microsoft and Netscape produced the two most widely used Web browsers (clients). Both Microsoft and Netscape are members of the W3C.

- a) Identify some feature available in one of the browsers but not in the other that indicates an adherence to (or lack of adherence to) a specific W3C Recommendation.

    Answer: At the time of this writing, interpretation of the Document Object Model (DOM) differs between the Microsoft and Netscape browsers. The W3C Recommendation for the DOM can be found at http://www.w3.org/DOM/.

    The differences between the Microsoft and Netscape DOMs are documented by the Web Standards Project (http://www.webstandards.org/).

LAB 12.1 SELF-REVIEW QUESTIONS

In order to test your progress, you should be able to answer the following questions.

1) It is important to distinguish standards from design.

    a) _____ True
    b) _____ False

Lab 12.1: Internet and WWW Standardization Activities

2) Which areas of the Web are mostly likely to be subject to standardization? Select all that apply.

a) _____ Protocols
b) _____ Underlying technology
c) _____ References
d) _____ Content

3) Which of the following is not an organization interested in developing standards for the Web?

a) _____ IEEE
b) _____ W3C
c) _____ ISO
d) _____ ANSI
e) _____ These are all organizations interested in developing standards for the Web.

4) How many functional areas is the IETF divided into?

a) _____ 5
b) _____ 6
c) _____ 7
d) _____ 8

5) Like the IETF, the W3C is a membership organization with a very impressive list of members from international hardware, software, electronic, governmental, and academic organizations.

a) _____ True
b) _____ False

Quiz answers appear in the Appendix, Section 12.1.

LAB 12.2

STRATEGIES FOR EVALUATING NEW TECHNOLOGIES

> ### LAB OBJECTIVES
>
> After this lab, you will:
>
> ✔ Understand the Importance of Standardization When Evaluating New Technology
> ✔ Understand When New Technologies Should Be Introduced in the Web Site Life Cycle

Users of the Web are frequently exposed to new technologies either implicitly or explicitly. For technical users, these new technologies often raise the question, "How did they do that?" followed quickly by "How can I do that?" Less technical users may be told that they must download a newer version of their client/browser or a new plug-in or helper application.

This onslaught of new Web technologies is likely to continue, so how can we learn about new technologies proactively—before they find us?

As we discussed earlier, the most reliable sources of information on new technologies are the standards organizations—the World Wide Web Consortium (W3C) and the Internet Engineering Task Force (IETF). The Web sites of these organizations will provide you with overviews of the emerging technologies, but will also tell you who the major players are in their development. However, the W3C and IETF can often get "bogged down" in technical details without giving you a real view of what the technology might offer. Much of the information they provide may only be of immediate interest to those people and organizations that are actively involved in the standardization development process.

TRUSTED SOURCES

You will need new technologies—your customers will demand them; your organization will expect them; your business will depend on them; and your hardware and software systems will require them. Keeping abreast of new Web technologies is "chasing a moving target."

The Web community is filled with persons and organizations that are technological fanatics. Being on the "cutting" or "bleeding" edge of technology is as much of an obsession for this community as the latest fashion is for high society. Such people or organizations are usually quite willing to give advice about "what's hot" and "what looks big on the horizon." But who can you trust or, perhaps more accurately, whose technology can you trust for your Web site?

It is important in this technological madhouse to establish a collection of "trusted sources"—sources with whom you feel comfortable and confident. Examples of trusted sources are

- The press
- Online sources—Web sites, mailing lists, etc.
- Conferences

THE PRESS

It's clear that the Internet and the Web make good press. Newsstands and bookstores often have separate sections dedicated to the latest magazines and newspapers. Most major newspapers have sections devoted to Internet and Web technology written by technology editors and columnists. There are dozens of free trade publications only too glad to give you a subscription in exchange for a completed questionnaire. Since most of these publications are in competition for your attention (and the advertising dollar), they try very hard to give you the latest information and industry gossip.

> Do not underestimate the value of industry gossip. A start-up company whose business plan includes a new technology or a company planning an IPO (initial public offering) might be worth watching—not for the investment possibilities, but rather for how the proposed technology is received.

Since it is impossible to read all (or even a significant portion) of these publications, it is important to identify a limited number to read and trust. Different publications address new technologies in different ways—some include tutorials, others address standardization, and still others review products or provide case studies. Each of these approaches can be invaluable in a new technology evaluation.

The following are a few examples of the press available to Internet and Web administrators. This list is not intended to be a recommendation, but rather some of the publications that this book author receives, regularly reads, and "trusts."

- *InformationWeek* (http://www.informationweek.com/)—This magazine is specifically (by its own admission) for business and technology managers, so it doesn't go into great technical detail. However, it is a very good source for Web technology case studies.
- *Inter@ctive Week* (http://free.intweek.com)—Addressing the Internet in general, *Inter@ctive Week* is short on technical content, but good for industry announcements and gossip. Information about new and emerging technologies comes from articles about the latest Internet start-ups.
- *InfoWorld* (http://www.infoworld.com)—While similar to *Inter@ctive Week, InfoWorld* often provides very good special reports on new technologies and articles about standardization activities. Bob Metcalfe, one of InfoWorld's regular columnists, often addresses new technologies and makes keen projections about future ones.
- *Beyond Computing* (http://www.beyondcomputingmag.com)—Billed as "The Magazine for Business and Technology Executives," it often includes concise articles about technological trends and good case studies.

One segment of the press often overlooked by Web administrators are those publications dealing with special technologies (skills, jobs, etc.) that are "subtechnologies" of Web site development and support. For example, there are very good publications for graphics designers or software developers that very often contain articles about current and new technologies affecting the Web. Examples of such publications are:

- *Publish* (http://www.publish.com)—Identifies itself as "The Magazine for Electronic Publishing Professionals."
- *NewMedia* (http://www.newmedia.com)—"The Magazine for Creators of the Digital Future"—need we say more?

ONLINE SOURCES

Online resources such as Web sites, portals, and mailing lists provide excellent means for tracking new technologies. "Ezines" often provide tutorials before many technologies become well known. The Web sites of the standards organizations (e.g., W3C) are essential for tracking the progress of technologies. (In the next lab, the essential references are online.) "Portals" addressing common or similar technologies (e.g., streaming media, scalable graphics) can be very helpful in comparing parallel technologies and learning who the "major players" are.

Mailing lists obviously allow interaction between persons interested in a technology. As was mentioned earlier, the IETF working groups are simply mailing lists—to become involved in the group's activity, you need only subscribe to the mailing list. The very active mailing lists can obviously contribute to greater volumes of email that you receive, so "trusted" mailing lists should be chosen carefully.

The following are several online resources that the author finds useful and that were active at the time this book was written. Their listing here should not be interpreted as an overall endorsement of the resource's goals and content.

- *HotWired Newsletter* (http://www.hotwired.com)—This is a very good resource. The mailing list informs subscribers of new content on the Web site.
- *Wired News* (http://www.wired.com/news/)—The WebMonkey often provides excellent tutorials and technological overviews.
- *E1.pub Weekly* (http://inf2.pira.co.uk/base02t.htm)—Originating in the United Kingdom, this list contains valuable links to a wide variety of announcements, tutorials, and other resources.
- *CNET Digital Dispatch* (http://www.cnet.com)—CNET is also a very good source for tutorials, standardization information, and well-written columns on forthcoming technologies.

CONFERENCES

While publications and online resources can be extremely helpful, nothing beats personal, face-to-face contact. Conferences allow you to meet other individuals who are facing the same technological and planning issues that you are encountering. Conferences allow you to hear presentations on technologies given by those involved in development. Conference tutorials allow you to ask questions and request examples.

On the negative side, the growth and importance of the Web has resulted in a large number of conferences—academic and commercial, broad-based to very focused. Since most of us can only attend a limited number of conferences and meetings, which ones should we choose and which ones should we trust?

The following are two conferences with which the author has been involved:

- The International WWW Conference Series (http://www.iw3c2.org/)—This is the original series of Web conferences. It is sponsored by the International World Wide Web Conference Committee (IW3C2) and is primarily an academic conference of refereed papers. What is unique about this conference series is its association with the W3C. The W3C always sponsors a "track" at these conferences to discuss current W3C activities. These conferences also help to satisfy part of the "meeting obligations" that the W3C has to its members. The conferences always include tutorials on a wide variety of new and important technologies and issues.

- Builder.Com (http://www.builder.com/)—Builder.Com, sponsored by CNET, brings together "high-end" Web designers and developers. Since this audience is always eager to be "on the cutting edge," presentations and tutorials concentrate on key forthcoming technologies.

A NEW TECHNOLOGY STRATEGY

Incorporating new technologies should be an element of the strategic plan for an organizational Web site. Figure 12.1 (adapted from Isakowitz, Stohr, and Balasubramanian) represents the significant steps that occur in the life cycle of a Web site. The functionality of a new technology can, most likely, be identified with one or more of the development/implementation steps in this figure. Therefore,

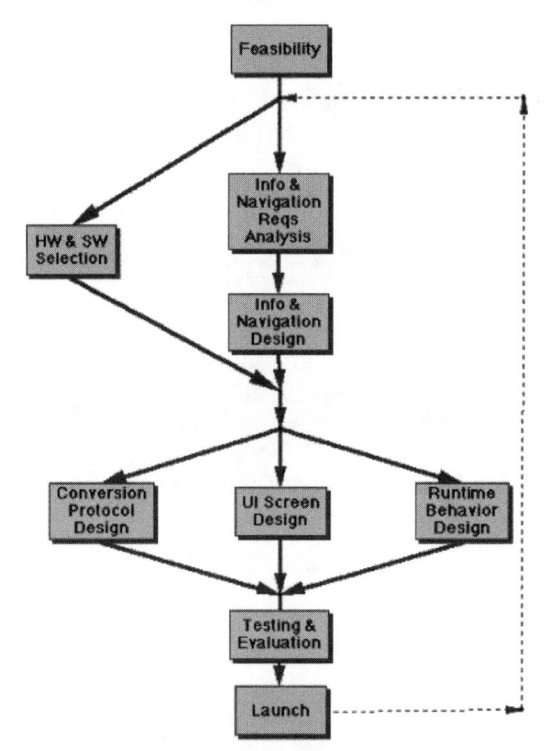

Figure 12.1 ■ **Web Site Development Life Cycle.**

new technologies should be incorporated into a Web site at the appropriate point (or the appropriate iteration) of that Web site's life cycle.

In general, a "sound" new technology strategy involves

- Identifying a technology of interest
- Tracking the technology's evolution, reception, and adoption (standardization)
- Integrating the technology into a long-term website strategy

"Research and assessment" are the keys to this strategy. One of the biggest potential mistakes that a Webmaster/Web administrator can make is the adoption of a new technology based on a "snap decision" motivated by the desire to be "on the leading (or bleeding) edge."

The following is a questionnaire/checklist that should be considered during the process of evaluating a new technology.

- Who or what motivated consideration of the new technology?
    - Was it the needs, desires, or expectations of the user/reader community?
    - Was it internally motivated by organizational technologists?
    - Was it in response to peers or competitors?
- Is the technology under consideration justifiable to the overall organizational Web site strategy? Does it add genuine benefit?
- Can the same (or similar) benefits of this technology also be provided using "old technology" (technology currently being used)?
    - If yes, what are the development requirements using the "old technology" versus those of the "new technology"?
- Is it possible to determine the total cost impact, development and otherwise, associated with the adoption of this technology?
- What would be the impact of the new technology on the readers/users of the Web site?
    - Would supplementary hardware or software be required?
    - Would user training be required?
- Is the organization willing and able to "back out" of the technology in the event of complications or unsatisfactory response? Is there a plan for accomplishing this quickly with minimal reader/user impact?
- Is the technology standardized or in the process of standardization? Are the major players and supporters of the technology converging or diverging in their support?

- What is the expected life span of the technology? Are frequent, significant revisions expected?
- Are there competing technologies?
  - What would be the impact of developing the new technology on current Web site support and development?
    - What is the staff impact?
    - What are the hardware and software requirements?
    - What existing resources can be shared by both the current and new technologies?
  - Are satisfactory resources available for support of the new technology?
    - Are staff training resources available? What is the learning curve for new or experienced staff?
    - Is technical support available?
    - Is adequate documentation available?
  - Are there new or additional Web site security considerations associated with the new technology?

LAB 12.2 EXERCISES

12.2.1 UNDERSTAND THE IMPORTANCE OF STANDARDIZATION WHEN EVALUATING NEW TECHNOLOGY

a) What impact should standardization have on the evaluation and/or adoption of a new technology?

12.2.2 UNDERSTAND WHEN NEW TECHNOLOGIES SHOULD BE INTRODUCED IN THE WEB SITE LIFE CYCLE

a) At what points in the life cycle of a Web site is the evaluation and/or incorporation of a new technology most appropriate? Why?

LAB 12.2 EXERCISE ANSWERS

12.2.1 ANSWER

a) What impact should standardization have on the evaluation and/or adoption of a new technology?

Answer: Efforts at the standardization of a new technology often reflect industry adoption and interpretation of the importance of the technology. Standardization efforts also represent some assurance that the technology will have a reasonable life span. Standardization usually indicates that a broad range of development and support tools is likely to become available and that a single vendor will not control the evolution of the technology.

12.2.2 ANSWER

a) At what points in the life cycle of a Web site is the evaluation and/or incorporation of a new technology most appropriate? Why?

Answer: New technologies should be considered and evaluated at any of the analysis, design, or selection phases of the Web site life cycle. New technologies should be incorporated into a Web site only at the end of its current life cycle. This strategy will ensure that it is a fundamental component of the new design and allow a simple reversion to the previous Web site design if the adoption of the new technology proves to be a bad decision.

LAB 12.2 SELF-REVIEW QUESTIONS

In order to test your progress, you should be able to answer the following questions.

1) What are "good" sources of information on new Web technologies? (Choose all that apply.)
   a) _____ Presentations at Web/Internet conferences
   b) _____ Reviews and articles in Web/Internet publications
   c) _____ Mailings from software vendors
   d) _____ Online sources

2) What are the three steps comprising a new technology adoption strategy?
   a) _____ Identification, tracking, integration
   b) _____ Identification, integration, maintenance
   c) _____ Identification, integration, tracking
   d) _____ Integration, tracking, maintenance

Lab 12.2: Strategies for Evaluating New Technologies

3) What are the key areas to be considered in the evaluation of a new technology? (Choose all that apply.)
   a) _____ Market share
   b) _____ Documentation and support
   c) _____ Availability of technology developers
   d) _____ "Coolness"

4) You should only rely on the standards organizations as the most reliable sources of information on new technologies.

   a) _____ True
   b) _____ False

5) Which of the following important segments of the press is often overlooked by Web administrators?

   a) _____ Online resources
   b) _____ Infomercials
   c) _____ Publications dealing with subtechnologies of Web site development and support
   d) _____ None of these

6) Which of the following is not a step in a new technology adoption strategy?

   a) _____ Identify a technology of interest
   b) _____ Test the technology using surveys and focus groups
   c) _____ Track the technology's evolution, reception, and adoption
   d) _____ Integrate the technology into a long-term Web site strategy

7) Research and assessment are the keys to adopting a new technology strategy.

   a) _____ True
   b) _____ False

Quiz answers appear in the Appendix, Section 12.2.

LAB 12.3

NEW TECHNOLOGIES TO WATCH

> **LAB OBJECTIVES**
>
> After this lab, you will:
> - Understand the W3C Functional Domains
> - Understand the Collaboration Between the W3C and the IETF

Looking into the future and speculating on significant Web technologies is a risky endeavor. It is easy to be reminded of some of the technologies of the past that appeared to be so promising but have slipped into oblivion. For example, in Fall 1995, "push" technology was the "buzz" of the industry. The companies that were founded to advance push technology have quietly (or maybe not so quietly) moved to other technologies in order to survive.

At the time of this writing (Fall, 1999) there are several new technologies that promise to enhance the Web and for which there is significant support. In this lab, we will discuss some of these technologies. The intention is not to offer a complete description of the technology, but rather to introduce the important concepts, establish a working vocabulary, and provide the capability for future consideration and research.

EXTENSIBLE MARKUP LANGUAGE (XML)

XML adheres to the philosophy that data belongs to its creators and that content providers are best served by a data format that does not bind them to particular script languages, authoring tools, and delivery

> engines, but provides a standardized, vendor-independent, level playing field upon which different authoring and delivery tools may freely compete.
>
> —Janus Boye

It would be unreasonable to have a discussion about new Web technologies and not mention *XML,* the Extensible Markup Language. In fact, it appears likely that XML will have greater impact on the future of the Web than any technology to date.

However, XML is not a markup language per se, but rather a metalanguage that lets Web authors/designers define their own markup languages. Extensible by definition, it specifies the syntax for tags, not the tags themselves. Therefore, the author/designer is able to define a markup language specifically for the type of document being written.

XML is not intended to be a replacement for HTML, but rather to augment it. Both have roots in SGML—HTML is an instance of SGML (if you don't know what that means, refer to Volume 1); XML is a "streamlined" version of SGML ("SGML-lite"). XML differs from HTML in three major respects:

1. Information providers can define new tag and attribute names at will.
2. Document structures can be nested to any level of complexity.
3. Any XML document can contain an optional description of its grammar for use by applications that need to perform structural validation.

XML is not backwards compatible with existing HTML documents, but documents conforming to HTML 3.2 can easily be converted to XML, as can generic SGML documents and documents generated from databases.

XML enforces the difference between document "content" and "structure/presentation." While HTML describes how to present a document's data, XML defines the data's actual content. For example, an HTML tag such as <H1> specifies a certain font and size either by means of a client/browser setting or a stylesheet. XML, on the other hand, describes the content that appears within the tags, what the content represents. A good example of this ambiguity in HTML is the frequent use by authors to designate document chapters using the <H1> tag. This might yield the desired results, but there is, in reality, no logical association between <H1> and the concept of a chapter. By separating presentation from content, XML adds structure to documents and allows them to be displayed/printed on various output devices without having to be rewritten specifically for each device. Theoretically, a single file authored in XML could be output to a wide variety of media, for example, Web browsers, newspaper printing presses, cellular telephones. The XML evangelists like to speak of "write once and publish everywhere."

XML is also designed to improve searching capabilities on the Web. For instance, if a student were doing a school report on the planet Mars, a search for "Mars" on a search engine would probably return references on the planet, the Greek god of war, and the candy company (and maybe even some others). When XML is in widespread use, that same student would be able to find only the documents that are relevant to his or her study because the relevant pages would include the markup:

```
<PLANET>Mars</PLANET>
```

The customized tagset capability of XML can also be used in multiple ways. For example, the tag

```
<AUTHOR>George Bernard Shaw</AUTHOR>
```

would enable an author's name to be displayed in a certain manner as well as provide a mechanism for external applications to scan documents for author references in order to create other documents such as an author list or index. This ability to use XML documents with other applications makes its usage quite literally endless. Likewise, applications that are able to output XML files (which is made easy by the fact that XML files are text/ASCII files), means that this output can be used/processed quite easily by other applications that are able to accept XML as input.

CONCEPTS

XML comes in two flavors: well-formed and valid. Well-formed is the easier standard to meet. It just requires that a document has an XML prologue, that all elements be nested cleanly, and that all start tags have matching end tags. "Empty" tags like IMG, which don't normally have closing tags, may end with a "/>" instead of receiving a full end tag. For instance, the HTML:

```
<IMG SRC="mygif.gif">
```

will become

```
<IMG SRC="mygif.gif"> </IMG>
```

or

```
<IMG SRC="mygif.gif"/>
```

The XML prolog is the most obvious change from either SGML or HTML:

```
<?XML VERSION="1.0" RMD="NONE" ENCODING="UTF-8"?>
```

The VERSION attribute should always be included, to protect documents against changes in the standard. RMD is short for Required Markup Declaration and announces which, if any, document type declarations (DTDs) should be applied to the document. For well-formed documents this will be "NONE." Valid documents may use "INTERNAL" or "ALL." ENCODING tells the parser what kind of character set the document will use. UTF-8, a subset of Unicode, is the default. (XML parsers must support the full 16-bit Unicode standard for international character encodings, however.)

These minimal changes to the world of mark-up make life much easier for parser developers, who no longer have to support poorly coded HTML missing half its end tags. Before a document can call itself well-formed XML, it has to meet minimum requirements. This requires some extra effort from those creating documents but makes it possible for programmers to build much more reliable systems with much less effort.

Valid documents must be accompanied by a document type declaration (DTD) that defines their structure. The DTD may be included as part of the document itself, or it may be stored in a separate document. Most complex DTDs will probably be stored as separate documents. A DTD is basically a list of element, entity, and attribute declarations in a simplified SGML declaration style.

WEB APPLICATIONS OF XML

The applications that will drive the acceptance of XML are those that cannot be accomplished within the limitations of HTML. These applications can be divided into four broad categories:

1. Applications that require the Web browser/client to mediate between two or more heterogeneous databases.
2. Applications that attempt to distribute a significant proportion of the processing load from the Web server to the Web browser/client.
3. Applications that require the Web browser/client to present different views of the same data to different users.
4. Applications in which intelligent Web agents attempt to tailor information discovery to the needs of individual users.

The alternative to XML for these applications is proprietary code embedded as "script elements" in HTML documents and delivered in conjunction with proprietary browser/client plug-ins or Java applets.

Significant Dates in XML Development

11/96:	The initial XML draft presented at the SGML'96 Conference
1/97:	The first XML parser developed
3/97:	The first XML Conference held in San Diego
4/97:	The initial XML Linking Working Draft
2/98:	W3C recommends XML as a standard

References

The main W3C XML page:	http://www.w3.org/XML
W3C Recommendation:	http://www.w3.org/TR/REC-xml
XML Linking draft:	http://www.w3.org/TR/WD-xml-link
XSL Style Proposal:	http://www.w3.org/TR/NOTE-XSL.html
XML Data Note:	http://www.w3.org/TR/1998/NOTE-XML-data-0105/
Microsoft's XML Page:	http://www.microsoft.com/xml

SYNCHRONIZED MULTIMEDIA INTEGRATION LANGUAGE (SMIL)

With SMIL . . . , anyone can make multimedia for the Web. Using your own digital snapshots and audio commentary, SMIL, and a simple text editor, you can make multimedia presentations that can immediately go live.

—Philipp Hoschka, Chair of W3C's Synchronized Multimedia (SYMM) Working Group

It has been said that the *Synchronized Multimedia Integration Language* (SMIL) is to synchronized multimedia what HTML is to hyperlinked text. Pronounced *smile,* SMIL is a simple, vendor-neutral markup language designed to let Web authors/designers schedule audio, video, text, and graphics files across a timeline without having to master development tools or complex programming languages. SMIL has this generalized capability because it is an XML application.

HTML allows the inclusion of multimedia content (audio, video, etc.) in Web pages but does not allow for their synchronization. This means that the Web author/designer cannot specify any timing information associated with the display of the multimedia. The lack of this capability severely limits the use of the Web for applications such as guided tours, presentations, online education, and so on. However, using SMIL and including simple XML tags allows a Web author/designer to specify such complex task sequences as "play audio file A five seconds after video file B starts and then show image file C."

SMIL marks a significant step toward making it easy to create low-bandwidth, TV-like content on the Web. It offers a new level of control over synchronized multimedia by allowing individual components of a presentation to be choreographed across a timeline in relation to each other. It also lets you control the layout, appearance, and exit time of each file.

What makes SMIL different from other multimedia presentation tools is that instead of forcing each component into a single video file, the text-based SMIL file merely references each file by its URL. Since the media files exist outside of the SMIL file, they retain their individual file sizes; therefore file size has minimal impact on download and presentation times.

Since SMIL is an XML application, the SMIL files contain only text information. Therefore, SMIL-defined multimedia presentations are easy to edit. If you want to change when an audio component within a complex presentation begins, you can just edit the SMIL file. You don't have to rewrite the entire presentation.

CONCEPTS

As was said earlier, SMIL is an XML application, so we would expect to see it composed of a tagset capable of describing an environment and actions associated with a synchronized multimedia presentation. Aside from the use of this tagset, a SMIL file looks similar to an HTML or XML file.

Most of SMIL's core functionality lies in its use of three tags:

- <PAR>
- <SEQ>
- <LAYOUT>

<PAR> is the abbreviation of "parallel," and <SEQ> is the abbreviation of "sequence." The <PAR> tagset contains references to media that should begin to be displayed simultaneously (or in parallel). For example, a slide show should begin at the same time as the audio file that describes it.

The <SEQ> tagset contains references to media that should be displayed in a sequence. For example, part one of a presentation must/should come before part two. The concepts of "parallel" and "sequence" are quite simple in their application of a presentation, but more of a challenge when considering technical issues such as download time of the media being presented.

It is possible to nest these two tagsets, such that you could have a subsequence that begins in parallel with several other media objects, or you could have several objects that play in parallel within a sequence.

The <LAYOUT> tagset defines the appearance of the playback window in which the media objects will play. It first defines the size and color of the entire SMIL presentation window. It then defines the areas within the window where the media objects are to be displayed. This also includes the use of the `<REGION>` tagset.

SMIL media types are expressed differently than in HTML. An image is expressed almost identically to the way it is in HTML, but as with all XML tags that don't have a second, closing tag, a backslash is added to the initial tag to ensure correct parsing. So:

```
<img src="http://www.prenhall.com/images/bebo.gif">
```

becomes

```
<img src="http://www.prenhall.com/images/bebo" />
```

Note that the explicit indication that the media object is a GIF image is not included. SMIL handles that independently, deriving that information from either the server, operating system, or from the "type" attribute in SMIL. Valid media types include audio, animation, `a` (the anchor tag), `ref` (a generic term for a media type, to be used when the media type is uncertain), `img`, text, textstream, video, and of course, the `par` and `seq` tags.

The following excellent example of a SMIL file is adapted from Larry Bouthillier of *WebTechniques*:

```
<SMIL>
    <HEAD>
        <LAYOUT>
            <ROOT-LAYOUT height="425"
                         width="450"
                         background-color="black"/>
                <REGION id="title"
                        left="50"
                        top="150"
                        width="350"
                        height="200"/>
                <REGION id="full"
                        left="0"
                        top="0"
                        height="425"
                        width="450"
                        background-color="#602030"/>
                <REGION id="video"
                        left="200"
                        top="200"
                        height="180"
```

```
                            width="240"
                            z-index="1"/>
            </LAYOUT>
        </HEAD>

        <BODY>
            <SEQ>
              <!-- This img tag displays the title screen
              -->
                <text src="title.rt"
                      type="text/html"
                      region="title"
                      dur="20s"/>
              <!-- This section displays the animated map
              with an audio soundtrack -->
                <PAR>
                    <AUDIO src="map_narration.ra"/>
                    <IMG src="map.rp"
                         region="full"
                         fill="freeze"/>
                </PAR>
              <!-- This section contains the video-
              annotated slideshow -->
                <PAR>
                    <IMG src="slideshow.rp"
                         region="full"
                         fill="freeze"/>
                    <SEQ>
                      <VIDEO src="slide_narration_
                             video1.rm"
                             region="video"/>
                      <AUDIO src="slide_narration_
                             audio1.ra"/>
                      <VIDEO src="slide_narration_
                             video2.rm"
                             region="video"/>
                    </SEQ>
                </PAR>
            </SEQ>
        </BODY>
    </SMIL>
```

Significant Dates in SMIL Development

1/97:   SMIL Working Group is formed
11/97:   W3C publishes first public draft of SMIL specification

6/98:   W3C publishes SMIL 1.0 Recommendation
7/98:   RealNetworks releases RealSystem G2 beta 1 with partial SMIL support
8/99:   W3C publishes SMIL "Boston" Specification

References

The SMIL 1.0 Specification:	http://www.w3.org/TR/REC-smil/
The Main W3C SMIL Page:	http://www.w3.org/AudioVideo/#SMIL
Just SMIL:	http://www.justsmil.com/
Working With SMIL:	http://www.developer.com/journal/techworkshop/092498_smil1.html
CWI SMIL Page:	http://www.cwi.nl/SMIL/
SMIL Mailing List:	http://lists.w3.org/Archives/Public/www-smil/

PORTABLE NETWORK GRAPHICS (PNG)

Ever since images were first supported on Web pages, JPEG (Joint Photographic Experts Group) and GIF (Graphics Interchange Format) have been the primary file formats used and supported. Other formats such as Bitmaps (BMP) have been used to a lesser extent. In late 1994, Unisys Corporation shocked the Web community by announcing that since it held the patent on GIF technology, it would begin to require authors of GIF-supporting software to pay a royalty. This action spurred the development of an open format, which eventually led to *Portable Network Graphics* (PNG). Pronounced *ping*, PNG is a true image format that tends to compress better than GIFs and is lossless unlike JPEG.

> Unofficially, the Portable Network Graphics (PNG) acronym stands for *PNGs Not GIFs*. This sums up the general attitude that went into creating the patent-free standard.

Not only does it not require a fee from programs that support it, PNG improves upon many of GIF's limitations.

CONCEPTS

GIF images support up to 8-bit color, but PNG is a true-color format, supporting up to 48-bit color. The W3C estimates that the file size of an 8-bit PNG image will be 10 to 30 percent smaller than that of the same image saved as a GIF. In addition, PNG's advanced interlacing method incrementally loads an image onto the screen in both horizontal and vertical directions, resulting in faster downloads.

PNG also offers features that GIF completely lacks, such as 256 levels of transparency using alpha channels. GIF's binary transparency allows pixels only two options: They can be transparent or opaque. PNG's varying degrees of transparency mean that an image of a lake, for example, could show the water as being semitransparent. Alpha channels also let images appear seamlessly over any background for improved anti-aliasing; GIF files require separate anti-aliasing for each background color.

Gamma correction, or cross-platform control of image brightness, is another bonus for PNG. GIFs can appear differently on different systems, but PNG insures that images created on one platform will look exactly the same on all platforms.

Significant Dates in PNG Development

12/94:	Unisys demands royalties on GIF technology
1/95:	The first PNG draft was developed
10/96:	PNG Specification issued as W3C Recommendation
10/96:	MIME type for PNG approved
11/97:	Microsoft Internet Explorer 4.0 becomes the first browser to natively support PNG

References

The PNG Specification:	http://www.w3.org/TR/REC-png.html
The Main W3C PNG Page:	http://www.w3.org/Graphics/PNG/
The PNG Home Page:	http://www.cdrom.com/pub/png/

SCALABLE VECTOR GRAPHICS (SVG)

Today, Web designers have to pick a width and height in pixels and save their work in some image format like JPEG. SVG will let the designer keep that vector flexibility and superior quality for delivery on the Web.

—Chris Lilley, W3C Graphics Activity Lead
and Chair of the SVG Working Group

Most images on the Web today, including GIFs and JPEGs, are raster images (or bitmaps) that record the color of each pixel individually. Since these images are "locked" into a static resolution, raster graphics resize and print poorly, but are well-suited for photographs, where each pixel needs to be defined.

Vector graphics, on the other hand, record images as mathematical descriptions of lines, Bezier curves, and other geometric shapes. This object-oriented approach means they're not locked into an exact pixel count, and graphic artists can access each object independently. Best of all, this means that such images can be resized easily without appreciable loss of resolution or clarity. Vector file sizes are also significantly smaller than traditional bitmap graphics, resulting in faster-loading pages. They're easily editable since you can access each object within the image individually, and they lend themselves to simple animation.

Since a move is afoot to provide Web content on a variety of devices—from television to cellular telephones—the scalability of images is of critical importance.

Graphics designers currently create vector graphics with common illustration programs, such as Adobe PhotoShop, but those graphics must be converted to raster format for native support in Web browsers/clients. Any Web documents including vector formats have required plug-ins such as Flash because no official, vendor-neutral standard exists. An official vector graphics standard would give a big boost to vector graphics on the Web, eliminating the need for proprietary plug-ins and fixing the problems of existing raster formats, such as the lack of scalability. *Scalable Vector Graphics* (SVG) promises to provide that standard.

SVG is an XML application and therefore benefits from XML's strengths and increasing popularity. Any existing XML parser can read SVG, and thus interchange will be easy. SVG is currently a working draft at the W3C, with working group members coming from key industry leaders such as Adobe, Hewlett-Packard, IBM, Macromedia, Microsoft, Netscape, Quark, Sun, and Visio.

In addition to faster download speeds, SVG also comes with many end user benefits. Some of the nice features of SVG are high-resolution printing, high-performance zooming and panning inside of graphics without reloading, gradients, animation, filter, kerning, masking, scripting, and linking.

Since it is based on XML, SVG is entirely text-based, which will mean that search engines will be able to index SVG images, and users will thus be able to search for text within images (e.g., search for a button text or a streetname on a map). With its text-based nature, it is also possible to create SVG images dynamically (e.g., with a database backend).

CONCEPTS

SVG contains the following six predefined objects: rectangle, circle, ellipse, polyline, polygon, and line. The usage of these objects is shown in the following example taken from the *SVG Working Draft Section 12: Other Vector Graphic Shape:*

```
<?xml version="1.0"?>
<!DOCTYPE svg PUBLIC "-//W3C//DTD SVG July 1999//EN"
  "http://www.w3.org/Graphics/SVG/svg-19990706.dtd">
<SVG width="4in" height="3in">
  <DESC>This is a blue circle with a red outline
  </DESC>
```

```
<G>
<CIRCLE style="fill: blue; stroke: red"
  cx="200" cy="200" r="100"/>
</G>
</SVG>
```

This will draw a blue circle with a red outline.

If you want to draw your own unique shape, you can basically draw anything you want with the `<path>` tag, which works like drawing on a piece of paper.

When you have your drawing ready, you can add text to it by using the text element. This could be useful for buttons, organizational charts, or maps.

By adding one extra line to the previous example, the blue circle now says "Hello World":

```
<?xml version="1.0"?>
<!DOCTYPE svg PUBLIC "-//W3C//DTD SVG July 1999//EN"
   "http://www.w3.org/Graphics/SVG/svg-19990706.dtd">
<SVG width="4in" height="3in">
  <DESC>This is a blue circle with a red outline</desc>
  <G>
  <CIRCLE style="fill: blue; stroke: red" cx="200" cy="200" r="100"/>
  <TEXT x=".5in" y="2in">Hello World</text>
  </G>
</SVG>
```

In addition to text drawn in a straight line, SVG also includes the ability to place text along the shape of a `<path>` tag. This could be a curving path, or any path defined by the designer, and then the base line of the text would follow this path.

SVG parallels the print world, in the sense that the designer will be able to create SVG graphics with whatever fonts he or she cares to use, and then the same fonts will appear in the end user's browser when viewing an SVG drawing, even if the given end user hasn't purchased the fonts in question.

SVG also supports the insertion of images. For example, you could insert a PNG or JPEG image into your SVG file. This is all done using SVGs `<image>` tag that is used in much the same way as the HTML tag `<img>`.

An example of how shapes, text, and images could be combined into an interesting SVG application could be an interactive map. For example, a city Web site could show the reader/user an initial map, and then the user would be able to dive into the map and find specific locations. The map could then have embedded images of points of interests.

Significant Dates in SVG Development

2/99:   First Public Draft
8/99:   Sixth Working Draft

References

W3C Scalable Vector Graphics (SVG): http://www.w3.org/Graphics/SVG/

Scalable Vector Graphics (SVG) Specification W3C Working Draft 06 July 1999: http://www.w3.org/TR/SVG/

Scalable Vector Graphics (SVG) Requirements W3C Working Draft, 29 Oct 1998: http://www.w3.org/TR/WD-SVGReq

Adobe on SVG: http://www.adobe.com/svg

RESOURCE DESCRIPTION FRAMEWORK (RDF)

Metadata is "information about information." A traditional metadata example would be a library's online catalog system—typically an electronic version of the old card catalog system. You could use this system to find a book that you're looking for—searching by metadata such as title, author, or subject matter to identify its location in the stacks—or you could search through every book in the library one by one until you found it. Obviously, the metadata approach would help you find the book much more quickly. RDF—the *Resource Description Framework*—is a foundation for processing metadata.

Currently, many (though not enough) Web authors/designers use the HTML <META> tags to describe their pages. Web robots/spiders indexing the Web are able to use this meta information in building their searchable databases. But this method often leads to ineffective search results; a single search may return many references to pages that have nothing to do with the search terms.

While RDF's potential to improve searching on the Web is reason enough to consider using it, that's not the only way metadata will improve the Web. In addition, it will describe individual elements such as pages, images, and multimedia files and describe the relationships between these items, thereby making site maps easy to create. RDF provides interoperability between applications that exchange machine-understandable information on the Web. RDF emphasizes facilities to enable automated processing of Web resources. RDF metadata can be used in a variety of application areas such as

- *resource discovery* to provide better search engine capabilities
- *cataloging* for describing the content and content relationships available at a particular Web site, page, or digital library

- *intelligent software agents* to facilitate knowledge sharing and exchange
- *content rating*
- describing *collections* of pages that represent a single logical "document"
- describing *intellectual property rights* of Web pages
- *digital signatures* as keys to building the "web of trust" for electronic commerce, collaboration, and other applications

> Discussions on resource description first began within the W3C with the development of the *PICS* (Platform for Internet Content Selection) technology. PICS is a mechanism for communicating ratings of Web pages from a server to browser/clients. These ratings, or rating labels, contain information about the content of Web pages. Examples of PICS usage could indicate whether a particular page contains a peer-reviewed research article, or was authored by an accredited researcher, or contains sex, nudity, violence, foul language, etc. Instead of being a fixed set of criteria, PICS introduced a general mechanism for creating rating systems.

CONCEPTS

RDF consists of three components—RDF Data Model, RDF Syntax, and RDF Schema—that provide the underlying structure for encoding, exchanging, and reusing human-readable and machine-understandable metadata on the Web.

The *RDF Data Model* is used for representing named properties and their values. These properties serve both to represent attributes of resources (and in this sense correspond to usual attribute-value pairs) and to represent relationships between resources. The RDF data model is a syntax-independent way of representing RDF expressions.

The *RDF Syntax* is for expressing and transporting this metadata in a manner that maximizes the interoperability of independently developed Web servers and browser/clients. The syntax uses the Extensible Markup Language (XML).

Finally, *RDF Schemas* are a collection of information about classes of RDF nodes, including properties and relations. RDF schemas are specified using a declarative representation language influenced by ideas from knowledge representation, e.g., semantic nets, frames, and predicate logic, as well as database schema representation models such as binary relational models and graph data models.

RDF in itself does not contain any predefined vocabularies for authoring metadata. It is expected that standard vocabularies will emerge; after all, this is a core requirement for large-scale interoperability. Anyone can design a new vocabulary; the only requirement for using it is that a designating URI is included in the metadata instances using this vocabulary.

Consider Figure 12.2—the graph says that "John Smith is the author of the document whose URL is http://www.bar.com/some.doc." In RDF syntax, this relationship is represented as

```
<?xml:namespace name=http://www.prenhall.com/
bibliography-info/ as="BIB"?>
<?xml:namespace name="http://www.w3.org/TR/WD-rdf-syntax#"
as="RDF"?>
<RDF:RDF>
    <RDF:Description RDF:HREF="http://www.bar.com/
    some.doc">
        <BIB:Author>John Smith</BIB:Author>
    </RDF:Description>
</RDF:RDF>
```

In this example, *syntax* represents the named properties and their values (the *Data Model*), using the *schemas* in the first two lines, that will provide you with more information about the different classes (Author and Description).

The first two lines tell the browser/client that the schemas (or vocabularies) from the two URLs will be used. The first URL is the host server and contains information about the tags that have been created and added to RDF. The next line is the W3C schema, and it contains the tags that are recommended by the W3C. The schemas tell the browser/client which tags are legal and what they mean.

The RDF tag container contains the appropriate metadata. The description line tells the browser/client that this is a description of a document at http://www.bar.com/some.doc. The author line tells the browser/client that John Smith is the author of that document.

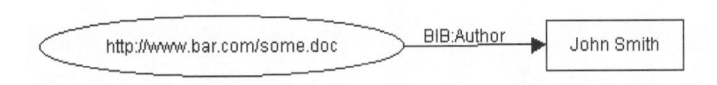

Figure 12.2 ■ **RDF Description as a Directed, Labeled Graph.**

The *Dublin Core* is a set of fifteen metadata elements (such as Title, Subject, Publisher, etc.) used to describe resources on the Web. A committee of librarians and experts from the computer networking and digital library research communities defined these elements. The Dublin Core is intended to be usable by noncatalogers as well as by those with experience with formal resource description models.

This next example illustrates how the RDF syntax can be used to encode Dublin Core metadata within an XML document.

```
<HEAD>
<XML>
<?namespace href = "http://www.w3.org/schemas/rdf-schema" as = "RDF">
<?namespace href = "http://www.purl.org/RDF/DC/" as = "DC">
<RDF:RDF>
<RDF:Description
    RDF:HREF="http://purl.org/metadata/dublin_core_elements"
    DC:Title = "Supporting Supplementary Technologies"
    DC:Creator = "Bebo White"
    DC:Subject = "Standards, XML, SMIL, PNG, RDF"
    DC:Description = "Webmaster book series"
    DC:Publisher = "Prentice-Hall"
    DC:Format = "text/html"
    DC:Type = "Book"
    DC:Language = "en"
    DC:Date = "1999-09-30" />
</RDF:RDF>
</XML>
</HEAD>
```

Significant Dates in RDF Development

10/96: W3C recommends PICS, leading to general discussions of resource description
10/97: Draft of RDF released
8/98: Working drafts of RDF published
2/99: RDF Model and Syntax Specification released as a W3C Recommendation
3/99: RDF Schema Specification released as a W3C Proposed Recommendation
8/99: RDF Interest Group organized

Lab 12.3: New Technologies to Watch

References

Introduction to RDF Metadata:	http://www.w3.org/TR/NOTE-rdf-simple-intro
W3C Resource Description Framework (RDF) Model and Syntax:	http://www.w3.org/TR/WD-rdf-syntax
Frequently Asked Questions about RDF :	http://www.w3.org/RDF/FAQ
Netscape RDF press releases:	http://home.netscape.com/newsref/pr/newsrelease488.html
	http://home.netscape.com/newsref/pr/newsrelease501.html

LAB 12.3 EXERCISES

12.3.1 UNDERSTAND THE W3C FUNCTIONAL DOMAINS

In the description of the W3C, we identified four functional areas of interest: User Interface, Technology and Society, Architecture, and the Web Accessibility Initiative.

a) In which of these areas would you expect to find the activity associated with the new technologies discussed—XML, SMIL, PNG, SVG, and RDF?

_____

_____

12.3.2 UNDERSTAND THE COLLABORATION BETWEEN THE W3C AND THE IETF

a) Identify IETF involvement in any of the new technologies discussed—XML, SMIL, PNG, SVG, and RDF.

_____

_____

LAB 12.3 EXERCISE ANSWERS

12.3.1 ANSWER

In the description of the W3C, we identified four functional areas of interest: User Interface, Technology and Society, Architecture, and the Web Accessibility Initiative.

a) In which of these areas would you expect to find the activity associated with the new technologies discussed—XML, SMIL, PNG, SVG, and RDF?

Answer:

- XML: Architecture domain
- SMIL: User Interface domain
- PNG: User Interface domain
- SVG: User Interface domain
- RDF: Technology and Society domain

12.3.2 ANSWER

a) Identify IETF involvement in any of the new technologies discussed—XML, SMIL, PNG, SVG, and RDF.

Answer: XML is not directly an Internet issue. However, the IETF is interested in XML Digital Signatures (http://www.ietf.cnri.reston.va.us/ids.by.wg/xmldsig.html). There are also some proposed protocols based on XML.

There is currently an IETF Draft for a SMIL mediatype.

The original specification for PNG was released by the IETF as RFC 2083.

The IETF is currently debating the appropriate mimetype for SVG. Since it is an XML instance, should it be image/xml?

There are presently no IETF efforts addressing RDF.

LAB 12.3 SELF-REVIEW QUESTIONS

In order to test your progress, you should be able to answer the following questions.

1) Ultimately, XML will become a replacement to HTML.

  a) _____ True
  b) _____ False

2) XML is not backwards compatible with existing HTML documents, but documents conforming to HTML 3.2 can easily be converted to XML, as can generic SGML documents and documents generated from databases.

   a) _____ True
   b) _____ False

3) Which of the following is not true of XML?

   a) _____ Applications that require the Web browser/client to mediate between two or more heterogeneous databases will drive the acceptance of XML.
   b) _____ XML is designed to improve searching capabilities on the Web.
   c) _____ XML enforces the difference between document "content" and "structure/presentation."
   d) _____ Information providers can define new tag and attribute names at will using XML.
   e) _____ These are all true of XML.

4) Using SMIL and including simple XML tags allows a Web author/designer to specify such complex task sequences as "play audio file A five seconds after video file B starts and then show image file C."

   a) _____ True
   b) _____ False

5) Most of SMIL's core functionality lies in its use of which three tags?

   a) _____ <PAR>, <SEQ>, and <REGION>
   b) _____ <PAR>, <SMIL>, and <LAYOUT>
   c) _____ <PAR>, <SEQ>, and <LAYOUT>
   d) _____ <REGION>, <SEQ>, and <LAYOUT>

6) SVG is an XML application and therefore benefits from XML's strengths and increasing popularity.

   a) _____ True
   b) _____ False

   Quiz answers appear in the Appendix, Section 12.3.

LAB 12.3

CHAPTER 12

TEST YOUR THINKING

1) Using the format followed in Lab 12.3 (Introduction, Concepts, Significant Dates, and References), write descriptions of these new technologies:
   a) DOM
   b) HTTP-NG
   c) P3P
   d) XHTML
   e) XSL

2) The Webmaster at a moderately large organizational Web site (approximately 2,000 pages) is considering the adoption of Cascading Stylesheet (CSS) technology. The current key design issues are:
   a) The organizational pages require a common "look and feel."
   b) The pages are "authored" by many individuals spread throughout the organization.
   c) The pages make extensive use of HTML tables to accomplish page layout.
   d) The readers/users of the organization Web site are known to use exclusively the Netscape and Microsoft browser/clients. However, they may be using different versions of the software.

   Conduct an analysis of the pros and cons of adopting CSS in this organization. If adopted, what would be a reasonable strategy for introducing this new technology?

3) In a recent well-known design magazine, a columnist discussing the future of HTML wrote,

   Currently Flash (Macromedia) is our best weapon. Drop HTML, pick up Flash, and really learn it—then push it. It offers the most robust authoring environment around, and it's backed by a single company that is focused on creating great tools. If Java had this kind of dedication behind it, I'd recommend it as well. But for all of Java's strengths, it lacks a great nontechnical authoring environment and that's what unleashes creativity and gives a new medium a life of its own.

   Your manager, upon reading this article, asks you why you aren't using Flash or why you aren't considering using it. This manager is fairly nontechnical, but immediately senses the columnist's enthusiasm. How do you respond?

APPENDIX

ANSWERS TO SELF-REVIEW QUESTIONS

CHAPTER 1

Lab 1.1 ■ Self-Review Answers

Question	Answer
1)	a, b, d
2)	c
3)	a
4)	b
5)	e

Lab 1.2 ■ Self-Review Answers

Question	Answer
1)	b
2)	d
3)	a, 4; b, 1; c, 3; d, 2; e 5
4)	c
5)	f

Lab 1.3 ■ Self-Review Answers

Question	Answer
1)	a
2)	d
3)	a, c
4)	a
5)	b, d

Lab 1.4 ■ Self-Review Answers

Question	Answer
1)	b, c, d
2)	a, 1; b, 3; c, 2
3)	a
4)	a, b, d
5)	b

Lab 1.5 ■ Self-Review Answers

Question	Answer
1)	a, b, c
2)	a, 3; b, 1; c, 2; d, 4
3)	c
4)	d
5)	f

CHAPTER 2

Lab 2.1 ■ Self-Review Answers

Question	Answer
1)	a
2)	d
3)	b
4)	a
5)	a, c, d

Lab 2.2 ■ Self-Review Answers

Question	Answer
1)	a
2)	a
3)	b, c
4)	b
5)	d

Lab 2.3 ■ Self-Review Answers

Question	Answer
1)	a
2)	c
3)	a, c
4)	a, b
5)	b

Lab 2.4 ■ Self-Review Answers

Question	Answer
1)	b
2)	a
3)	b
4)	b
5)	a

Lab 2.5 ■ Self-Review Answers

Question	Answer
1)	d
2)	b
3)	a
4)	a
5)	b, c

CHAPTER 3

Lab 3.1 ■ Self-Review Answers

Question	Answer
1)	b
2)	b
3)	c
4)	a
5)	d

Lab 3.2 ■ Self-Review Answers

Question	Answer
1)	b
2)	a
3)	c
4)	c
5)	d

Lab 3.3 ■ Self-Review Answers

Question	Answer
1)	b
2)	a
3)	a
4)	b
5)	b

Lab 3.4 ■ Self-Review Answers

Question	Answer
1)	a, 2; b, 1; c, 3
2)	b

Appendix: Answers to Self-Review Questions

3) b
4) b
5) b

Lab 3.5 ■ Self-Review Answers

Question	Answer
1)	a
2)	a
3)	c
4)	b
5)	a

Lab 3.6 ■ Self-Review Answers

Question	Answer
1)	a, b, d: TCP; c, e: UDP
2)	b
3)	a, c, d
4)	b
5)	b

CHAPTER 4

Lab 4.1 ■ Self-Review Answers

Question	Answer
1)	c
2)	a
3)	b, d
4)	a, b
5)	b, c

Lab 4.2 ■ Self-Review Answers

Question	Answer
1)	b
2)	c
3)	d
4)	a
5)	b

Lab 4.3 ■ Self-Review Answers

Question	Answer
1)	a
2)	b
3)	b
4)	a
5)	b

Lab 4.4 ■ Self-Review Answers

Question	Answer
1)	c
2)	c
3)	b
4)	a, b, c, d
5)	f

CHAPTER 5

Lab 5.1 ■ Self-Review Answers

Question	Answer
1)	a, 2; b, 1; c, 4; d, 3
2)	b
3)	a
4)	a
5)	b

Lab 5.2 ■ Self-Review Answers

Question	Answer
1)	a, N; b, Y; c, Y
2)	a
3)	a
4)	a, d
5)	b, c, d, e

Lab 5.3 ■ Self-Review Answers

Question	Answer
1)	b
2)	a
3)	b
4)	a, b, d
5)	b

CHAPTER 6
Lab 6.1 ■ Self-Review Answers

Question	Answer
1)	a
2)	b
3)	a, 3; b, 1; c, 4; d, 2
4)	a, c, d
5)	a, b

Lab 6.2 ■ Self-Review Answers

Question	Answer
1)	b
2)	c
3)	a
4)	b
5)	b

Lab 6.3 ■ Self-Review Answers

Question	Answer
1)	a
2)	a
3)	b
4)	a, b, d, e, f
5)	c

Lab 6.4 ■ Self-Review Answers

Question	Answer
1)	a, b, d
2)	b
3)	a
4)	e
5)	a, d

CHAPTER 7
Lab 7.1 ■ Self-Review Answers

Question	Answer
1)	b
2)	b
3)	a
4)	d

Lab 7.2 ■ Self-Review Answers

Question	Answer
1)	a
2)	b
3)	a
4)	c
5)	c

Lab 7.3 ■ Self-Review Answers

Question	Answer
1)	b
2)	a
3)	d
4)	c

Lab 7.4 ■ Self-Review Answers

Question	Answer
1)	b
2)	a

3) b
4) a
5) b

Lab 7.5 ■ Self-Review Answers

Question	Answer
1)	a
2)	b
3)	d
4)	d

Lab 7.6 ■ Self-Review Answers

Question	Answer
1)	a
2)	b
3)	b
4)	d

Lab 7.7 ■ Self-Review Answers

Question	Answer
1)	a
2)	a
3)	c
4)	d

CHAPTER 8
Lab 8.1 ■ Self-Review Answers

Question	Answer
1)	b
2)	b
3)	a

Lab 8.2 ■ Self-Review Answers

Question	Answer
1)	c
2)	a
3)	b
4)	c
5)	a, c

CHAPTER 9
Lab 9.1 ■ Self-Review Answers

Question	Answer
1)	a
2)	b
3)	b
4)	d
5)	a

Lab 9.2 ■ Self-Review Answers

Question	Answer
1)	a, c
2)	a
3)	d
4)	b

Lab 9.3 ■ Self-Review Answers

Question	Answer
1)	c
2)	c
3)	d
4)	b
5)	a

CHAPTER 10
Lab 10.1 ■ Self-Review Answers
Question	Answer
1)	b
2)	a
3)	a
4)	c

Lab 10.2 ■ Self-Review Answers
Question	Answer
1)	c
2)	c
3)	b
4)	d
5)	d

Lab 10.3 ■ Self-Review Answers
Question	Answer
1)	c
2)	b
3)	d
4)	c, d
5)	b

CHAPTER 11
Lab 11.1 ■ Self-Review Answers
Question	Answer
1)	b
2)	f
3)	c
4)	d

Lab 11.2 ■ Self-Review Answers
Question	Answer
1)	d
2)	b
3)	c
4)	c

Lab 11.3 ■ Self-Review Answers
Question	Answer
1)	c
2)	c
3)	b
4)	b
5)	c

Lab 11.4 ■ Self-Review Answers
Question	Answer
1)	c
2)	d
3)	a
4)	b

CHAPTER 12
Lab 12.1 ■ Self-Review Answers
Question	Answer
1)	b
2)	a, c, d
3)	a
4)	d
5)	b

Lab 12.2 ■ Self-Review Answers
Question	Answer
1)	a, b, d
2)	a
3)	a, b, c
4)	b
5)	c
6)	b
7)	b

Lab 12.3 ■ Self-Review Answers

Question	Answer
1)	b
2)	a
3)	e
4)	a
5)	c
6)	a

INDEX

Acceptable Use Policy (AUP), 65
Access authorization, 221–225
   file and directory access, 223–224
   policies, 224–225
   restricting access, 221–222
   server access, 222–223
ack packet, 82
Active Server Pages (ASP), 256; see also ASP
ActiveX, 261
Advanced Streaming Format (ASF), 119
Amdahl Corporation, 65
American National Standards Institute (ANSI), 48, 335
Application Programming Interface (API), 255
ARPANET, 65
ASP, 298–304
   basic if-then statement, coding, 300–301, 303
   basic variables, outputting, 299–300, 302
   JScript, 298
   PerlScript, 298
   VBScript, 298
   while loop, coding, 301–302, 303–304
Asynchronous Transfer Mode (ATM), 87

BARRNET (Bay Area Regional Research Network), 65
Basic Rate Interface (BRI), 127
BBN (Bolt Beranek and Newman), 65, 151
Beyond Computing, 348
Bit, 70

Bridges, 53
Broadband, 117
Broadcast addresses, 89–90
Builder.com, 349–350
Bus topology, 15
Byte, 70

Cable modems, 138–142
Cable Modem Termination System (CMTS), 138
Card-sorting method, 214
Carrier Sense Multiple Access with Collision Detection (CSMA/CD), 47
CERN, 66
Certification/Certificate Authorities (CAs), 148, 151–152
   Bolt Beranek and Newman (BBN), 151
   Federal Information Processing Standard (FIPS), 151
   Personal Computer Memory Card International Association (PCMCIA), 151
Ciphers, 146
   RC4, stream cipher, 147
Circuit-switching
   and packet-switching, comparison of, table, 39
Client/server architecture
   and peer-to-peer, master-slave, advantages and disadvantages of, 44–45
   and peer-to-peer, master-slave, comparison of, 44
Client-side scripting, 261–268

Index   383

code, 240
  and server-side scripting, combining, 269–275
CNET Digital Dispatch, 349
Codec, 119
Cold Fusion, 305–312
  basic if-then statement, coding, 307–308, 310
  loop, coding, 308, 311
  variables, outputting, 306–307, 309–310
Cold Fusion Markup Language (CFML), 256
Common Gateway Interface (CGI), 255
Compression, 118
Connection, 81
Connectivity, 125–143
  options, comparison of, table, 140–141
Content, deletion and/or replacement of, 202
Cookies, 270

Daemon, 41
Decryption, definition of, 146
Denial-of-service attacks, 202
Digital certificates, 149–151
  barriers to adoption of, 150
  information in, 149
  levels of, 152
  types of, 150
Digital Subscriber Link. *see* DSL
Distributed load-balanced Web site architecture, 188–189
DNS, 100
DNS Round Robin Web site architecture, 187–188
Document root taxonomies, 214–220
  hierarchical file taxonomies, 215–216
  real and virtual file paths, 216
Document type declaration (DTD), 358
Domain Name System (DNS), 77–80; see also DNS
Dotted octal (base 8), 70
DSL, 127–128
  Asymmetric Digital Subscriber Link (ADSL), 127

  High bit-rate Digital Subscriber Link (HDSL), 127
  Rate Adaptive Digital Subscriber Link (RADSL), 127

ECMAScript, 261, 262
Electronic wallets, 158
Encryption, definition of, 146
Encryption systems, 146–154
  certificate authorities, 151–152
  digital certificates, 149–151
  public key cryptography, 148–149
E.1pub Weekly, 349
Ethernet, 47
  10Base-T technology and, 47
  100Base-T technology and, 47
  communication between computers on separate segments, diagram, 88
  FDDI, comparison with, 50
  and LANs, 21
  and MAC addresses, 89
European Center for High-Energy Physics (CERN), 42; see also CERN
European Computer Manufacturers Association (ECMA), 340
Extensible Markup Language (XML), 355–359
  concepts, 357–358
  references, 359
  significant dates, 359
  Web applications, 358
Extranets, 28–29
  components of, 28
  connections for, 29
  security and, 29
  types of, 29
Ezines, 348

FDDI, 48
  and LANs, 21
Fiber Distributed Data Interface (FDDI), 10, 15; see also FDDI
File path
  real, 216
  virtual, 216
File Transfer Protocol (FTP), 109
Firewalls, 162–163, 204

384 Index

Flash, 261
Form validation, 269

Gateway, 103
Gopher, 66
Graphics Interchange Format (GIF), 36, 363; see also GIF

Hardware virtual servers, 194
Hewlett-Packard, 65
High-speed Data Link Control (HDLC) protocol, 59
HotWired Newsletter, 349
.htaccess file, 224
HTTP, 100–107
Hypermedia, 117
Hypertext markup language (HTML), 36; see also HTML
Hypertext Transfer Protocol Daemon (HTTPD), 42
Hypertext Transfer Protocol (HTTP), 11; see also HTTP

IEEE 802.5 standard, 15
IETF RFC 821, 108
InformationWeek, 348
InfoWorld, 348
Integrated Services Digital Network. *see* ISDN
Inter@ctive Week, 348
International Organization for Standardization (ISO), 5, 8, 334–335
International WWW Conference Series, 349–350
Internet
　history of, 65–67
　IP and, 65–67
　WWW standardization activities and, 333–345
　　standards, 334
　　standards organizations, 334–335
　　Web standards organizations, 335–340
　　　European Computer Manufacturers Association (ECMA), 340
　　　IETF, 336–337
　　　Web Standards Project (WSP), 340
　　　World Wide Web Consortium (W3C), 338–340

Internet Corporation for Assigned Names and Numbers (ICANN), 68
Internet Engineering Task Force (IETF), 155, 336–337; see also IETF
　functional areas of, 336–337
　mission of, 336
　Request for Comments (RFCs), 337
　For Your Information (FYI) subseries, 337
Internet Message Access Protocol (IMAP), 108
Internet Protocol (IP), 65
Internet Service Provider (ISP), 21
InterNIC, 68
Intranets, 26–28
　architecture of, 26–28
　HTTP and, 26
　logical view of, 27
　TCP/IP and, 26
IP addresses, 70–76
　subnet masks, 71–72
ISDN, 126–127

Java applets, 261
JavaScript, 261
Java Server Pages (JSP), 256
Joint Photographic Experts Group (JPEG) format, 363
Jscript, 261

Language evolution, 323–328
　cost, 324
　off-the-shelf Web applications, 323
LANs, 20–21, 89
　benefits of, 23–23
Latency, 53
Line-of-sight technology, 132
Local Area Networks (LANs), 4; see also LANs
logfile, 204
Lynx, 101

MAC addresses, 87–92
　broadcast addresses, 89–90
　and Ethernet, 89
Mailing lists, 349
MANs, 20, 21
Media Access Controller (MAC). *see* MAC
Media Technologies, 119

Mega-indexes, 230
  simultaneous (parallel), 230
Metadata, 367
Metcalfe, Bob, 28
Metropolitan Area Networks (MANs). *see* MANs
Microsoft Internet Explorer, 101
Mosaic browser, 66, 101
Multiple servers, supporting, 193–199
  hardware, 194–195
  hardware virtual servers, 194
  software virtual servers, 195
Multiplexing, 117–118
  dense wavelength-division (DWDM), 118
  frequency-division (FDM), 118
  time-division (TDM), 118
Multipurpose Internet Mail Extensions (MIME), 108–109
Multi-threaded meta-indexes, 230

National Center for Supercomputing Applications (NCSA), 42, 66
National Science Foundation (NSF), 57–58
Neilsen, Jakob, 214
Netscape Navigator or Communicator, 101
Network Access Points (NAPs), 57–58
Network connections, 57–61
  ASPs, 57
  ISPs, 57
  Metropolitan Area Exchanges (MAEs), 57
  Points-of-Presence (POPs), 57
Network devices, 52–56
  bridge, 53
  functions and advantages of, table, 54
  router, 52
  switch, 53
Network interface card (NIC), 138
Networks, 3–7
  characteristics of, 3–4
    table, 6
  characterized by spatial distance, 20–25
    LANs, 20–21
    MANs, 20, 21
    WANs, 20, 21
  internetwork, 14
  packet-switched, 36–40

  technologies, telephone company advantages and disadvantages of, table, 130
  topologies, 14–16
    bus, 15
    ring, 15
    star, 15–16
    wireless, 132–137
Network security, 145–174
Network Solutions, 67
NewMedia, 348
New technologies, 355–373
  Extensible Markup Language (XML), 355–359
  Portable Network Graphics (PNG), 363–364
  Resource Description Framework (RDF), 367–371
  Scalable Vector Graphics (SVG), 364–367
  strategies for evaluating, 346–354
    IETF, role of, 346
    new strategy, 350–352
      questionnaire/checklist for evaluating, 351–352
    trusted sources, 347–350
      conferences, 349–350
      online sources, 348–349
      press, the, 347–348
    W3C, role of, 346
  Synchronized Multimedia Integration Language (SMIL), 359–363
Nonswitched line, 118

Open Systems Interconnection (OSI) model, 4–5, 8–13
  diagram of, 9
  Layer 1, physical, 10
  Layer 2, data link, 10
  Layer 3, network, 10
  Layer 4, transport, 10
  Layer 5, session, 9
  Layer 6, presentation, 9
  Layer 7, application, 9
Opera, 101

Packets, 36
Packet-switched networks, 36–40
  TCP and, 36
  UDP and, 36

386 Index

PC/SC Working Group, 169
PHP, 256, 313–322
  basic if-then statement, coding, 316, 319–320
  basic variables, outputting, 314–315, 318–319
  while loop, coding, 317, 320–321
PHP: Hypertext Preprocessor. *see* PHP
Plain Old Telephone Service (POTS), 21
Platform for Internet Content Selection (PICS), 368
Point-to-Point Protocol (PPP), 10; see also PPP
Port, 81
Portable Network Graphics (PNG), 363–364
  concepts, 363–364
  references, 364
  significant dates, 364
Portals, 349
Post Office Protocol 3 (POP3), 108
PPP, 58–59
Primary Rate Interface (PRI), 127
Privacy and data protection, 158–159
  TRUSTe, 158
Programming and scripting
  security issues, 277–295
  as security practice, 205
Proxy, 103
Proxy servers, 167–168, 189–190
Public key cryptography, 148–149
  elements of, 149
  steps in, 148
Publish, 348
Pulse code modulation (PCM), 128
Push and pull technologies, 113–116

Quality of service (QOS), 9

Real file path, 216
RealSystem G2, 119
Registration Authority (RA), 152
Request chains, 103
Request/response protocol, 103
Resource Description Framework (RDF), 367–371
  application areas, 367–368
  concepts, 368–370
    Dublin Core, 370

RDF Data Model, 368
RDF Schemas, 368–369
RDF Syntax, 368
references, 371
significant dates, 370–371
RFC 2616, 337; see also HTTP
RFC 2659, security extensions for HTML, 337
Ring topology, 15
Robot, definition of, 229
Robotic specialized search engines, 230
robots.txt file, 232
  disallow directive, 232
  user-agent directive, 232
Robustness, 283
Routers, 52

Satellite links, 132
Scalable Vector Graphics (SVG), 364–367
  concepts, 365–367
  references, 367
  significant dates, 367
Scripting, user *vs*. Webmaster, 290–294
Scripting language evolution, 297–329
Search engines
  definition of, 229
  types of, 229–230
    mega-indexes, 230
    robotic specialized, 230
    simultaneous (parallel) mega-indexes, 230
    subject directories/portals, 230
    "true," 230
Searching and indexing issues, 228–236
  robots, spiders, and indexers, 229
  search engines, types of, 229–230
  Web robots/robotics, 231–232
Secure Electronic Transaction (SET), 150; see also SET
Secure Sockets Layer (SSL), 29; see also SSL
Security
  at-risk elements, 201
  good practices, 203–207
  intrusions, what to do in the event of, 207–208
  limitations, 223
    CGI scripts, 223
    document interception, 223

IP addresses, 223
  usernames and hostnames, 223
  logfile, strategies, 205
  programming and scripting issues, 277–295
  server, 200–213
  tools, 206
  tradeoffs, 278–282
  validating user input, 283–289
Security exploit, 206
Security incident, definition of, 200
Serial Line Internet Protocol (SLIP), 58
Server security issues, 200–213
  good security practices, 203–207
    firewalls, 204
    limiting server services, 204
    programs and scripts, 205
    security tools, 206
    server administration, 204–205
    server maintenance, 206–207
  intrusions, what to do in the event of, 207–208
  potential security areas, 201–203
    deletion and/or replacement of content, 202
    denial-of-service attacks, 202
    installation of unauthorized resources, 202–203
Server-Side Includes (SSIs), 255
Server-side scripting, 254–260
  and client-side scripting, combining, 269–275
  reasons for writing, 240–244
Session, 81
SET, 156–158
  and credit card companies, 156
  Secure Hypertext Transfer Protocol (SHTTP), 157
Shockwave, 261
Simple Mail Transfer Protocol (SMTP), 108
Single server Web site architecture, 187
Small office/home office (SOHO), 127
Smartcards, 168–169
Sniffers, 163
Sockets, 81–84
Software virtual servers, 195
SSL, 150, 155–156
  code, 155–156

X.509 digital certificates, 156
Standard Generalized Markup Language (SGML), 335
Stanford University, 65
Star topology, 16
  10Base-T Ethernet, 16
Streaming media, 117
Streaming multimedia, 117–122
Streaming video, 118–119
Subject directories/portals, 230
Subnet masks, 71–72
  host number, 71
  network number, 71
Supplementary technologies, 331–374
Switches, 53
Synchronized Multimedia Integration Language (SMIL), 359–363
  concepts, 360–362
  references, 363
  significant dates, 362–363
Synchronous Optical Network (SONET), 87
syn packet, 82

Taxonomy, definition of, 214
T-carrier service, 128–129
TCP, 67, 81–86
  sockets, 81–84
TCP/IP, 41
Thinking Machines (Boston), 66
Time-division multiplexing (TDM), 128
Token ring, and LANs, 21
Traceroute (tracert), 97
Transmission Control Protocol (TCP), 10; see also TCP
"True" search engines, 230
Tunnel, 103
UDP, 93–96
  reasons to use, 93
Unauthorized resources, installation of, 202–203
Uniform Resource Identifier (URI), 102
  Uniform Resource Locator (URL), 102
  Uniform Resource Name (URN), 102
Uniform Resource Locator (URL), 36; see also URL
University of Minnesota, 66
UNIX, 66
URL, 100, 101, 102

Index

User Datagram Protocol (UDP), 10; see also UDP

Validating user input, importance of, 283–289
VBScript, 261
Virtual domains, 103
Virtual file path, 216
Virtual hosting, 103
Virtual private networks. *see* VPNs
Virtual servers
   hardware, 194
   software, 195
VPNs, 168
   extranets and, 28
   extranets and wide-area intranets, 168
   Layer 2 Forwarding, 168
   Point-to-Point Tunneling Protocol (PPTP), 168

WAIS (Wide Area Information Service), 66
WANs, 20, 21
Web application design, 3-tiered, 245–251
   business logic layer, 246
   persistence layer, 246
   presentation layer, 245–246
Web client/server model, 41–46
Web robotics, 231–232
   co-existing with, 231
   four laws of, 231
      error reporting, 233
      exclusion standards, 232
      identification, 231–232
      polite indexing, 233
Web security toolbox, 206
Web server
   evaluation issues, 177–186
      case study, 180–183

server implementation strategies, 177–178
   dedicated server support, 180
   hosting services, 178–179
   turnkey solutions, 180
support, 175–237
Web site service models, 187–192
   advantages and disadvantages of, 190–191
   common architectures, 187–190
      distributed load-balanced, 188–189
      DNS Round Robin, 187–188
      proxy servers, 189–190
      single server, 187
Web Standards Project (WSP), 340
Wide-area microcellular data network, 132
Wide Area Networks (WANs), 4; see also WANs
winipcfg utility, 74
Wired News, 349
Wireless networks, 132–137
   connection options, diagram, 134
   line-of-sight technology, 132
   satellite links, 133
   use of radio-frequency (RF) or infrared (IR) waves in, 132
   wide-area microcellular data network, 132–133
World Wide Web Consortium (W3C), 338–340
   defined domains, 338–339
   mission of, 338
   publications of, 339–340
      Notes, 340
      Proposed Recommendation, 339
      Recommendations, 339
      Working Drafts, 339

Z39.50 standard, 66

See It! Hear It! Do It!

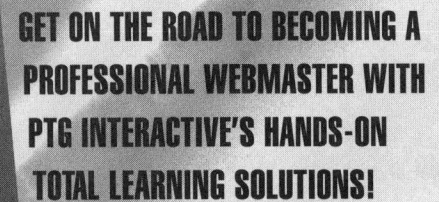

GET ON THE ROAD TO BECOMING A PROFESSIONAL WEBMASTER WITH PTG INTERACTIVE'S HANDS-ON TOTAL LEARNING SOLUTIONS!

These interactive multimedia Training Courses on CD-ROM feature easy-to-use browser-based interfaces and fully integrated print books and searchable e-books.

- **Listen** to hours of expert audio describing key administration tasks
- **Watch** the digital videos showing a pro administrating a system and creating Web interfaces
- **Practice** your knowledge with hundreds of interactive questions and practice exercises

There's simply no better way to learn!

WOW WEB SERVER TRAINING COURSE
LARSON AND STEPHENS
©2001, Boxed Set, 0-13-089437-0

WOW WEB DESIGN TRAINING COURSE
HUBBELL, WHITE, WHITE, AND REES
©2001, Boxed Set, 0-13-040760-7

www.phptr.com/phptrinteractive

ORDERING INFORMATION:

SINGLE COPY SALES
Visa, Master Card, American Express,
Checks, or Money Orders only
Tel: 515-284-6761 / Fax: 515-284-2607
Toll-Free: 800-811-0912

GOVERNMENT AGENCIES
Pearson Education Customer Service (#GS-02F-8023A)
Toll-Free: 800-922-0579

COLLEGE PROFESSORS
Desk or Review Copies
Toll-Free: 800-526-0485

CORPORATE ACCOUNTS
Quantity, Bulk Orders totaling 10 or more books.
Purchase orders only — No credit cards.
Tel: 201-236-7156 / Fax: 201-236-7141
Toll-Free: 800-382-3419

INTERNATIONAL ORDERING:

CANADA
Pearson Education Canada, Inc.
Phone: 416-447-5101
Toll Free Tel: 1-800-567-3800
Toll Free Fax: 1-800-263-7733
Corporate and Gov Tel: 416-386-3633

PEARSON EDUCTION LATIN AMERICA
Attn: Lynnette Kew
815 Northwest 57th Avenue
Suite 484
Miami, FL 33126
Tel: 305-264-8344 / Fax: 305-264-7933

UNITED KINGDOM, EUROPE, AFRICA & MIDDLE EAST
Pearson Education
128 Long Acre
London WC2E9AN
United Kingdom
Tel: 01-44-0171-447-2000 / Fax: 01-44-0171-240-5771
Email: ibd_orders@prenhall.co.uk

JAPAN
Pearson Education
Nishi-Shinjuku, KF Building
8-14-24 Nishi-Shinjuku, Shinjuku-ku
Tokyo, Japan 160-0023
Tel: 81-3-3365-9224 / Fax: 81-3-3365-9225

ASIA Singapore, Malaysia, Brunei, Indonesia, Thailand, Myanmar, Laos, Cambodia, Vietnam, Philippines, China, Hong Kong, Macau, Taiwan, Korea, India, Sri Lanka
Pearson Education (Singapore) Pte Ltd
317 Alexandra Road #04-01,
IKEA Building, Singapore 159965
Tel: 65-476-4688 / Fax: 65-378-0370
Cust Serv: 65-476-4788 / Fax: 65-378-0373
Email: prenhall@singnet.com.sg

AUSTRALIA & NEW ZEALAND
Pearson Education Australia
Unit 4, Level 2, 14 Aquatic Drive
(Locked Bag 507)
Frenchs Forest NSW 2086 Australia
Tel: 02-9454-2200 / Fax: 02-9453-0117

SOUTH AFRICA
Pearson Education South Africa Pty Ltd
P. O. Box 12122, Mill Street
8010 Cape Town, South Africa
Tel: 021-686-6356 / Fax: 021-686-4590
Email: prenhall@iafrica.com

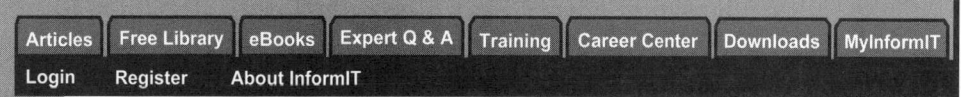

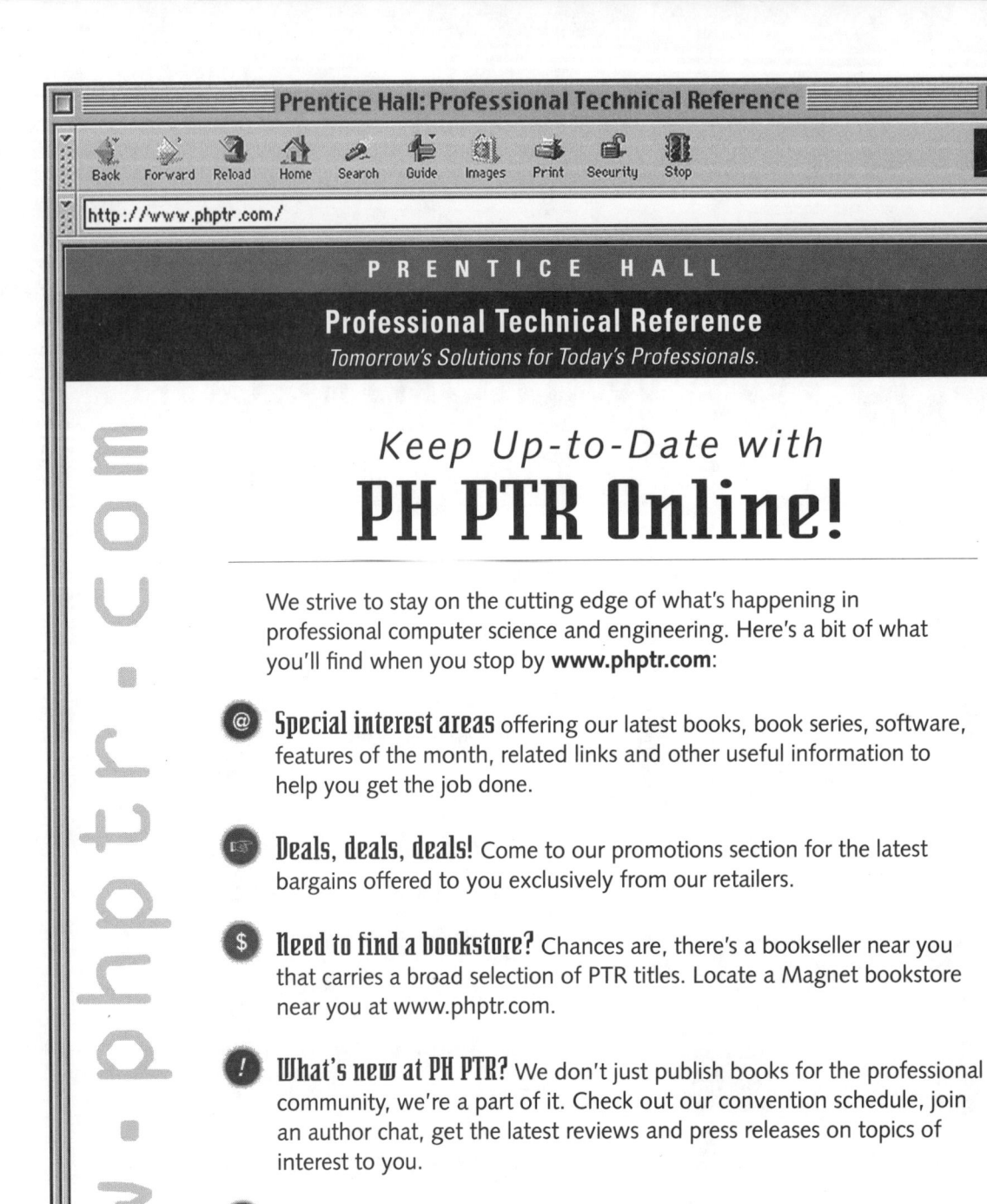

PRENTICE HALL
Professional Technical Reference
Tomorrow's Solutions for Today's Professionals.

Keep Up-to-Date with
PH PTR Online!

We strive to stay on the cutting edge of what's happening in professional computer science and engineering. Here's a bit of what you'll find when you stop by **www.phptr.com**:

@ Special interest areas offering our latest books, book series, software, features of the month, related links and other useful information to help you get the job done.

Deals, deals, deals! Come to our promotions section for the latest bargains offered to you exclusively from our retailers.

$ Need to find a bookstore? Chances are, there's a bookseller near you that carries a broad selection of PTR titles. Locate a Magnet bookstore near you at www.phptr.com.

! What's new at PH PTR? We don't just publish books for the professional community, we're a part of it. Check out our convention schedule, join an author chat, get the latest reviews and press releases on topics of interest to you.

Subscribe today! Join PH PTR's monthly email newsletter!

Want to be kept up-to-date on your area of interest? Choose a targeted category on our website, and we'll keep you informed of the latest PH PTR products, author events, reviews and conferences in your interest area.

Visit our mailroom to subscribe today! **http://www.phptr.com/mail_lists**